Narratives of the French & Indian War: 2

Narratives of the French & Indian War: 2

The Diary of Sergeant David Holden

•

Captain Samuel Jenks' Journal

•

The Journal of Lemuel Lyon

•

Journal of a French Officer
at the Siege of Quebec

•

A Battle Fought on Snowshoes

•

The Battle of Lake George

LEONAUR

Narratives of the French & Indian War: 2
The Diary of Sergeant David Holden
Captain Samuel Jenks' Journal
The Journal of Lemuel Lyon
Journal of a French Officer at the Siege of Quebec
A Battle Fought on Snowshoes by Mary Cochrane Rogers
The Battle of Lake George by Henry T. Blake

A LEONAUR ORIGINAL

Leonaur is an imprint of Oakpast Ltd

Text in this form and material original to this edition
copyright © 2008 Oakpast Ltd

ISBN: 978-1-84677-554-3 (hardcover)
ISBN: 978-1-84677-553-6 (softcover)

http://www.leonaur.com

Contents

The Diary of
Sergeant David Holden
February 20th—November 29, 1760

Introduction

David Holden, the writer, was the first sergeant in Captain Leonard Whiting's company. He was a son of John and Sarah (Davis) Holden, and born at Groton, on December 10, 1738. His family, in both its branches, had suffered much from Indian warfare. His grandfather, Stephen Holden, with his "two biggest sons,"—one of them David's father,—was taken by the Indians during the summer of 1697, and held in captivity for nearly two years; and his mother was a niece of John Davis, who was killed by the Indians, in his own door-yard, on October 25, 1704. The site of this tragedy is in the neighbourhood of the Groton School.

On July 13, 1761, David was married to Sarah, daughter of the Reverend Phinehas and Sarah (Stevens) Hemenway, of Townsend, who was born on October 25, 1739. There is a tradition in the family that the first time he ever saw his wife was while drilling a squad of men at Groton for the campaign of 1760. After his return from the army he lived during some years at Townsend, where most of his children were born. At the outbreak of the Revolution his sympathies were with the Crown; and so strong was the feeling in his neighbourhood at that period against the tories, that he was obliged to leave his home, when he took up his abode in Hollis, New Hampshire. His military service had laid the foundation for a loyalty to the King which did not swerve even at the cost of his personal popularity.

Captain Whiting, the commander of Sergeant Holden's company, was a native of Billerica, where he was born on March 27, 1734; but at the time of this campaign he was living at Westford.

The company was recruited from Middlesex County, largely from Littleton, Westford, Billerica, and Dunstable; and the muster roll is still preserved among the Massachusetts Archives (98) at the State House, in the volume marked "Muster Rolls, 1760-1761" (8. 313-315). During the Revolution Captain Whiting was a resident of Hollis, and he, too, was a tory. An account of his adventures with some patriotic women of the neighbourhood is given in Caleb Butler's History of Groton (pages 336, 337).

Mr. Holden died at Hollis, on August 8, 1803, aged 64 years, and his widow at the same place, on April 7, 1830, aged 90 years. He left a *Register* of his children, handsomely written by himself and framed, which is now in the possession of a great-grandson, William H. Bunton, of Boston. His children were as follows:

David, born June 28, 1763, died July 12, 1763; Sarah, born December 17, 1764, married Lieutenant Benjamin Cummings, of Brookline, N. H., July 20, 1786, as his second wife, and died in the year 1835; Betsey, born September 18, 1766, married David Hale, June 3, 1787, and died November 18, 1842; David, born July 31, 1769, married Bridget Atwell, January 1, 1789, and died October 13, 1823; Phineas Hemenway, born May 8, 1772, married Betsey Jewett, January 31, 1799, and died January 29, 1856; Lavinia, born June 30, 1774, married Andrew Bunton, of Pembroke, N. H., March 13, 1800, and died November 17, 1836; Artemas, born September 13, 1776, lived in Lowell, and died August 8, 1863; Sylvanus, born April 3, 1779, and lost at sea, February 5, 1811; and Joshua, born April 3, 1781, lived in Boston, and died December 17, 1852.

After the death of Sergeant David Holden, the Diary passed into the hands of a son, Phinehas Hemenway Holden, who left it to a daughter Mary, wife of Dexter Greenwood, of Hollis, by whom it was given, perhaps thirty-five years ago, to her cousin, Dr. Sylvanus Bunton (son of Andrew and Lavinia); and after Dr. Bunton's death the book came into the possession of his son, Henry Sylvanus Bunton, who has since given it to the Massachusetts Historical Society. According to an advertisement in *The Boston Weekly News-Letter*, July 3, 1760, forty-one companies had been mustered into the service of the Province during the campaign of 1760, up to July 1, either at Worcester by Commissary Anthony Wheelock, or at Springfield by Ensign Campbell, and then marched westward from those towns.

The *Diary* consists of sixty-four pages of a small blank-book, written in a legible hand; and 104 remaining pages are filled with the ordinary notes, usually found in a memorandum book, and extending through a period of twelve years. From these entries it appears that Sergeant Holden was a farmer and a cooper; and occasionally he let his horse or his cart and oxen to some of his neighbours to do work. In July, 1765, he has a charge of one pound for a "Pigg" against Archibald McIntosh, who ten years later was taken prisoner at the Battle of Bunker Hill, and who died in Boston jail. On September 2, 1765, he carts a "Load of cole from the battrey[1] to Tarbells mills," which were situated in Squannacook Village, now West Groton. In January, 1772, he opens an account with Henry Price, the first Provincial Grand Master of Masons in New England and North America, and he sells him some turnips and does some "hooping" for him.

There is also given "A List of the Schoolars in ye year 1772," at Townsend, which then had a population not far from 750 inhabitants. The list is as follows:

Isaac Kidder	David Patt
Lucy Kidder	Joshua Smith
John Kidder	Benja Ball
Jona Patt	Rachel Ball....10
James Patt	Rebeca Proctor
Sybel Patt	Rachel Proctor
Nathan Conant	Wm. Stevens
Jeremiah Ball	Molly Stevens
James Ball	Abel Gillson
Molly Ball	Daniel Gillson
Betty Ball	Henry Turner
Isaac Proctor	Benja Abbot

1. The neighbourhood of Battery Hill in the western part of Townsend, near the Ashby line. The hill was so called from a garrison house, which once stood near its base.

Elisabeth Proctor	Polly Price
Jacob Baldwin....20	Samuel Wyman
Rachel Read	Anna Wyman
Patty Read	Huldy Wyman
Levi Read	Uzziah Wyman
Howard Read	Polly Holdin
Joel Read	Sally Holdin
Benja Read	Betey Holdin
Jona Wallis	Ruth Baldwin
Suse Wallis	John Bauldwin
Sybel Wallis	Jonas Baldwin
Isaac Wallis....30	Joseph Willson....50
John Stevens	Juno Willson
Samuel Stevens	Sarah Willson

In connection with this *Diary*, see one kept by Lemuel Wood during the same campaign, and printed in the Essex Institute *Historical Collections* (Vols. 19.-21.); and also another by Samuel Jenks, in the Proceedings (second series, 5. 352-392) of the Massachusetts Historical Society for March, 1890.

DIARY

David Holdin's Book Bought at
Boston Apriel Ye 1st 1760
Price 14/
David Holdin his booke
If I it loose and you it find,
restore it me for it is mine
1760

The Diary of David Holden

On *Thursday Febuary ye. 20th* 1760 I, David Holdin inlisted with Captain Leonard Whiting in the expedition for the total reduction of Canada

March ye 10th, Past muster before Colonel John Bulkley[1] at Groton

Apriel ye 16th, Orders came from Captain Whiting that I should warn all the men that I had inlisted, and march them to Harvord the next Thursday, where I should join his company on their march to Worcester.

On *Thursday Apriel ye 24* 1760 I set out from Groton and marched with the men to Harvord to Captain Samuel Harskel's, where we met with Captain Whiting's company—Here we tarried all night.

25 We marched with eighty-two men to Captain Curtices' in Worcester, where we tarried all night.

26 We was all billited out at Worcester, though at sundry places. I with my party was billeted at John Curtices, about two miles from the town.

Sunday 27 and 28th, Companies kept coming in and some going out.

29 Orders came that Captain Whiting's company was to muster tomorrow morning at 8 o'clock.

---

1. Colonel Bulkley was a prominent inhabitant of Groton, who died on December 3, 1772, aged 69 years.

30 Captain Whiting marched to Worcester town with eighty-five men officers, included out of which seventy-five past muster and ten only was rejected.

We mustered before Anthony Whelock a regular officer

May ye 1 and 2nd. Companies coming in and marching out towards Albany

3 A great commotion among the officers, some they established, some they ground and sent home, took their men and put them under other officers. Some they sent home recruiting till the 20 of May.

Orders came that Captain Whiting's company should be in readiness to march the next morning— accordingly the captain payed off all his company their billiting and ordered them to prepare for their march the next morning

Sunday May ye 4th. Captain Whiting set out for Westford and Lieutenant (Nathaniel) Comings took the command of the company with Lieutenant (Joseph) Boynton. Took a team to carry our baggage and provisions and began our march with seventy-four men, officers included, and come about five miles and half to Lanlord Serjeant's in Lester where we went to dinner—and afterwards marched about ten miles to Lanlord Woolcut's in Brookfield where we tarried all night.

5 We marched about (twelve) miles to Lanlord Shaw's in Palmore and tarried all night. This day some of Captain Hutchins's company abused a woman and a young child— wounding both the woman and the child.

6 We marched about (nine) miles to Landlord Persons' on Springfield Plain where we tarried all night, and a woman belonging to Captain Hutchings's company was brought a bed with a stately soldier for the king

7 We marched to Springfield by 8 o'clock in the morning which was about six miles. Here we tarried all day Captain Whiting came up to us.

Four of Captain Hutchings's men was put in prison for abusing the people by the way

8 Past muster this morning before Lieutenant Campbell. Drew seven days' provision, took a team to carry our baggage in and marched about (ten) miles to Lanlord Captain Claps' in Westfield where we tarried all night

Here we left Jonas Butterfield (of Dunstable) lame at the Widow Ingolson's, under the care of Dr. Clapum

9 We marched four miles and half to the foot of the mount of Glasgow (Blandford), where our team left us and we was obliged to carry our packs on our backs to Shuffield. So we marched seven miles to Landlord Pees's in Glasgow where we tarried all night, here we left Freeborn Raimond and Thomas Hildreth (both of Westford) sick.

10 Marched through the Green-Woods to No. one (Tyringham) to Mr. Jakson which was about twenty miles and tarried all night.

11 Sunday we set out and came ten miles to Landlord Burgat's in Shuffield and tarried this night where Captain Hutchins's company tarried

12 Was detained till afternoon before we could empress wagons to carry our baggage after which we set out with Captain (Thomas) Beman's company and came about eleven miles to Landlord Lovejoy's, where we tarried all night.

13 We marched about (fifteen) miles To Landlord Follicumburrer's in Kinderhook where we left Benjamin Pollard (of Westford,) sick with the chiken pox and Abraham Taylor and Caleb Hustone (both of Westford) to take care of him. Captain Hammont's company came up and tarried with us.

14 It being a wet wet day did not march till 12 o'clock then set out and came about ten miles to the Half way House where Captain Whiting's and Captain Hamment's companies tarried all night. Myself and two others set out for Greenbush in order to git quarters for our company and came about seven miles and tarried at a Dutch Tavorn.

15 We came in to Greenbush and provided a place and barn for our company about three miles below the city of Albany—about one o'clock our company came in, here we tarried all night.

16 Orders came that we should march up the river to Colonel Ransley's, accordingly we did and there was about 600 men all assembled of the Massachusetts troops whereupon a detachment was sent to Half Moon consisting of one lieutenants, two serjeants, thirty men, of which five went out of our company, *viz.* Lieutenant Cumings took the command of the party Serjeant (Peter) Procter, Josiah Procter (both of Littleton), Samuel Fassetts (of Westford), Andrew Farmer (of Billerica).

After which we was ferried over the river to Albany, drew two days' provisions took seventy-nine battoes loaded them with twenty barrills provisions in each boat, with seven hands on board of each and set sail with a fair wind up the river—and came about six miles to Captain Vanornom's where we landed and tarried all night and it was very wet .

17 We set sail in the morning and came up the river about nine miles and encamped it being a wet night.

18 Sunday. We set out and came up very bad falls about two miles and half to the head of the falls where we was obliged to wade up all the falls and draw the battoes here we encamped, it being a wet night.

19 We set sail and came about one mile and half where we unloded our boats and tarried chief of the day. Towards night we hoisted sail and set out with a fair wind and came down to Half Moon in an hour and half this was nine miles. Here we drew a day's allowance and tarried all night, here we left Simeon Cumings (of Dunstable) ye lieutenant.

20 This was a wet morning . We stowed forty men in a boat and came down to Albany and drew four days' provisions.

Was ordered to load other boats and go another trip up the river with provisions accordingly we did and came up about a mile above the city and encamped. Abraham Taylor, Benjamin Pollard and Caleb Hustone came up to us, that we left at Kinderhook, also Samuel Hawood (of Billerica) and Timothy Twist (of Woburn) that we left at Worcester.

21 We set sail and came about a mile above the fort at Half Moon and encamped.

22 We came up the falls and encamped.

23 Set out and came to the landing place, unloaded our boats. Came down to Half Moon and tarried all night.

24 Here we left all our boats only just enough to carry the men in, and set out came down to Albany where we landed below the town and was forbid going into the city by reason of the small pox. Orders came that the Massachusetts troops should march, accordingly ten companies marched upon the hill above the city, containing 564 men, officers included ,were three other companies of the same corps was already encamped. Here we drew our tents and pitched them in order. A man of the second battalion Royal Hiland Regiment received 999 lashes for leaving his post when on sentry

25 Sunday A detachment of hundred men was sent out into the woods to look up king's oxen, seven sloop loads of men arrived here of the New York Rhode Island and Jersey troops. A party of about thirty men were sent to Crown Point under the command of Lieutenant Clark—two of which belonged to our company, *viz.* David Kemp (of Groton) and John Heald (of Townsend). Jonas Butterfield (of Dunstable) that we left lame at Westfield came up to us. A detachment of men was ordered to look up oxen, but it being a wet day they did not go.

26 Drew six days' provision, Serjeant Craggitt (Cragin, of Acton) of Captain Wm. Barron's company was taken sick with the small pox.

27 The serjeant was carried into the hospitle. Orders came that Captain (Daniel) McFaling's and Captain (John) Clapum's companies should march with a detachment out of each of the remaining companies to Fort Miller and Saratoga (twelve of which went out of Captain Whiting's company) under the command of Major Hawks *viz.* David Trull (of Littleton), Jonathan Hartwel, Joseph Hartwell (of Westford), Benjamin Worster (of Littleton), Thompson Maxwell (of Bedford), Timothy Priest (of Lincoln), Benjamin Allen (of Lincoln), Jona Peirce (of Woburn), George Hiber (of Littleton), John Robinson (of Dunstable), John Walker (of Lincoln), and Jona Lawrence (of Littleton). They were all paraded after which they was all dismissed and ordered to appear upon the parade tomorrow morning at daybrake.

28 General election at Boston. The men that was detached yesterday marched off, about 250 of them. A detachment were sent out after oxen the officers drew lots to see which of them should go down the country to look for deserters and it fell to Captain Whiting and Lieutenant King and they set out. This was a showery day.

29 Nothing remarkable.

30 Captain (Thomas) Ferringtons[2] and Captain Jinks marched with their companies and a detachment out of the remaining company in camp, some were sent back after they had set out. A corporal and four men went out of our company *viz.* Corporal Benjamin Baulding (Baldwin, of Billerica), Joseph Pollard (of Westford), Jonathan Pollard, Ephraim Johnson, David Rumrill and Ephraim Johson—Freeborn Raimond and Thomas Hildreth came up here that we left sick at Glasgow (Blandford). Took four days' provisions.

31 Orders that all the Massachusetts troops should be drawed up at the head of their encampment at 4 o'clock this evening and

---

2. Captain Thomas Farrington commanded a Groton company, of which a "Return of Men" is given in the Appendix.

at 5 o'clock his Excellency General Amhurst with a number of other officers came to view us after which we ware all dismissed.

A Return of all the fire arms was made that belonged to to the Massachusetts troops and ammunition was drawn

Sunday 1st June A man belonging to Captain Martin's company received fifty lashes for not doing his duty. Orders that 300 of the Rhode Island troops march up the river this afternoon, and that all the Massachusetts troops now encamped should strike their tents tomorrow morning at daybrake, and that the regiment of 1000 should be allowed provision, or the four pences in lieu of it, for four women each company and those of 700 for three women each company. A weekly return was made, our company at this time was reduced to forty-eight men, officers included.

2 Struck our tents and set out for Fort Edward, took one battoe to a company to carry the tents and officers' baggage and camp equipage and came up as far as Half Moon and encamped.

3 We took battoes to compleat the whole with seven men to a boat with provision corn and hay and came up as far as the foot of the falls below Still Water—unloaded our boats and encamped.

4 Set out and came up two pair of falls and then arrived at Still Water where we loaded our boats with thirty barrils of flour or twenty-five of pork, pees or rice—this was a very rainy day and a tedious time we had of it and the men chiefly tarried here all night but I with my boats crew came about five miles farther to the Great Fly so called and encamped.

5 We set out and came as far as the falls above Saratoga,—this was a very tedious rainy time and we encamped.

6 This also was a wet day unloaded part of the boats and took them up the falls—carried the provisions in wagons one mile and half

21

7 It still remains wet unloaded the remainder of the battoes and took them up the falls and encamped.

8 Sunday Dull, lowry still hangs over our heads. Loaded our boats and came up two miles and half to the carrying place opposite Fort Miller where we unloaded the battoes drew them out put them on wagon and carried them half a mile by land and the provisions, and launched them into the river again. Captain Whiting came up to us this day.

Here we left Freeborn Raimond in the room of Jonathan Pollard.

9 Loaded our battoes as usual and set out for Fort Edward and on the way we meet a number of the Hiland troops coming down the river in battoes who was a going to join General Amhurst. Arrived at Fort Edward and unloaded our battoes and encamped. Lieutenant James conch was broke and sent home. Several showers this day. Here we left Moses Shattuck (of Littleton).

(One leaf of the *Diary* here missing.)

16 Set sail and came to Crown Point Fort where we landed and pitched our tents. Had intelligence of Major Roggers's[3] fight within about fifty miles of St. Johns where they had a very warm engagement a party of about five or six hundred of the enemy fell upon three hundred of our Rangers and Provintials—fought them for considerable time and killed nine of our men on the spot and wounded thirteen more—ten of which died soon after. Captain Noah Johnson was killed at the same time. Tis thought they killed a large number of the enemy but never could find out how many for they being so numerous they carried off their dead. John Heald and David Keemp joined our company again that was sent from Albany the 25 of June (May) last. We had several very smart thunder showers here this day.

---

3. Major Robert Rogers, an officer of the French and Indian War, who commanded a famous body of troops known as the Rogers Rangers. He was a native of Dunbarton, N. H., where he was born about the year 1730, and died in England about 1800, after a life of singular adventures and vicissitudes.

17 Four of Captain Ferringtons' men joined our company *viz* David Sawtell, Jonathan Holdin, Nathaniel Green and Ephraim Keemp (all of Groton).

Likewise Peletiah Whittemore (of Dunstable) and Henry Foster (of Billerica) that we left at Green Bush sick came up to us detachments of men for fatigue till there was scarsly a man left in camp.

A number of Rhode Island troops arrived and encamped here

18 A small light was discovered on the other side of the lake just before sunset whereupon Major Skeen, Captain Brewer, and Captain James Roggers of the rangers with about thirty men went out in two battoes and one whale boat on the discovery and was gone all night. Captain Hutchins of the Provintials also went out

19 This morning the party came in. Brought in two English prisoners that was taken last winter who ran away from the Indians and built a light that they might be discovered by the garrison.

This day Captain Foot came in with about 116 other prisoners in the brig with a flag of truce from. the French who give account that ye French are so short of provision they could keep them no longer. Two companies of the Massachusetts troops arrived here, *viz*. Captain Wintsworth's and Captain Jakson's.

20 An express went to Ticonderoga a small party of men went down the lake with Major Skeen .

21 Wet day Captain Whiting inlisted carpenters to work in the fort Captain Jefford's company arrived here.

22 Sunday. Nothing remarkable.

23 This was a wet day, Major Roggers arrived here from his scout at Saint Johns, brought in twenty-five prisoners.

24 A man of the Massachusetts received hundred lashes for his insolent language to his ensign the cremonal's name was John Bunker (of York).

25 A party was sent down the lake to bring in the remainder of the prisoners five companies of the Massachusetts troops arrived here

26 Orders that a party should be sent down to Putnum's Point for cutting timber

27 Colonel (Joseph) Ingersoll, Major (Caleb) Willard, three captains, nine subalterns, nine serjeants and 300 of the Massachusetts troops embarked for Putnum's Point—a return of the Gunners was made—a rainy day.

28 Captain Jonas's company with a detachment from the Massachusetts and Rhode Islanders was ordered away as gunners and marched down to the water side and encamped.

29 Sunday. The three whale boats came in that went down the lake after ye prisoners.

30 A command consisting of one captain, two subalterns, four serjeants and a hundred provintials to proceed to the saw mills with sixteen battoes for provisions in eight of them and eight to be loaded with boards. Two men carried out of camp sick with the small pox.

1st July. A party consisting of two subs four non-commissioned officers and fifty-eight provintials, were ordered down the lake to relieve the same number of regulars on board the sloops. Leonard Butterfield and Jonas Butterfield (both of Dunstable) went out of Captain Whiting's company.

2nd. Orders that no sutler should (sell) any liquor after gunfire. Ensign Emerson Willcutt and (Joseph) Hatfield (both of Brookfield), joined Captain Whiting's company.

3 Captain Silas Brown with a hundred men were sent up to join Colonel Ingersoll at Putnum's Point. George Morris of the market and the ranging sutler had their liquor stove for disobeying orders. Orders that the sutler of the rangers and George Morris of the market that had their liquor stove this day to quit Crown Point immediately, if they hereafter are found in the camp or in any post between this and Albany they will be whipt and drummed out—a very smart thunder shower this evening.

4 One of Captain Bailey's men was carried out of camp with the small pox. Brigadier Ruggles arrived here this day. Peter Jones (of Boston) of Captain Martin's company received fifty lashes for refusing to do his duty and for insolent language confined by Captain Abiel Peirce

5 A bark canoe was brought in with six Indians, and said they came from General Johnson across the woods from Oswego. and had a French scalp.

6 Sunday. Sent the six Indians in a battoe with a serjeant and seven men to the landing place at Ticonderoga

7 A party consisting of one captain, two subalterns, four serjeants and hundred men of the provintials were sent up to the saw mills with sixteen battoes for provisions and to return again as soon as possible— this was a very hot day

8 This morning about sunrise a party of the rangers being at work was fired upon by the enemy and in ye scrummage one man was killed and six wounded. It lasted about half an hour— Major Roggers with a party of the rangers and light infantry went in pursuit after them. Being regimented Captain Whiting's company comes into the 2nd battalion in Brigadier (Timothy) Ruggles's regiment commanded by Lieutenant Colonel Ingersoll moved and pitched our tents in Regimental order

9 Major Roggers came in with the party but could find nothing of nor any sines of them.

10 One of the provintials received hundred lashes for neglect of duty.

11 A man received fifty lashes for using the word to one of his sergeants "dam ye to hell" and wishing him there.

12 A man of ye Massachusetts troops received five hundred lashes for inlisting twice and deserting afterwards

13 Sunday. One of the regulars was confined to our quarter guard by one of the Provintial officers for his misbehaviour to him and passing the sentry without order,—whereupon immediately a mob was raised by the regulars and came to reprieve the prisoner at the guard house and knocked down the sentries at the guard house dore and let out ye prisoner— whereupon immediately the piquet was all raised and pursued them and fired two guns upon them took some prisoners—the Rhode Islanders caught the prisoner.

14 This morning four of Captain Jenks's men confined by their captain for forging orders against him and ill treatment— was brought to the post one received 250 lashes, one 150, one 50 the other was set free by the Brigadier.

15 An exceeding dry time for ye season one of ye regulars was flogged for striking one of the provintials at ye spring and braking two of his ribs.

16 Nothing remarkable happened this day, the train threw several bombs to p(r)actise at a mark.

17 A dull time for news in camp

18 A very smart thunder shower was drawed up and after role calling had prayers of one of ye provintial chaplins which was ye first prayers we have had since we came in camp

19 Major Hawks's party arrived here—twelve of which joined Captain Whiting's company that was draughted from it at Albany.

20 Sunday Began to do serjeant major's duty.

21 The brig and sloop came in from Ticonderoga.

22 150 men were sent to Ticonderoga in battoes for provisions, came back this evening.

23 A boat came in from ye sloops.

24 A rainy day. two sloops came in from ye advance guard.

Captain Hutchings arrived here from General Amherst and joined the rangers.

25 A detachment of 400 regulars, provintials and rangers excluding officers were sent to the saw mill in battoes for provisions.

26 A rainy day.

27 Sunday. Had preaching.

28 No extraordinaries happened this day.

29 A command of about eighty provintials and forty Rhode Islanders excluding officers were sent towards No 4 with two days' provisions in order to meet ye New Hampshire Regiment who by intelligence of two men that came from them and arrived here last night was like to suffer for want of provision.

30 A party of one serjeant and twenty-four men were sent to Ticonderoga for sheep.

31 The party came in with ye New Hampshire Regiment and encamped near the grenadiers' encampment.

August ye 1 Very wet in ye morning, orders that all the boats to be delivered to the respective regiments of regulars, as well as provintials in order to examine the same and fit them better if possible, notwithstanding no orders yet arrived determining the time of embarcation, therefore the following detachment was ordered out to fit and secure them, *viz*. six captains, nineteen subalterns, fifty-two serjeants and 523 men from all the corps. Lieutenant Wm. Holdin arrived here.

A follower of the army received 1000 lashes[5] for stealing and was drummed out of camp with a halter about his neck and his crime wrote and pind upon his brest and so sent to Albany.

2 A detachment consisting of 1 captain, three subalterns, five serjeants and 111 seamen of the Massachusetts and Rhode Islanders to embark on board his Majesty's brig the *Duke Cumberland*.

---

5. This number seems incredible, but the figures are perfectly plain. See also entry of August 10.

3 Sunday A party consisting of 200 men excluding officers went with Major Burk over to ye other side ye lake to cutting timber. Ye New Hampshire Regiment past muster before Lieutenant Small.

4 Peter Linsey (of Boston) of Captain Martin's company received 250 lashes for making an attempt to desert. Richard Gattoway[6] (of Boston) of ye aforesaid company received forty lashes for making a disturbance in Mr Hubby's markee and using ye adjutant with insolent language. One of Captain Hart's men received twenty lashes for refusing to go on duty when ordered by his serjeant.

5 A detachment of hundred men was sent to falling trees towards the block houses with Major Hawks—a man carried out of camp with ye small pox.

6 An express came in from General Amherst to Colonel Haverland, also money to pay off the soldiers' part of their wages.

7 Making ready as fast as possible for an embarcation in order for a trial at Isle au Noix or St. Johns.

8 Orders that the army should hold themselves in readiness for an embarcation at the shortest notice. Major Burk's party came in, and Colonel Ingersoll's from Putnam's Point. Three Indians seen on the other side the lake

9 Several detachments was ordered out this day. Forty men of the Massachusetts joined the artillery. Was in the greatest preparation for an embarcation

10 Sunday. Richard Galloway of Captain Martin's company received 900 lashes for fighting, striking and threatening officers and for abuseful language to them &c. The recrutes came in *viz* Colonel Whitcombe's regiment from ye Massachusetts. An express came in from the brig. Orders that the army should strike their tents tomorrow morning and embark in order to pass Lake Champlain, also how they should proceed, and in what form they should go and in what position they should form to land.

---

6. See entry under August 10, where the name is written Galloway.

11 Loaded our boats with five barrills of flour and three of pork, and upon ye sygnal of a gun from the artillery park the general beat, upon which the army struck their tents and put them on board their battoes, and upon the sygnal of a second gun, the army assembled and marched down to their boats and embarked— But not put off from ye shore and the sygnal was made on board the *Leginear* rideau (radeau) upon which the army set sail—But with a contrary wind.

The number of vessals and boats the fleet consisted of is as follows *viz*. One brigenteen, four sloops, three rideaus (radeaux), three prows, two large boats, 263 batteaus large and small, forty-one whale boats, twelve canoes and proceeded about six miles and landed on the west shore, advanced a piquet according to former order and encamped.

12 Embarked in ye morning set sail with a contrary wind and came about eight miles and came too in Butten Mole (Button Mould) Bay and encamped on ye shore.

13 This morning a council was held upon Captain Shores and he was broke and sent back to Crown Point for his misconduct in times past, although the sentence was past upon him before, yet it was not revealed to him till now.

Set sail but the wind still holds very contrary and we came about ten miles and encamped near Legenier (Ligonier) Bay Harbour on the west side the lake.

14 We set sail with a very fair wind but stormy and very ruff wether and arrived at Schyler Island which day's sail was about thirty odd miles and on our voyage this day one man was drownded another accidentally shot himself and tis to be feared very mortally wounded.

Had further intelligence of several boats being cast away and the men lost some of which belonged to ye rangers

15 The wind still holds fair but not so boistrious as yesterday. Yet several boats was cast away and some stove on the shore we came about thirty-five miles and encamped on Isle la Motte.

Orders came how the army should proceed—and in what form they should go—and how they should form to land,—and above all it is highly recommended that we should pay no regard to popping shots from ye shore and that no man should fire out of any boat. Also it is recommended that nothing be done in a hurry which will prevent confusion. Cleaned our fire locks, and compleated ye men with ammunition.

16th About 3 o'clock this morning we all embarked and set sail for Isle au Noix which was about ten miles and came and landed on the East shore about 1 o'clock within about two miles of the fort without any great matter of mollistation. The French fired several shots at our rideau (radeau) and sloops and our people fired some at them. We encamped and made a brest work, half ye men up and ye other to lay on their arms this night, we hove several bombs in the night.

17 Sunday. Pritty calm this morning about firing. About 8 o'clock Captain Clagg belonging to the train on board of a small artillery rideau, bore away towards the fort whose orders was to go on till fired upon,—accordingly he did and by a six pounder had both his legs shot off— after which ye captain soon died,— five more wounded, one of which had both his legs shot off, the other four— one leg apiece—soon after one or two died Corporal Majory of Captain Bailey's company was broke and whipt 300 lashes for denying his duty. Kept on fortifying clearing a road, &c. very calm and but little firing the remainder of this day— one man carried to Crown Point with ye small pox.

18 Fired several cannon at the men at work opposite ye fort, but to little purpose also fired upon our rangers and killed one with their small arms in a boat
Pritty calm and but little firing
Began to build our battries for bomb and cannon.

19 Moved our encampment and encamped opposite the fort, in about half a mile of it, in a very thick place of woods and made a brest work. Both in front and rear was fired upon from the fort but received no damage.

20 A deserter came from the French and resigned himself to our guard this morning about daybrake. He gives us an account that there is about 1500 men in the fort and that they are short of ammunition and have but nine pieces of cannon in the fort. Fired very hot on our men at work at the battries. Detachments were sent to work at the battries all night. This was a rainy day.

21 Landed part of our artillery, was fired upon at the battries—had seven or eight men wounded—two false alarms in the night, one of which was a little before daybrake and our men fired from one end of ye lines to the other but no enemy was near to oppose us.

22 A man carried out of camp with ye small pox. kept on building and repairing the battries as fast as possible in order for a warm reception. Three French prisoners was brought in that was taken between St Johns and Montreal, for which the men that took them had fifty guineas reward—ye party consisted of a serjeant and six men.

23 Opened three of our battries at 3 o'clock this afternoon upon the sygnal of a gun from the artillery and which time the drums and fifes beating a pint of war from one end of ye lines to the other,—after which we blazed away very smartly from our battries—one man was killed and sculpt by ye the Indians, two more killed and two wounded.

24 Sunday. Began to erect a new battrey below ye fort to prevent the French going off, as we perceived they was making ready for an escape. The party that was at work at the new battrey was fired upon from the fort by their cannon—wounded fifteen of our men,—some tis to be feared mortally. This was a lowry wet day.

25 Cleared off—we blazed very hot upon them all this forenoon. Took three vessals from them *viz* one rideau, one topsail schooner and a sloop and thirty odd men on board of them who gave intelligence that there was about 150 men killed this day by our cannon bombs and small arms—and that there was a regiment of brigades joined them had one man killed at ye lower battrey this day with a cannon ball from ye French. He belonged to Captain Barrons's company. Made a trial last night to cut away the boam that the French had fixed across the lake from the fort to the east shore to prevent our shipping going past the fort.

26 Orders for a number of men to go on board the prize vessals consisting of 165 men, officers included, to go voluntiers from the provintials, also for forty-one men to list out of the Massachusetts regiment to join Major Roggers as rangers in lieu of that number of the New Hampshires that was not fit for rangers. Thompson Maxwell, of Captain Whiting's company listed a ranger and Serjeant (Jonas) Parker (of Chelmsford), Samuel Treadwell (of Littleton), Thaddeus Read (of Westford) and John Robinson (of Dunstable) went on board the prizes.

27 This was a thick foggy morning and the more so by the smoake of the cannon and bombs—both of the French and English— for they played very smartly on both sides, but ye French threw no shells at us, but the cannon cracked as though the heavens and earth was coming together for chief of the day.

A ball from the enemy came through one of our amberzoers (embrasures) and into a magazean where was many shells and cartridges— and set it on fire and brew it up broke about twenty shells which killed two men and wounded two more very bad,—one of those that was killed belonged to the Massachusetts, the other to the 17th Regiment. The French played very smartly with their cannon all this day.

28 Last night the French deserted the fort, took of all their baggage which they could carry on their backs and made their escape off as fast as they could. Left a number of their sick and wounded but the exact number I cannot tell. About twenty French regulars came and resigned themselves. We took posses-

sion of their fort and hoisted King George's colours on the walls, sent our flour to be baked in their ovens, had French bread and pork to our allowance. Seven of the rangers pursued the army and took one from their rear and got considerable plunder. Four of the Light Infantry brought in two French prisoners that they took near St Johns. Began to embark our artillery and fix as fast as possible in order to make a push upon St Johns.

As to the situation of ye Isle Au Noix it is situate and lying very low in the centre of the lake and has a very strong fortress on it and is very strongly picqueted in all round and contains about — acres though very low and swampy great part of it and chiefly cleared up.

29 Embarked all our artillery that was thought necessary to carry along with us. Orders that boats should be took over to the island and loaded with five barrills of provisions and brought back again to the side next our encampment and that ye tents should be struck tomorrow morning half an hour after reveillie beating and the army to be ready to embark when ordered.

30 Struck our tents this morning and put them with our baggage on board the battoes after which the army soon embarked and set sail with a fare wind for St Johns. Our orders was to keep in the same position as former ordered and to form a line to land in the same manner when ordered, which was to be told us and which shore we should land on. Left all our sick and wounded at the island with officers and soldiers draughted from the provintials in order to keep the fort.

When ye front of our army came in sight of St Johns Fort, and the grand *Jeoble* (*Diable*) that we took at Isle au Noix had fired one or two shots at it, the French set it all on fire and made their escape as fast as possibly they could. Major Roggers with his men overtook some of them and had a scrummage with them. Lost two men and one or two more wounded one of which was Lieutenant Stone who was shot through the foot. The rear of our army landed about 2 o'clock and encamped.

31 Sunday. Major Roggers took and brought in seventeen prisoners amongst which was one major and 1 captain of ye French army. Orders came last night for the army to throw up a brest work in the front of our encampment, accordingly we began it this morning. Soon after which orders came to the contrary. St Johns is situate on ye west side the lake (river) and according to appearance it was a pritty strong fortress and butifully situated before it was consumed.

There is considerable cleared ground but few improvements. Orders came that the army should strike their tents tomorrow morning a quarter after revallie beating in order to go to St Therese. Colonel Haverland sent a packit to General Murray very cold for the time of year.

1st September. Struck our tents according to orders and put them on board. Orders that as the army is now going into the inhabitant part of the country, therefore it is ordered that none of the inhabitance are plundered or ill used on any pretence. Whoever are detected disobeying this order will be hanged and that we should take nothing without being regularly paid for this is done to induce the inhabitance to stay in their villages, and good usage will prevent their men from joining their French army. The army embarked about 3 o'clock in the afternoon and set sails and as our battalion is the rear guard we came about two miles to the head of the falls and encamped but ye regulars and those in ye front went down ye falls and arrived at St Therese this night.

2 Set out this morning and came down ye falls without much difficulty and arrived at St Therese which is about six miles from St Johns. Here was on the west side the lake a little snug fortress before it was consumed but there was the stockade and pikets standing, and a beautiful little trench round it—here we encamped on the west shore and began to throw up a brest work at the front of our encampment Major Roggers brought in two French prisoners.

3 This was a wet day, we finished our breast work. Here was two or three French families who came in and traded with us and past and repast without any mollistation they exchanged green peas and other comodities for salt pork and salt which was very scarce among them and hard to be got—bought horses from them and had their assistance in drawing our artillery.

4 Cleared off—a detachment of about 200 men were sent to Fort Chambelle (Chambly) in order to lay siege and take it with some artillery— accordingly this day about 2 o'clock in the afternoon they surrendered only at ye discharge of two cannon and two shells being hove into ye fort. They sent in this night about 12 o clock seventy odd French prisoners.

5 A detachment of 400 men were sent down to join them at Chambelle. A detachment consisting of one captain, four subalterns, five serjeants and sixty rank and file took ten battoes and set out for ye Isle au Noix for provisions. A party of Captain Hazen's rangers came in with an express from General Murray they left the army last night in about twelve miles from Montreal—some French officers came in with them with horses.

6 A detachment was sent to meet those at St Johns that went to the Isle au Noix yesterday for provisions and meet them and returned here with ye provisions. All the French and wagon they could raise were set to carrying the provisions to Chambelle all this day and have been three trips and seem to be very cheerful in serving their new master. The battoes was all sent to the island opposite the stockaded fort and moored of in the stream—drew six days' provisions.

7 *Sunday* Orders came and the army marched for Montreal excepting the sick and them we left on the island. Some was sent to Chambelle. The French carried our baggage and artillery with their carrages and horses we marched to Chambelle which is four miles from thence we marched till about 10 o'clock at night and encamped in the woods as to the situation of Chambelle and the fort it is finely situate on the south side the River Surrell (Sorel)—and a little snug fortress wholly built with stone and lime, and many fine settlements round it. One thing more I

shall just remark which is something strange though of but little consequence which is that there was ice at Chambelle near eight inches thick which has been since last winter.

8 We marched and arrived at Montrol which is about twenty-five miles from Chambelle and encamped on the east side the River St Lawrence opposite the city of Montreal which was surrendered to General Amherst this very day. Here was General Amherst's army encamped on the west side the river above the town, and General Murray's army on the same side encamped below the town. But the town surrendered without much bloodshed for I believe they thought it was but little worth their while to stand any rangle with us General Amherst's army had a spat with the Light Horse about fifteen miles above the city of Montreal opposite the town of the Cocknawagon (Caughnawaga) Indians, but received but little or no harm from them.

On our march from Chambelle to Montreal there was very fine settlements all the way and very civer usage we received from them; The town of Deprare lies on the east side the river about six miles from Montreal. The French treat us on our march with utmost civelity. Moreover our army was very cautious in not abusing any of them or their substance. General Amherst returns the troops under his command abundance of thanks for their so strictly observing his orders.

9 A man belonging to Captain Bailey's company died very sudden after he had eat his dinner.

As to ye situation of Montreal ye city lyeth on the west side ye river and is very butifully situated close along upon ye water—and the suburbs or other settlements lay up and down the river for many miles in length—and a very butiful level place as ever I saw, and appears to have many very fine farms on both sides the river and fine churches.

10 Orders came that the provintial troops proceed as fast as possible to Crown Point under ye command of Brigadier Ruggles. Accordingly the army marched but the sick was sent in battoes by water to Chambelle where they was to meet the army. I being unable at this time to march went by water, so we set sail ten battoes of us and came down the river about six leags and landed and tarried all night at a French village and they used us very cively.

11 We set sail this morning with a fair wind and a very brisk gale and came to a place called Surrell (Sorel) where we took in an English prisoner that had been two years with them this Surrell lyeth fifteen leags below Montreal, here the River Surrell empties itself into ye River St Lawrence. St Lawrences River from Montreal to this place runs a N N: East pint, and all the way upon both sides the river there is very fine villages and churches. We set sail up the River Surrell and came five leags and encamped. St Franciways (François) lies five leags below Surrell.

12 Here we took in a little girl of five years of age, (a daughter of the Widow Johnsons that was taken with her but was parted) and brought it along with us, and came about six leags and encamped.[7]

13 Set out and came up the river about four leags and arrived at Chambelle where we joined the army again who lay there waiting for us, here we put our baggage into wagons and marched to St Therese and encamped.

14 Sunday Embarked and came to St Johns where Samuel Herrin of Captain Martin's company was very much hurt by his powder horns catching a fire full of powder about his neck. Embarked and set out with a very contrary wind and arrived at ye Isle au Noix and encamped, this was a wet night.

15 Took in our sick people, and left a detachment, Colonel Thomas tarried here to keep the fort: And we set out but the wind still holds contrary and encamped on the west shore.

---

7. Susanna Johnson, daughter of James and Susanna Johnson, who was captured with her parents by the Indians at Charlestown, N. H., on August 30, 1754. At this time she was ten years old, but her mother was not a widow.

16 Set sail with a fair wind and came about thirty leags and encamped on the east shore.

17 Set sail, but a very foggy morning and came about four miles and arrived at Crown Point and encamped on our old encamping ground.

18 400 men was detached and sent to work on the other side ye lake under the command of Major Burk. A number of men sent for fatigue.

19 The New Hampshires threaten to desert for which reason all the serjeants of the provintials was ordered as a guard all night.

20 The rangers arrived here from Montreal in order to take battoes down the lake for the regulars to come in— very cold for the season.

21 Sunday. Nothing remarkable.

22 The rangers set off down the lake in battoes to fetch the regulars over.

23 The Royals arrived here this night.

24 Nothing remarkable happened this day.

25 Very rainy last night and today. The grand *Deoble* arrived here this morning.

26 Men carried out of camp with the small pox more or less everyday.

27 A very sickly time in camp.

28 Sunday. A detachment of provintials and rangers was sent to the saw mills in battoes for provisions.

29 A very cold storm, a very sickly and dying time, fatiguing very hard. A party was sent to Ticondaroga.

30 A party was sent to Ticondaroga. The rangers joined their respective corps

Oct 1st A party was sent to Ticonderoga or saw mills.

2 Some regulars arrived here from Montreal. One of the provintials received hundred lashes for deserting a fatiguing party.

3 Colonel Haverland arrived here with a number of regulars.

4 Sir William's men arrived here that came with General Amherst. A mighty discord amongst the regulars this night disputing who had the best right to a woman and who should have the first go at her—even till it came to blows, and their hubbub raised all most the whole camp.
Some men deserted from the provintials this night.

5 Sunday. Had preaching. Nothing remarkable.

6/7 Major Schean set off in a whale boat for Montreal with a serjeant and eight provintials to carry two French ladies down there.

8 Some men deserted from ye provintials.

9 Some of the deserters was brought back and confined to the Pervoo Guard

10 A number of sick was sent home by the way of Albany. Men die very fast in the hospitle.

11 Nothing remarkable.

12 Sunday. Had preaching. The small sloop arrived here from St Johns. Very pleasant for the season.

13 Nothing strange.

14 General Amherst arrived here from Montreal this evening.

15 A sickly time and many die.

16 More men was added to the works until all got on duty. Nine of our provintial deserters inlisted with the regulars in the Inniskilling Regiment, to clear themselves from other punishment.

17 A man of Captain Martin's received hundred lashes for insolent language to his officer and persisting in it after he was confined and calling his officer a black guard.

18 Nothing remarkable.

19 Sunday. Very rainy and cold.

20 Two sloops arrived here from the Isle au Noix.

21 All the sick was viewed by Mr Mun Row.

22 Nothing remarkable.

23 A large number of invalids was sent home by the way of No 4 (Charlestown, New Hampshire.)[8]

24 More sick was sent home by the way of Albany.

25 Two men carried out of camp sick with the small pox.

26 Sunday All the rangers was sent home only Captain Ogden's company. Fifty of them went by No 4, and the rest by the way of Albany.

27 Wm. Matthews of the New Hampshire regiment was sentanst 500 lashes for mutiny and disobedience of orders which was proved against him, and to receive them this day before the mounting of the Guards this morning: 100, at Whitmore's, 100, at the Inniskilling, 100, at ye Massachusetts, 100, at ye Rhode Islanders, 100, at the New Hampshire regiment— and to be drummed out of the army with a halter about his neck— and to be set over on the other side the lake with provisions to carry him to No 4. A surgeon was also to attend. Accordingly the prisoner was brought to the post to receive his punishment and received twenty odd lashes— and was taken with fits that he dropped for dead— that they could not proceed to give him his punishment so the prisoner was conveyed to the guard

28 General Amherst went to winter quarters. Cold wether comes on a main.

---

8. At the period of the French and Indian War the four townships on the east bank of the Connecticut River, before they received their names, were numbered in their geographical order, and known by their numbers alone. They come now within the state of New Hampshire, township No. 1 being known as Chesterfield; No. 2, as Westmoreland; No. 3, as Walpole; and No. 4, as Charlestown.

29 Fatigues are very hard, to that degree we cannot compleat the parties required.

30 Colonel Thomas with a detachment that was left at the Isle au Noix arrived here this day.

31 A very tedious time for colds and coughs in camp.

November 1st. Finished raising the new wooden barrack in the new fort of 120 feet in length.

2 Sunday Nothing remarkable happened.

3 Colonel Willard set sail in order for home. Colonel Ingersoll sent part of his baggage.

4 I took sick with a tedious cold.

5 Gun powder treason (Guy Fawkes's day.)
A mighty firing throughout the camps this night. a corporal was sent with a file of men through the lines to patrol the camps in order to confine the men that fired.

6 and 7 Nothing remarkable.

8 Dull lowry wether and looks like a storm of rain.

9 A very rainy day Sunday.

10 Fired twenty-one cannon in honour to the day it being King George's birthday.

11 The sick was all drawed up and viewed by Mr Munrow

12 A large number of invalids sent home by the way of No 4.

13 A number of the feeblest of the invalids was sent home by the way of Albany.

14 A snow storm began last night and snowed about three inches deep, after which is tedious cold blustering wether. Twenty-seven cannon was fired

15 As the carpenters was shingling the stone barrack one of the stages broke and three men fell from the roof and was very much bruised. A party was sent to Ticonderoga for flour.

16 Sunday Orders that all the carpenter should return in all their tools tomorrow and was paid off for their work the same day. A party was sent to Ticonderoga for flour. Captain Page with sixty men set off for No 4.

17 Orders that the Massachusetts and Rhode Islanders should strike their tents tomorrow morning at day brake and return them in to the commissary; and march to Ticondaroga where we are to receive provisions to carry us to No 4. this was joyful news to us, as the weather was then cold. Brigadier (Timothy) Ruggles with his attendance marched for home by the way of No 4.

18 We struck our tents according to order and began our march for Ticondaroga (Lieutenant Colonel Ingersoll took the command of the first and second battalion's) and we arrived there the same day and drew eight days' provisions to carry us to No 4. and was carried over the lake and encamped on the other side Captain Whiting set sail for Albany.

19 We began our march through the woods.

23 Sunday Arrived at the Connecticut River about sunset and was ferried over and encamped on the other side.

24 Marched into the town of No 4. where the regulars abused some of our men we was drawed up; and drew allowance and every man took their own way home this was a wet day.

25 Two men that was confined for burying a man alive in No 4 woods received their punishment, one received 500 lashes, the other 100.

Set out from No 4. and came eighteen miles and encamped in the woods till the moon arose and then set out and came to Keen about daybrake; which is thirty miles from No 4.

26 Tarried here till afternoon and came about ten miles and encamped till the moon arose; and then set out and arrived at Lanlord Elexander's in Dublin where we slept till day this was a very snowy night.

27 Set out and came to Peterborough and tarried at Mr Swan's this was a rainy day.

28 Set out and came to Townshend and tarried all night at Jonas Stevens's.

29 Set out and arrived at Groton.

And blessed be God who has preserved me in health this campaign also who has covered my head in the day of battle and returned me in health to my friends again.

Appendix 1

Orders

The following orders, found on loose sheets, have since been placed in the *Diary*, where they originally belonged. One sheet or more is gone, which will account for the abrupt beginning:

. . . . company's, and will send in a return of what ammunition they want that they may receive carabine ball, powder, paper and thread to make up thirty-six rounds compleat each man.

The provoss guard to be reduced to a corporal and of four men

The 2nd battalion Royal Highland Regiment and Montgommery's to receive three days' provision which will compleat them to the 27 inclusively.

Allexander Donaldson

Adjutant

2nd battalion R. H Regiment and of the day

Albany

May ye 25

After orders
Parole Crown Point

The twelve companies of the Massachusetts troops encamped to receive provisions tomorrow morning at five o'clock to the 29th inclusively

Monday May ye 26th Parole, Rockinggum.

Tuesday May ye 27th Parole, Dartmouth

CAMP NEAR ALBANY
PAROLE YORK SHEIR
THURSDAY MAY YE 29TH

The companies of Montgommery's regiment to march tomorrow morning at 5 o'clock, they will receive their wagons in proportion to their number allowed to carry camp equipage and baggage to Schenactada by applying To Colonel Bradstreet, All the men on duty of that regiment to be relieved this evening and their colours to be lodged in the fort in the same manner as those of the Royal. Major Campbell will receive his orders from the general.

The order given the fifth of may last year at Albany, relating to the grenadiers and light infantry telling of the battalions and posting of officers the serjeants taking fire locks instead of holbords.

And only one drummer being allowed each company the rest put in the ranks.

No women being permitted to go with the regiment or to follow them.

The method of marching the regiments are to practice the orders for the front and flanque and rear and flanque. Platoons are to be all the duty observed this campaign, and as more baggage then is absolutely necessary for the officers is an encumbrance to officers and men and must be an obstruction to an army in this country. Each officer must take a small tent, blanket, bear skin and port mantle, they will take no sashes into the field. The regiments that have gorgats will wear them when on duty, and each officer will take care that the men don't load themselves with any thing more then is necessary.

A Koknawago (Caughnawaga) Indian is suspected to be strolling about the town or camp, every officer or soldier who sees any Indian who is not known or cannot give an account of himself will bring him to head quarters. The Massachusetts troops to receive four days' provisions to the second of June inclusive. A return of the state of each company to be given in immediately.

May ye 29th

REGIMENTAL ORDERS

The commanding officer of each company in camp will take care that no strong spirits even cyder are sold by the soldiers nor small beer, unless liberty first obtained from the quarter master.

The role of each company to be called every morning in the presence of a commissioned officer at six o'clock, and at sun set.

Whatever soldier shall be found easing himself in camp will be severely punished. The New York, New Jersey and Rhode Island troops will receive provisions to compleat them with what they have already to the second of June inclusive.

GENERAL ORDERS
PAROLE ALBANY
FRIDAY MAY YE 30TH 1760

The court martial ordered this morning to set at the orderly room so soon as the prisoners is marched in for the trial of the soldiers of Montgommery's accused of burning Mr Tinbrook's[1] out house.

Mr Graham President: Captain Montereef Deputy Judge Advocate, all evidence to attend in case the court martial should not be over by the time Sir Allen McLain's com-

---

1 See *postea*, where the name is written TimBrooks.

pany marches. Which company is to march at two o'clock this afternoon, the evidences a corporal and six men to march the prisoners.

The commanding officers of the companies of Montgomery's regiment having desired to take their colours into the field they are to take them accordingly. all the regiments are immediately to clear their men to the twenty fourth of Apriel. Afterwards at the end of every two months agreeable to former orders. One sergeant, two corporals guard of six men each, are to be posted by Lieutenant Coventry along the fence which runs at the bottom of the hill to Holland House; to prevent that fence being destroyed and the cattle gitting out. Two sergeants and thirty-six men to be ordered from the provintials for the service of the scows and to remain till further orders.

AFTER ORDERS

Captain Baker's, Captain Hawkton's, and Captain Plats's companies of the Second New York Regiment to be compleated with arms according to the returns given in this afternoon by applying to Colonel Williamson tomorrow morning at five o'clock.

The First and Third Regiments of New York to be compleated with arms tomorrow morning according to the returns given in by applying to Colonel Williamson.

The First Regiment to receive theirs at half after five. The Third at six o'clock.

GENERAL ORDERS
PAROLE BARLIN
SATURDAY MAY YE 31ST 1760

The field officers of the provintial troops who are arrived here, and have commissions to send a return of their ranks, and dates of commissions to the adjutant general at orderly time.

Colonel Thomas or officer commanding the Massachusetts troops will send in a report from what company,s the several detachments of the Massachusetts troops sent up Hudson River, are taken as the companies are not formed in battalions, he will give in this return at five o'clock this evening.

The general will see what provintial troops are in camp, at the head of their encampment at five o'clock this evening they are to be drawn up in two ranks, all those that have arms are to appear with them, and those that have powder horns and bullet pouches will put them on.

A court martial of enquiry consisting of one major and four captains of the New York troops to set at the court house at eight o'clock tomorrow morning to examine into the accusations against Peter McCoy who is confined by Lieutenant Muyncher on suspicion of heaving a man overboard and drowning him.

Lieutenant Colonel Ingallson is to remain here to receive the Massachusetts troops as they come in. Which he will report as they come in— the regiment of 1000 will be allowed provisions, or the four pences in lieu of it, for four women each company, and those of 700— for three women each company.

This allowance to be paid to the women by Lieutenant Coventry at Albany and the commanding officer of each regiment is to send in a list of the women of each company of the regiment who are recommended for this provision, which he will sign and transmit to the major of brigade who will give the list to Lieutenant Coventry and give in their names to the matron of the hospitle, that if they should be required for the attendance of the sick they may attend or otherwise be struck off the allowance.

The general court martial of which Major Graham is president is dissolved

And Donald McKinson private soldier of Montgomery's

regiment tried on suspicion of having maliciously and wilfully set fire to Mr Tinbrooks[2] out house is found not guilty of the crime laid to his charge and is acquited Captain Cameron will take him to join the regiment.

---

2. See *ante*, where the name is written Tinbrooks.

Appendix 2

Captain Farrington's Company

The following "Return of Men," etc., mentioned in the foot-note for June 30, is found among the manuscripts of the Massachusetts Historical Society, given by me, on October 1, 1895. The papers came into my possession from General A. Harleigh Hill, of Groton, Vermont, a descendant of Captain Ephraim Wesson, who more than a hundred years ago carried the name of the Massachusetts town into the Green Mountain region.

The men were enlisted by Captain Thomas Farrington, who raised a company in Groton and neighbourhood, which served during the campaign of 1760. In the copy of the return, here given, I have omitted some of the headings, such as "When Inlisted," "By whom," and "What Regiment." With the exception of James Frye and Philip Barker, both of Andover, who joined a company in Colonel Osgood's command, they were all enlisted in the regiment of Colonel William Lawrence, of Groton. The date of enlistment covered a period extending from February 14 to April 9, 1760. "Barzzealer" (Barzillai) Lew, son of Primus, was a negro, and belonged to a well-known coloured family of that day, somewhat noted for their musical attainments. In early times the sturdy yeomanry of Massachusetts often stood in military ranks shoulder to shoulder with the black man; and it was never thought that this juxtaposition lowered their dignity. The surnames Kemp and Kendall are written "Kimp" and "Kindall," showing how the words then were generally pronounced.

The *Return* is found on two separate sheets, each bearing the endorsements of the mustering officers. There is reason to think that there is still a sheet missing, which made up the complete *Return*.

A Return of Men Inlisted for His Majesty's Service for the Total Reduction of Canada 1760

Men's Names	Where Born	Where Resident	Age	Names of Fathers of son under age and Masters of Servants
Silous Kimp	Groton	Groton	18	Hezekiah Kimp
Sampson Blood	Do	Do	27	
Abijah Parker	Do	Do	17	the Scelectmen
Lemuel Ames	Do	Do	17	William Lawrance
Zachreah Parker	Do	Do	21	
John Gragg	Do	Do	19	Jacob Gragg
Aaron Blood	Do	Do	21	
Joseph Page	Do	Do	20	Joseph Page
John Boyden	Do	Do	25	
Stephen Pirce	Do	Do	21	
James Fisk	Do	Do	22	
Joseph Gillson	Do	Do	21	
William Parker	Do	Do	19	William Parker
Nathaniel Green	Do	Do	18	William Green
Hezekiah Kimp	Do	Do	22	
Robert Blood	Pepperall	Pepperall	25	
John Trowbridge	Groton	Groton	21	
John Erwin Jun.	Do	Do	21	
John Erwin	Do	Do	42	
Andrew McFarland	Do	Do	18	Margrat McFarland
Abel Kimp	Do	Do	17	Hezekiah Kimp
Oliver Hartwill	Do	Do	20	Scelectmen
Jona Boyden	Do	Do	17	Josiah Boyden
Josiah Blood	Do	Pepperall	18	John Shattuck
Abijah Warren	Weston	Groton	22	
William Hubart	Do	Pepperall	18	Sheb. Hubart

Ebenezer Nutting	Groton	Groton	17	Thos Farrington
James Frye	Andover	Andover	20	Colonel James Frye
Philip Barker	Dover	Do	19	Isaac Blunt
Isaac Nutting	Groton	Groton	21	
William Lasley	Do	Do	18	Robert Parker
Jonathan Holden	Do	Do	24	
Ruben Woods	Do	Do	18	Ruben Woods

33

(Endorsed "Farrington's Roll.")

A RETURN OF MEN INLISTED FOR HIS MAJESTY'S SERVICE FOR THE TOTAL REDUCTION OF CANADA 1760

Men's Names	Where born	Where Resident	Age	Names of Fathers of son under age and Masters of Servants
William Brown	Ireland	Stow	31	
Obidiah Perry	Weston	Groton	35	
Josiah Stevens	Townshend	Do	18	Martha Stevens
David Sartill	Groton	Do	33	
Moses Keazer	Haverall	Groton	45	
John Archerbill	Groton	Do	18	John Archerble
William Pirce	Do	Do	17	Elijah Rockwood
Joseph Parker	Do	Do	16	Ephream Ware
Jonas Nutting	Do	Do	16	Scelectmen
Joshua Pirce	Weston	Do	18	Jonas Stone
Benjamin Willson	Groton	Townshend	19	Benjamin Wilson
Nathan Harrington	Lexenton	Shirley	19	Richard Harrington
John Farnsworth	No 4	Groton	18	David Farnsworth
William Farwill	Groton	Do	17	Olever Farwill
Richard Sartill	Do	Do	22	
William Stevens	Stow	Stow	29	
Jabez Kindall	Groton	Pepperall	18	Jabez Kindel
Ephream Kimp	Do	Groton	18	Samuel Kimp
Ebenezer Woods	Do	Pepperall	31	
Josiah Fish	Do	Do	26	

Oliver Shead	Do	Do	21	
William Shead	Do	Do	22	
William Farnsworth	Do	Do	22	
Jonathan Williames	Pepperall	Do	22	
Lemuel Patt	Townshend	Do	18	John Patt
John Avery	Do	Do	17	Edmand Bancroft
Barzzealer Lew	Groton	Do	18	Primous Lew
Oliver Ellott	Do	Do	24	
Henery Willord	Lancester	Do	30	
Solomon Parker	Suresbury	Groton	17	Simon Parker
Peter Gillson	Groton	Do	27	
Abner Turner	Lancester	Do	16	Eliab Turner
James Lasley	Groton	Pepperall	25	
Benjamin Rolf	Do	Do	18	Benjamin Rolf
Stephen Gates	Canterbuary	Litleton	17	Stephen Gates

35

Captain Samuel Jenks' Journal
of the Campaign in 1760

Introduction

At a meeting of the Massachusetts Historical Society, held March 13, 1890, the Reverend Henry F. Jenks communicated a diary kept in 1760, during the French and Indian War, by his great-grandfather. Captain Samuel Jenks, which covers the same period as the diary of Sergeant David Holden, already printed by the Society.[1]

Samuel Jenks was born in Lynn, Mass., March 12, 1732. He learned his trade (that of a blacksmith) from his father, and wrought at it successively in Chelsea (on Point Shirley), where the journal following shows that he was residing in 1760, when he started on the campaign which it records, and in Medford, Newton, where his son William (H. C. 1797, and member of our Society for many years) was born, and in Boston. In the "Boston Directory" of 1789, the first published, his name appears, "Jenks, Samuel and Son, blacksmiths and bellows makers, at the sign of the bellows, Gardner's Wharf, Ann Street"; and in that of 1796, which appears to have been the next one published, his residence is given on Cross Street, where he was known to have been living in 1787, when the same son entered the Boston Latin School. He died at Cambridge, June 8, 1801.

"He was twice," says his son,[2]" engaged in military expeditions, being in the Canadian campaigns of 1758 and 1760, in the latter of which he was the youngest captain in the provincial

---

1. See 2 Proceedings, vol. 4.
2 *N. E. Hist. General Reg.*, vol. 9., July, 1855.

army; and the late Governor Brooks assured me that the instruction which he derived at Medford from my father's experience and military knowledge was of essential service to himself at the opening of the Revolutionary contest."

In the *Mercury and New-England Palladium*, of Friday, June 12, 1801, was published the following obituary:

Died at Cambridge, on Monday, Samuel Jenks, Esquire, aged 70, late of this town, a captain of the provincial service of 1760, and an active officer in the campaign of 1758. In the character of this upright and worthy man were combined those qualities which render piety amiable and virtue engaging. His mind was enlightened and candid. The leisure of a laborious and useful life was employed in furnishing it with various information. Convinced of the truth and importance of the Gospel, he was a rational, sincere, and practical Christian, and experienced in the closing scenes of life that peace of mind and hope of future happiness which it alone can confer. As a friend, a brother, a husband, and a father, he was tender and affectionate. As a citizen, he was blameless, and governed his whole conduct by the strictest rules of equity. He was a lover of order and good government, and an ardent friend to his country. To society he has bequeathed an exemplary pattern of honesty, integrity, and Christian meekness; to his children a rich legacy, the inestimable treasure of an unblemished reputation.

He was buried in Saugus, and his gravestone is but a few steps from the gate in the burying-ground.

Journal of the Campaign in 1760

Point Shirley, *May the 22nd,* 1760. Then set out on a campaign for the total reduction of Canada.

Wednesday, 28th of May. Arrived at Albany to the camp; found my company encamping in good health.

Thursday, 29. Sent a letter home by the post. Received orders to be ready for command up the river and to leave my tent standing.

Friday, 30th of May. Received orders from General Amherst to proceed to Fort Miller with a number of battoes loaded with provisions and a command of fifty men.

Monday, June 2nd , 1760. Onload the battoes at the rifts above Half Moon, and proceed with empty battoes to Still Water.

Tuesday, 3rd June. Received 240 barrels flour and drew two days' allowance to carry to Fort Miller.

Wednesday, 4th June. Arrived at Fort Miller at night and landed the provisions, and am here stationed for the transportation of provisions from hence to Fort Edward.

Thursday, 5th. Drew five days' allowance to bring my men up to the time of others on station draw.

Friday, 6th of June. Captain Smith arrived to relieve me and for me to proceed forward with my own company. This day proud wet, and a sorry party of the Massachusetts troops arrived. We were hurried in transporting the provisions and battoes across the carrying place.

Saturday, 7th . Continued at ye station in gitting over battoes and provisions.

Sunday, 8th. Orders for my company to proceed with the party that is ready for Fort Edward; myself to tary till Colonel Thos arrives for my orders to proceed. This day my company put of in battoes for Fort Edward, and I have received orders to follow them in the first boats.

Monday, June 9th. Imbarqued on board Captain Dunbar's battoe for Fort Edward; arrived there before night; found my company encamped on the plain; went to view the fort, which I think is well built, but not well situated for to stand a siege.

Tuesday, 10th . Received orders to march to Lake George, and marched off about 10 o'clock a. m. in one colum. Arrived at Lake George, and encamped before night.

Wednesday, 11 June. Remained encamped; went to view the works; drew two days' allowance to carry us to Ticondaroga.

Thursday, 12 June. Sent a letter home by Mr Dix. This morning struck our tents, and decamped at revallie beating, then marched down to ye battoes and imbarqued for Ticondaroga. The wind blowing hard a head, we put a shore at a small distance from ye fort on ye east side ye lake; the wind abating, we set off and came to the first narrows on a small island and stopt to cook, having come twelve miles. The land on each side is exceeding mountainous, and abounds with vast number of rattlesnakes; our people killed six or eight on this small island. Then put off, as soon as the rear came up and refreshed themselves, to another island near Sabbath Day Point, and camped.

Friday, 13th June. We got our breakfasts; then the colonel gave orders to put off for Ticondaroga. Got there about three o'clock p. m. and landed, and the colonel went with a small escort to the fort and returned; gave orders for the troops to march and encamped at the saw mill about a mile from ye landing, which was accordingly done; here all the officers that had never been on this land had to pay their entrance.

Saturday, 14th June. Remained encamped at the mills. Here great numbers of the camp ladys came down from Crown Point on their way to Albany; some of them interceding to be taken back. Here we are like to draw arms, having marched all the way hither without. Expect to march for Crown Point tomorrow, having detached Lieutenant Pope and twelve men to tarry at Ticondaroga with Lieutenant-Colonel Miller, who has a detachment of 300 men to stop there.

Sunday, 15th June. This morning we drew our arms and six cartriges a man. After delivering out the arms and ammunition we imbarqued on board battoes, thirty-two in each, for Crown Point; set off, and passed by the fort at Ticondaroga, which is very pleasantly situated on ye Lake Champlain, and commands the Narrows and the entrance of South Bay. Here lay the Great Reddoe and two sloops waiting for a wind to proceed to Crown Point. It being late in the day, we could not reach Crown Point. The colonel ordered the regiment to encamp near a block house, which is two miles from the main fort. The land on each side this lake is level, and looks like good land, and all looks pleasant and agreeable.

Monday, 16th June. Decamped early this morning, and arrived at Crown Point; landed above the fort, and encamped. This day it rained and thundered pretty much in ye forenoon. Went to view the works, which I think, when finished, may be justly styled the strongest place the English has on the continent. Here, I believe, is our station for this campaign, for there is an immense sight of work to be done before these forts are compleated.

Tuesday, 17th June. This morning I was ordered off with 200 men across the lake in order to git some spruce. Captain Brewer of the Rangers went to pilot us; when we got ashore we marched with front, rear, and flank guards. Returned without any molestation from ye enemy; brought a fine quantity of spruce. The commanding officer on the station gave us his thanks for the service we had done.

Wednesday, 18th June. This day I was off duty. At the evening we espied a fire[3] made on the west side the lake about six miles down. Immediately a party and some of our pequit guard was sent in two battoes and a whale boat for to discover who they be. As Rogers is out with a large party tis supposed it is some of his returning.

Thursday, 19 June. This day, Major Skeen, who went out to see what the fire was made for, returned about 9 o'clock a. m., and brought in two of our men that run away from the French; they had been without provisions six day, living on strawberrys and roots. About noon we discovered several boats coming up the lake from toward St Johns, which proves to be some of our people that have been in captivity; there is about 130 in all. They bring us the agreeable news of the French being obliged to raise the siege of Quebec in the greatest confusion, with the loss of 3,500 men, and all their artillery, and all their camp equipage, and that the country is all in confusion.

Friday, 20 June. This day the train are carrying the shot and shells in great numbers out of the fort down to the wharf, in order to ship on board the vessels; and great numbers are at work in preparing cartriges and other necessaries for the expedition which I believe will be formed her against the fortified island and St. Johns. This day I wrote several letters to be ready to send by some of the prisoners that are going home to New England. This afternoon a whale boat was sent off with dispatches to Major Rogers, &c.

Saturday, 21 June. This day proud rainy. We spent the day in our tent writing letters and disputing some points of consequence. At evening we drank to our wives and sweethearts, &c.

---

3. See *Sergeant Holden's Journal*, 2 Proceedings, vol. 4.

Sunday, 22nd June. This day proved very pleasant. I was off duty. Should be glad to have some news from home to amuse myself. No regard is paid in general here to sacred time. This day I heard a band of music at the commanding officers tent while they were dining, which was very delightful, though in my opinion not so seasonable on such days of sacred appointment.

Monday, 23 June. This day was very rainy and wet. I kept in my tent most of the day. Toward night it cleared off. Some of Major Rogers party arrived from a scout. At nine o'clock in ye evening the major came in himself, and twenty-six French prisoners with him, taken about three miles from St. John's Fort. He has destroyed a small pequited fort and several houses, and a great quantity of provisions. This was effected without any bloodshed or firing a gun.

Tuesday, 24. This day fair and pleasant. I had the care of a hundred men to work in the King's Garden, which is the finest garden I ever saw in my life, having at least ten acres inclosed, and mostly sowed and improved. This day one of our pretenders to a commission was whipt a hundred lashes at post for disobeying orders and insolent language.[4]

Wednesday, 25 June. This morning Captain Harris's company came up to ye encampment; brings no news or letters. This day, about 9 o'clock a. m., a flag of truce arrived from Canada. There is a general officer in the flag of truce, and they was sent down directly to General Amherst, who we hear set of three days ago from Shenaetada.[5] I hear, by Captain Harris, that Mr. Samuel Berry is stationed at Fort Edward; is got so far promoted as to have a second lieutenancy with Captain Henry Brown.

Thursday, 26 June. This day I took a quantity of stores of Mr. Forsey in order to supply my men. I received a letter from Boston with Lieutenant Richardson's commission in it. Went directly to the sutlers to wet it, so it might wear well without cracking.

---

4 *Sergeant Holden's Journal* gives the name of John Bunker. 2 Proceedings, vol. 4.
5. Probably Schenectady.

Several battoes arrived here with provision from Ticondaroga. The weather clear and pleasant.

Friday, 27 June. Today Colonel Ingersoll and Major Willard and four captains and 300 men, were sent up the lake in order to cut timber to finish the works.[6] Today I am off duty; went to see the detachment imbarque. This day the prisoner that were sent here by the enemy went off for New England and N. York.

Saturday, 28 June. Today I detached seven men of my company to go in the artillery under the command of Captain Jones. Went out to walk round to see the land; could see where the Indians used to carry our people in order to burn. I am told great numbers of them have been carried there to suffer to satisfy their insatiate love of blood and cruelty. At night we followed the old custom of drinking to wives and sweethearts.

Sunday, 29 June. Today the weather is quite pleasant, a rare thing in this part of the word. I see no regard paid to this day, without it is to put more men on duty. Can hear no news from home at all, no way.

Monday, 30 June, 1760. This day I have the pequit guard. Sent the lieutenant and thirty-six men across the lake to git some bark for the hospital. The weather showery. I wrote a letter home, having an opportunity to send it directly to Boston. Today two men belonging to our troops was carried to the hospital, being taken with the small pox.[7] I am in hopes it won't spread, for all possible care is taken to prevent it, the hospital being two miles off the encampment; and our colonels have not had it; so they will, I trust, take the more care that it don't spread.

Tuesday, 1st July, 1760. This day am off duty. This morning the brig came up the lake from a cruise. She is a fine looking vessel, and it seem much as if I were at home, seeing a brig come in and come to anchor. We are mending the battoes, and every-

---

6. Colonel Joseph Ingersoll and Major Caleb Willard. *Holden's Journal* makes a trifling difference in the numbers sent. See 2 Proceedings, vol. 4.
7. *Ibid.*

thing looks likely we shall move forward in about twenty days. Today my first lieutenant and Sergeant Martin and three privates my company went down the lake to relieve the regular troops stationed down there in the sloops. There went about sixty of the Provincials and Rhode Island troops in the party. Today Ensign Newhall of my company is on duty at drawing timber in to the fort. He has command of eighty men.

Wednesday, 2nd July. Today I have the care of 280 men to work in the fort. Today Joseph Eaton of Captain Hart's company died senseless, and in the evening one of Captain Jackson's men at roll calling answered to his name, but before they had done he was dead. Colonel Willard came to camp today from New England.

Thursday, 3rd July. Today I am off duty; went to view the works. There is a seller here has not obeyed the general orders, but sold his liquors to the soldiers, and several of the regulars got drunk, and one of them broke open a markee and was whipt one thousand lashes. His liquors were seized and taken out of his store, to the number of one pipe of Bristol beer and three quarter casks of wine, and stove to pieces, and all the liquor lost; and another sutler for the like offence had five or six casks of liquors stove in like manner. So we have wine and strong beer running down our street.[8] In the evening we had very sharp thunder and lightning. The clouds run very low. I was never so sensible of the thunder being so nigh in my life. We have rain here almost every other day, otherwise there would nothing grow, for the ground is almost all clay, and in two days' time if it be clear sunshine, it will bake so hard that no grass can grow.

Friday, 4th July, 1760. Today I was ordered to hold a court martial at my tent, myself president, for the trial of Peter Jones a private in Captain Martin's company, confined by Captain Abial Peirce for denying his duty and insolent language. The mem-

---

8. See *Sergeant Holden's Journal* of the same date. One of the sutlers was named George Morris. 2 Proceedings, vol. 4.

bers, being four lieutenants, were assembled. The prisoner was brought, and the crime read. He pleaded ignorance of the facts alleged against him, as also his being in liquor and knew not what he did. Captain Peirce was then called, who proved the fact by Captain Hart, who was present and heard him deny and abuse Captain Peirce. The prisoner's own officer then came and said that the said Jones was very apt to be deprived of his reason by the smallest quantity of spirituous liquor. The prisoner was then sent back to the guard house. The court after having debated and considered on the nature of the crime and the man's constitution, they resolved he should receive fifty stripes on his naked back with a cat nine tails. The result being carried to the commanding officer, he approved of it as just and right. There was myself and two other of the court had never been on court martials; we went and was showed according to custom. This evening at relieving the pequit the said Jones received his punishment. Today Brigadier General Ruggles arrived here from New England.

Saturday, 5th July. This day was very sultry, hot. I took a walk round the encampment. There came in six Oneida Indians,[9] and brought in one scalp. There is a rumour in camp that there is 300 Canada Indians a coming to join us, being discouraged with the bad luck the *Monsieurs* have. I hear likewise that our General Murry at Quebec hangs all without distinction who were in the capitulation last year at the surrender of Quebec, and that have assisted the French at the late attempt on that fortress. Today I heard that Colonel Montgomery has had a skirmish with the Cherokee Indians, and killed hundred of them, and burnt three towns. At night we concluded by drinking to wives and sweet hearts, which is as duly observed here as any of our duty. There is one more of Captain Hart's men dead today. Through God's goodness, I haven't lost one man of my company yet, nor is any of them sick; it is a general time of health in camp. Can hear no news from home. Yesterday was

---

9. These Indians are mentioned by Sergeant Holden, Ibid.

in company with the gentlemen commissioners from old York, who are well acquainted with my relations there, who were all well when they set off.

Sunday, 6 July. Today it is extreme hot. I took a walk about two miles in the wood to see the carpenters; returned and wrote two letters to send home. We have no appearance of any divine worship in our camp, and I can see no difference in regard to the day. I spent most of the day in my tent writing and reading. Ensign Newhall is on duty drawing timber. I hear two of our New England men are dead of the small pox at the hospital, and I hear that the French will give up Montreal without fighting any more. The news about Colonel Montgomery is confirmed.

Monday, 7th July. Took a walk down to the landing. Returned to breakfast, and received a letter from my brother Jenks, dated 9 June, 1760, with the agreeable news of their being all in health at that time. Today I begun to build me a booth, but before it was finished I had orders to move to the right of the encampment, being in the first battalion of Brigadier General Ruggles's regiment, and so must move my booth or loose all my labour. There is eleven companies in the first battalion, and ten in the second. Colonel Richard Saltonstall commands the first battalion under the Brigadier.

Tuesday, 8 July, 1760. This morning we were alarmed about 6 o'clock by the enemy, who fell upon a party of Major Rogers' rangers, just by their encampment on the other side the lake, all in sight of our encampment, and they have killed one on the spot and wounded six more, who are brought over to the hospital. I have been down to see them, and four of them are mortally wounded, two shot through their bodies, and one shot through his head, the other through both thighs; the two others may, with good care, git well. It was a very affecting sight to see the poor creatures lay weltering in their blood and fainting with death in their countenance.[10]

---

10. Cf. *Holden's Journal* of the same date, 2 Proceedings, vol. 4.

Immediately Major Rogers with his rangers ran out of their breast work and pursued the enemy, who are almost all French, but very few Indians among the party. 'Tis supposed there was 300 in their party, and the regular light infantry and several large parties of regulars to intercept them; and a subaltern of our troops and twenty-five men was sent down to the sloops to give them intelligence. It was a bold action, right in plain view of our forts and camps, and but a little way from Major Rogers encampment, and on the same side the lake; we have seen part of the rangers return, but what news I cannot learn. The same day we were settled and regimented, and I am in Colonel Saltonstall's battalion, which is the first in the regiment, commanded by Brigadier General Ruggles. We then struck our tents and encamped on the right of all the Massachusetts troops. Both the brigadiers battalions, Colonel Thos' regiment on the left and Colonel Willard in the centre. Those captains belonging to the first battalion, after our being ranked, all went to the sutlers and drank to our better acquaintance, and then returned, mutually satisfied with our lots; and I am exceedingly rejoiced that it was my lot to fall amongst such agreeable officers.

Wednesday, 9 July. This day am off duty, and have built us a fine booth. At the door of my tent, the weather extreme hot. Took a walk after dinner. Can hear no news in camp, only disputing of rank amongst officers, and whipping sutlers and soldiers. At evening had a letter from Lieutenant Richardson, who is well, but not content with his station. Major Rogers is returned without overtaking the enemy; the wounded men are all alive yet, but I don't think they can live long.

Thursday, 10th July. This day is very sultry, hot. I am off duty, building me another booth. Ensign Newhall is on a court martial. I let the president hold his court at my tent, because his had no booth finished for his convenience. I find this climate vastly hotter than I ever expected. I think it has been much hotter this six or seven days than I ever knew so many together in New

England. Two of the wounded men of the rangers is dead; and Jacob Hallowell, that was wounded in Rogers' fight before, is also dead of his wounds.

Friday, 11 July, 1760. Continues very hot and dry. I am on duty, and Ensign Newhall with me; we were drawing timber out in the wood; have hundred men; and we all carry our arms out since the enemy fell on Rogers's working party. Today I received a letter from my own partner, the only one I have received from her since I left home, dated 8 June, and one from brother Nathan, dated 9 June, with the most agreeable news of their being in health. Lieutenant Pope came up from Ticondaroga, and brought these letters and a number of others from New England. Expect soon to move forward.

Saturday, 12 July, 1760. Continues extreme hot and dry. Today I found that James Casey and Wm Delarue had got orders on the sutler and forged my name to them and taken a considerable up. I immediately sent them under guard, and acquainted Colonel Saltonstall of their crime, who advised me not to send their crime in as forgery, because then they must come to a general court martial and be tried for their lives, and it is death by the martial law for a soldier to counterfeit his officers hand; but told me to send in their crime as ill behaviour and insolent treatment, which I accordingly did, and by that means hope their lives will be saved by trying them by a regimental court martial. Today Mr. Furnance, our brigade major, arrived from New England. I sent two letters for home by Sergeant Fullinton, of Captain Harris's company, who has orders to go to Albany. At night we drank to wives and sweethearts, and so concluded the day. More news of going forward.

Sunday, 13 July. This morning I went to the sutlers and searched all my orders, and found that Henry Bony and Jacob Hasey had orders on him that was counterfeit. I immediately sent the gentlemen under guard, and the Brigadier ordered a court martial on them; but I got him to put it off until tomorrow. Today Lieutenant Richmond confined a regular to our guard for abusive language, and just as our pequit was relieved and gone to their tent, there came about forty of the grenadiers with clubs and forced our quarter guard and took away the prisoner. The guard pursued as fast as possible, and pequit was turned out, and all pursued, and recovered two of the mob; they fired two guns at the grenadiers; I believe wounded some. This affair put the whole of the line in commotion; all the regular regiments were turned out in an instant and drawn up in order, supposing it was an enemy; however, we were soon in quiet. two of the offenders was secured, and will no doubt meet with a punishment adequate to their crimes. I can see no distinction paid to the day except the flags flying and more men put on duty, and almost always some devilish prank played, &c.

Monday, July 14th. This day, about 7 o'clock a. m., there was a regimental court martial held at the presidents tent, who was Captain Chadbourn; after the prisoners was brought and examined, Casey and Delarue confessed they were guilty of the facts, but the other two pleaded not guilty; but Hasey owned he saw Delarue sign his order, but it appeared Bony knew nothing of his signing his. The court sentenced Casey 250 stripes, Delarue 150, and Hasey 50; which the Brigadier approved off as just. At relieving the quarter guard, these fellows was brought forth and received their punishment.[11] I ordered the serjeants to turn out all my company to see them go through the operation, to deter any from such vile practises. I had rather lost twenty dollars than such affairs should a happened in my company. Ensign Newhall has been on command up to Ticondaroga today. Lieutenant Richardson sent of for stores which I sent him. Heard a rumour of Esquire Goldthwaits coming up paymaster of our troops; I fear too good news to be true.

Tuesday, July 15. The weather continues extreme hot and dry. I have the care of a hundred men for to make fachines and gabions and erecting a fachine battery in order to practise the men as

---

11. The record of this and the preceding two days amplifies the account of Sergeant Holden, under date of July 14, 2 Proceedings, vol. 4.

Lord Louden did at Halifax. I had an easy tour, for I went out at 5 o'clock in the morning and returned at 8, and then went out again at 5 in the afternoon and return in at gun firing. We have continual whipping of some or other in the line. Today Colonel Saltenstol told me my friend Esquire Goldthwait was certainly coming up to pay of our troops.

Wednesday, 16 July. Today am off duty. Got sundry of stores of Mr. Hobbey for my company. We had news in camp that there was 12,000 French coming up the lake, and that they had taken our three sloops that are cruising down the lake, camp news, I believe. Today I read a New York paper of the 30 June, and find the news exactly true that ye prisoners brought in here the 19th of June concerning the raising the siege of Quebec. In the afternoon went to see the train practise in throwing shells. They hove twelve in all; it was a pleasant sight to see them flying in the air. Our people has caught two fawns alive in the lake, and there is plenty of them in these parts.

Thursday, 17th July. Today am off duty. The weather continues hot and dry. I spent most part of the day in my tent a overhauling orders and settling accounts, and seeing that my company's tents well barked over the bottom, according to Brigadier General Ruggles order. In the afternoon walked round the camp to pass away time and to divert ourselves. Hear that General Amherst set off from Oneida Lake the 9 instant for Oswago, and expect to move forward in about twelve days from here. Today Ensign Newhall is on pequit.

Friday, 18th July, 1760. Very hot and no signs of rain, which is very much wanted here, for if it continues such weather a few days longer, all the fine gardens we have here will be entirely dried up, and all the fruits perish. This morning Captain Hart and I went to view the fachine battery, which is a most finished and looks very beautiful. Returned and have been calculating how far we are from home, and find it by the best judges 190 miles to Boston by No. 4. So then I am nearer home than when I was at Albany, although I have travelled a 100 miles from Albany. Today the train are practising their mortars in throwing shells, and our troops have drawn six rounds per man in order to fire at a mark. In the afternoon we had a fine refreshing shower. Cleared up and quite cool and pleasant. There was two of the regular officers fought a duel with pistols. They made two trials, but did not wound neither. This evening we was drawn up on the parade and had prayers performed by a chaplain[12] from New England. He is the only one of that cloth that has joined us yet.

Saturday, 19th July, 1760. This morning went to see the train practise throwing of shells. They made several very good shots. Returned and went to view the fachine battery. This day about 500 troops went across the lake to git spruce; nothing material happened. This day there is a post arrived from Oswago. At night we concluded by drinking to wives and sweethearts, which is as constantly observed as any duty we have in camp. Pleasant weather today.

Sunday, 20 July. Today am off duty. It has been my luck as yet not to be on any duty of a Sunday. Today I wrote a letter to send home, and spent most of the day in my tent writing and reading. The weather very hot; much hotter than is used to be in New England. At night we had prayers in the camp. No news from home, which is the scarcest of any thing in camp; for we have ladys enough in town, and they are walking out with the regular officers to take ye evening air every night.

Monday, 21st July. Today I have the care of a party of men to work in the fort drawing the timber up on the walls. Was very agreeably entertained on the works by the company of a regular officer who lately came from captivity in Montreal, and reading the *Spectator*. Towards night the brig[13] came down from Ticondaroga, having been up to clean and grave. The weather pretty pleasant. I have a bad boil on my right wrist, which is very troublesome.

---

12. See *Sergeant Holden's Journal*, 2 Proceedings, vol. 4.
13. See *Sergeant Holden's Journal*, 2 Proceedings, vol. 4.

Tuesday, 22nd July. The large English sloop has come down last night, and all things preparing to proceed down the lake. Went this morning with Captain Hart and Ensign Newhall down to the wharf to see the shipping and the preparations going on. In returning to camp Ensign Newhall is taken very ill with a vomiting. I immediately by his desire got the doctor to come to him, and he has gave him something which I hope by God's blessing will carry off his illness. Went after dinner to view the fachine battery. Rogers's men are practising at shooting at marks. We have very hot dry weather, the days much hotter than in New England, but the nights are as cold as we have in September, for I cannot lay warm in my blanket towards day, but in the day can hardly bear any cloaths on. By the best information I can git we shall move forward in first week in August. We are preparing all things necessary to forward the operations. This evening Ensign Newhall is much better.

Wednesday, 23rd July, 1760.[14] This morning there is a general court martial, held at Brigadier General Ruggles' tent, himself president, for the trial of all prisoners that are brought before them. Lieutenant Richmond of Colonel Thomas's regiment is brought on trial, confined by the commanding officer Colonel Havertin for disobedience of orders. This morning Ensign Newhall is got pretty comfortable again; he has had a very sharp turn, but hope is out of danger of being sick. In the afternoon had a letter from Lieutenant Richardson from on board one of the sloops that are down the lake, with news of their being all well that belong to me I prepared a quantity of stores to send them down, but am informed they are ordered up; so I deferred sending them. The brig has been firing two rounds to clear her guns. The train and rangers and all the troops except the provincials are practising.

Thursday, 24th July, 1760. Today am off duty. Went to see where they have been throwing bombs. They have measured out a 1000 yards, and set stakes at every fifty yards with the

14. See Notes end of *Diary*.

number on them. Here is one of my men that was stationed at Ticondaroga, come up with a setler who has brought up a very fine mistress with him. On their passage they fell into disputes. At length he struck her, which enraged her so that after several fits and efforts jumped overboard. This cooled her courage, for her sweetheart held her under water until she was almost expiring. They then took her in, stript off her cloaths and dressed anew, and so the fray ended. I wish it were the fate of all these sort of ladys that follow the army. She appeared pretty likely and was very well dressed. This day proves rainy, which is very much wanted in this dark corner of the earth. At night two of our sloops came up from a cruise. I hear Lieutenant Richardson is on board one of them.

Friday, July 25th, 1760. Went this morning on board the sloop where Lieutenant Richardson and part of my company is. Found them all in good health. Brought the lieutenant on shore. The news in camp is that General Amherst, attempting to go down a falls, was attacked by the enemy and lost 1000 men and is now coming back to go this way. I likewise heard the French had blown up the fortified island and gone, and that General Murry had laid siege to Montreal, and that it is a established peace at home, &c.

Saturday, July 26th, 1760. This day off duty; the weather rainy. I kept chiefly in my tent. Ensign Newhall remains ill. Lieutenant Richardson on shore, wee all practising drinking to wives and sweethearts, and I am warned this evening to go on command to Ticondaroga tomorrow for provisions. A regular captain commands the whole detachment. Nothing occurred today remarkable.

Sunday, 27th July, 1760. This morning was on the parade at revallies beating for go with the detachment to the mill for provision. It rained pretty much, but the wind is fair. We set off about 7 o'clock a. m.; had a fine gale all the way, but much rain. Got there about noon. There was about 500 in the party. We could not git boats enough for the whole, so came back ten in battoe. We rendavoused at Ticondaroga fort. I went to view the fortifications. They are advantageously built and very strong and pleasantly situated. We all set of again about 5 o'clock p. m. The weather is cleared up quite pleasant and calm. We all made the best of our way for our station. I arrived about nine o'clock at night at my tent. This is the first Sunday I have been on duty up here. There was divine service performed in camp today. But I have not had the luck of hearing one sermon since I left home. I hear today that the recruits raised in our province are on their march. Query, will they arrive before December?

Monday, 28th July. This morning went down to the landing for to see the boats unloaded. The weather is fair, serene, cool, and pleasant, with a fine breeze to the westward. I spent most of the day in walking round the fort landing and places adjacent. The fleet is fitting out with all expedition and makes a very fine appearance. I hope we shall soon pay *Monsieurs* a visit at the Ile aux Noix. No extraordinaries happened today.

Tuesday, 29th July, 1760. Today am off duty. Lieutenant Richardson has sailed again down the lake on a cruise to relieve the other sloop. Today there was a large pekerell found on the shore. It measured four feet five inches in length and weighed, as is reported, 35 lb. Towards night the sloop that was stationed down the lake came up. Most part of this day I spent in walking round the camp and forts. There is a party sent to carry provisions to the Hamshire troops.

Wednesday, 30th July. Today am off duty. Spent most of the day in the tent in writing and posting of my accounts. This afternoon a drove of cattle came from No. 4. At the evening wrote a letter to send home by the drovers. Ensign Newhall is got quite well again. No news from home, although there comes plenty of letters in camp, yet none for me.

Thursday, 31st July. Today wrote letters and made up two packquets for my men to send home to New England. Have spent part of the day with Captain Hart in his tent and several other gentlemen disputing on the carriage and different disposition of the fair sex. This afternoon the Hamshire troops are arrived. They were obliged to quit the road and come forward because they could not git a supply of provisions that way.

Friday, 1st of August, 1760. This morning I awoke and found my tent all flood with water, about four inches over the floor. I got a number of my men to dig a trench to drain off the water. Today have ye care of a party of men to take the number of battoes that are issued to our battalion. We received eighty battoes for all the Massachusetts troops, and brought them to a convenient place and sunk them for to keep them tight, and set a guard over them.

Saturday, 2nd August. Today am off duty. There is about 120 seamen draughted out to go on board the brig[15] and sloops; they are this day sailed on a cruise down the lake. It's said they are to take post at an island seven miles a this side Ile aux Noix, and a rumour prevails that we shall send a 1,000 men down there to encamp till the whole arrives. At evening we followed the delightful custom of remembering wives and sweethearts.

Sunday, 3rd August. 1760. I find tis the Lords Day by the flags flying, as its the only visible sign of the day amongst us. Went to view the Hamshire encampment and the mark that is made to fire cannon shot at. The weather very hot today. Captain Aaron Willard arrived from No. 4. I hear the recruits are on their way up here a this side Albany. Today divine service was performed at our parade by one of our chaplains.

Monday, 4th August. 1760. This morning lowry and rainy. I am off duty today; spent my time in tent writing and reading and posting of accounts. I have twelve of my men detached this morning to go over the lake to cut timber. In the afternoon it cleared up quite pleasant. As I walked out to amuse myself down to the landing and round the encampment, I heard of

---

15. The name of the brig was *Duke Cumberland*. See *Sergeant Holden's Journal*, 2 Proceedings, vol. 4.

the approach of the recruits; hope to have news from home by them. I expect them here this week.

Tuesday, 5th August. I understand that Mr. Farrington has agreed to ride as post to New England, to carry letters at six pence, Yorke currency, a piece; he purposes to make two trips this campaign. I wrote several letters to send by him. I went over the lake to see Rogers's encampment which is very pleasant. There is a fine hospital raised today for our troops. The afternoon spent in walking out, and writing in my tent. Have nothing extraordinary today.

Wednesday, 6 August. 1760. Today am off duty; went to see the artillery practise at firing shot. Today, about noon Esquire Goldthwait arrived from New England; he is, as I understand, paymaster general of our troops. He brought me the most agreeable news I have heard in camp; that is, I mean the news of my wife and friend being in health. I received three letters, one from her, one from brother Jenks, and one from brother Nathan Sergant.

Thursday, 7th.[16] Today am off duty; spent most of the day in camp. I hear the recruits are all on their way up here; some of the officers are arrived all ready. We have orders to be ready to imbarque a Sunday next for St. Johns. I hope to be able in short time to give a good account of some part of Canada if its the will of God, and my colonel orders me to move on with the troops. No extraordinaries today. Shipping shot and shells.

Friday, 8th August. Today wrote a letter, and sent it in Mrs. Goldthwait's by Mr. Farrington, who set of today for Boston, and is to return immediately after his business is done. Mr. Goldthwait intends to begin paying the soldiers tomorrow morning. This evening all the detachments are coming in, except those all ready gone forward, in order to prepare themselves for to imbarque.

Saturday, 9th August, 1760. This morning all my men received one dollar a piece that desired it, to git them some

16. See Notes end of *Diary.*

necessaries to carry with them down the lake. I have been packing up mine and giting some stores for me on the lake, if I am ordered. It is not known who goes or stays as yet. At night we drank to wives and sweethearts. I hear Lieutenant Colonel Hawkes is to tarry behind.

Sunday, August 10th, 1760. Orders to be ready to imbarque tomorrow morning. I spent most of the day in packing up my things. I left my coat and jacket and all my writings with Esquire Goldthwait and one *johannas* in cash, to be kept till I return; or if I am not to return, to be sent home. I lost two of my best shirts today by a washer woman.

Monday, 11th August. This morning at 10 o'clock a.m., we struck our tents and marched down to the battoes, in order to imbarque for St. Johns. The Brigadier led the whole of the Massachusetts troops. At noon we set of in three colums; the wind blew pretty fresh ahead. We rowed till about sunset when the signal was made to form to the left, or west, shore, and then we landed and the pequit made the guard. We have come about six miles.

Tuesday, 12 August. The morning very calm, only a small breeze to ye southward. We set off in order about sunrise; I had very hard lodging on the barrels in the battoe last night. After rowing about three or four miles, the wind came right ahead, so that the *Ligoneir* was obliged to anchor the rest of the fleet. Kept along until the wind blew pretty fresh; orders came to cross the lake to the east side, where we all came to land in a bay called Button Mold Bay, where we are to tarry all night. Here Captain Shores[17] got his dismission from his Majesty's service to return to New England.

Wednesday, August 13th , 1760. We tarried in the morning a while for the *Ligoneir* to come up; set of about 8 o'clock a. m. having come about eighteen miles from Crown Point, we passed through the Narrows, which is very mountainous on the west

---

17. See *Sergeant Holden's Journal* under date of August 13, 2 Proceedings, vol. 4.

side, but very plain, flat land on the east. We proceeded forward till about noon, when the wind sprung up quite fresh ahead; we kept on until about 4 o'clock p. m., when we landed on the west side the lake. We are now about twenty-eight miles from Crown Point. Here we have news from the brig and sloops; they have had a brush with the *Monsieurs*, and drove them back to the island. I lodged much better last night than ye night before.

Thursday, 14th August. This morning the wind came fare and the *Ligoneir* came up. We put of about sunrise, and stood along down the lake with all sail spread, and made a fine appearance. We kept on till about 11 o'clock a. m., when the wind blew quite hard, and rained very much. We were obliged every one to shift for themselves; a prodigious sea and hard wind obliged us to make a harbour on ye north side of an island called Scuylers Island. We have lost seven rangers[18] two by the canoe splitting, and two of the recruits fell over and was drowned; one killed by accident, and there is several battoes missing, I fear in bad circumstances. We came today about forty-five miles.

Friday, 15th August. This morning is lowry, and the wind pretty fresh, but fair; we set off about sunrise and made all sail, as much as we could suffer, a prodigious sea going. The land is all flat and level, hardly any hills or mountains to be seen, and what is at a great distance. Expect to be amongst bad neighbours before night. God grant we may behave ourselves like men, and play the man for the city and people of our God, and let him do as seemest him best. I lodged these two nights past very comfortably in my battoe; most of the troop lodged on shore by large fires.

Saturday, 16th August. We set of from an island called Ile a mot[19] it is about eighteen miles to the fortified island from here. I lodged in the battoe very comfortable. It was about the dawning of the day when we put off; after rowing across a large bay we formed the line, two boats abreast. I believe the whole

---

18. *Ibid.*

reached four miles, and made a very beautiful appearance. The weather quite pleasant with a small breeze in our favour. Thus Providence seems to smile on our proceedings. After entering the Narrows, which is not more than a musket shot across, and very intricate, the enemy's schooner and reddow came out to meet us, but was drove back. We formed for landing in about a mile and half from the enemy's fort, with all our battoes a breast, to land on the east shore. As soon as the signal for landing was made, we all rowed right to shore, and landed in extreme good order without any molestation at all. The *Ligoneir* reddows[20] and prows kept a fire on the enemy's fort and vessels, to favour our landing; after which we marched up and formed a line, and set out our pequits. The land we marched through exceeding wet and miry. I went sometimes almost up to my middle in mud and water, and obliged to run most of the way to keep up with the front. We then set about making a breast work which was compleated in a little time, as the men are in high spirits. The vessel keeps firing on the French; but *Monsieurs* are not so complaisant as to answer them, which we impute to their want of men or ammunition. We having a little rum, we made some toddy to keep up the custom of Saturday night health.

Sunday, 17th August. I lodged last night on the ground without my blanket, only a few bushes to cover me, and as wet as could well be, but through Divine goodness rested very well. No enemy to molest us in our breastwork, which was kept well manned all night. One of our reddows going to reconnoitre the forts was fired on by the enemy, and Captain Graye[21] of the Royal Artillery was killed, and five or six more lost their legs. One of these unfortunate men belongs to my company, and has his leg cut off; I hear he is like to recover. The rest of the day spent in fixing a shed to lodge under. I have not had my cloaths of since I left Crown Point; am obliged to lay with my arms and ammunition all on, to be ready in case of need.

---

19. Ile a mot is Ile au Noix. See *Sergeant Holden's Journal*, 2 Proceedings, vol. 4.
20. Probably radeau, mentioned *Ibid.*
21. Clagg, according to *Sergeant Holden's Journal*, *Ibid.*

Monday, 18th August. 1760. Last night I had the pequit, and kept one quarter of it standing sentry at a time all night. I had two subalterns who took care of the pequit, and I lay in my bower till break of day, and slept comfortably; in the morning was ordered out to cover a party of fachine makers in the woods, about half mile from the breast work. The enemy have fired several cannon today at our people, but done no execution. We have taken possession of a point of land right opposite the island, and within musket shot of the fort where we are erecting batteries. At night was relieved by Captain Barnard.

Tuesday, 19th August. Last night I had my tent set up, and lay like a minister all night; this morning we had orders to pack up every thing for to move on to the Point to cover the batteries. Marched off about 11 o'clock a. m., through extreme bad way, to the Point, and built a fine breastwork in front, and begun one in the rear. The enemy heard us encamping, and they kept firing cannon at us, but hurt none of the men, though our camp is not half cannon shot from the enemy's fort, and nothing to hinder but only the trees, and them not very thick.

Wednesday, 20th August. 1760. Last night rained some. I lay in my tent all night without any molestation. The enemy have not fired a gun all night. This morning there came one of the enemy to our people, and what story he tells I cannot learn, I hear it so many different ways; but by all I think the enemy very scant of men on the island. In the afternoon they fired very briskly on our men, but did no great damage, only wounded one man with a grape shot slightly. We go on briskly with our batteries, and hope in a few days to give *Monsieurs* a salute; for they begin to grow very quarrelsome of late, and won't let us live in peace by them.[22]

Thursday, 21st August. Last night it rained pretty much. However, it did not hinder our people from working on the battery. Today I am ordered to assist the engineer; I have a party of

22. Compare the entries for 19th and 20th August with those of *Sergeant Holden's Journal* for the same date. 2 Proceedings, vol. 4.

150 men, two subalterns, four sergeants in carrying timber to the batteries; there is 800 of the provincials of us on fatigue in building batteries today, under the care of Colonel Saltonstall. The enemy kept a constant fire on us most part of the day, firing twelve, nine, and six pound shot and langrege; they wounded ten men, five of which, I believe, mortally, the other not bad. I escaped myself very narrowly several times. I think it very remarkable that the enemy have not killed great numbers, when we are so much exposed. Our reddows have fired several shot on them today.

Friday, 22nd. Last night just as I had got to bed, being much fatigued, the whole army was ordered to arms immediately, having discovered a large party of the enemy set off from the island in battoes and putting over towards us. After we had put out all fires in camp and manned the breast work, there came orders to return to our tents, except the pequit; for the enemy, finding they were discovered, returned back without firing a gun. However, we lay in readiness to receive them if they should attempt it again; and about an hour before day, a regular sentry, supposing he heard some of them, fired his piece, as did three or four more, which alarmed us again, and all turned out and manned the breast work, waiting for them. In a few minutes, the captain of the pequit, thinking he saw a man without the lines, challenged it three times, and nothing answering, fired his piece; and somebody at the same time gave the word to fire, when the whole of our battalion mostly discharged their pieces, which spread almost the line, it being impossible to stop our men from firing, although there was no enemy near us. We soon found our mistake, and returned to our tents.

We have got a fine breast work, both in front and rear, and have cut all the trees and cleared them out of our camp to prevent our being hurt by the limbs falling that are shot of by ye enemy's cannon. This morning we are clearing a road through our camp to draw cannon across below the enemy's fort, to erect a battery on a point of land in order to cut off all communication between them and St. Johns. We have landed all our mortars and got them up to the bomb-battery, and are gitting the cannon on shore and drawing them to the batteries, and hope to have three batteries opened by night. I hear a scout of our rangers have taken four prisoners this morning. Nothing material has happened today; the enemy have been pretty quiet, and haven't fired above five or six cannon today and a few small arms, and done no damage, as I can hear. There was a man of Captain Harriss taken up for dead, hurt by a tree falling on him.

Saturday, 23rd August. 1760. Last night we had no molestation from the enemy. Our batteries are almost compleat, and the brig has sent on shore to git fachines to hang over on her sides, so as to attack the fort at the same time the batteries are opened. The enemy have killed and scalped one of our men last night where we first landed; a party of our rangers fired across to the island last night and killed four of the French. I hear the batteries opening will be preceded first by all the drums beating a point of war, next by a band of music, followed by all the provincials singing psalms. About 3 o'clock p. m., all our batteries was opened and gave the French a fine salute, which *Monsieurs* did not return; the artillery kept playing constantly, and did great execution. A little while after, one of our soldiers fired his piece; Colonel Saltonstall immediately ordered a court martial on him, which fell to be my tour of duty. I, immediately after the members was assembled, held it at my tent. I ordered the prisoner to be brought, who pleaded ignorance of the guns being charged; on ye whole the court sentenced him forty stripes, which was approved of by Colonel Saltonstall. But when he was stript and brought to ye post, the colonel was so good as to forgive his punishment.

Sunday, 24th August. This morning I wrote a letter and sent it to Crown Point to Esquire Goldthwait, to acquaint him I was well, and desiring him to write that I was so in his letter. I had no sleep last night, for our people was cutting away the boom, and the enemy would fire volleys of small arms on them, and then our battery would return it with grape shot, and the mortars was kept going all night, which made it seem that the elements was all fire and smoke. Our people has almost effected cutting away the boom. The French has not fired a cannon since our batteries was opened this morning. Nine of the French battoes was seen going off towards St. Johns, and two more went last night, so I believe the enemy will all leave ye island shortly.

Monday, 25th August. 1760. Last night I had the pequit. In the evening Ensign Warren of Captain Jones' company was shot in his back by a musket ball; the ball lodged in his body. A serjeant of ye Massachusetts had both his hands shot away at the same time, and several more wounded. One of my company has received a ball in his arm; the ball was cut out, the bone is not hurt. I kept up all night walking round our battalion to keep the sentry right; for if any disorder happens, the blame would lay on me. The night quite pleasant and bright moonshine; the battery would fire a round about once an hour and throw shells about as often. In the morning I sent a serjeant and eight men to carry Ensign Warren to ye hospital, who I don't think will live 24 hours longer; he has been a very good officer and behaved well.

About 9 o'clock we heard a great number of small arms firing down along the lakeside, and some cannon. Immediately all the pequits was turned out to assist Major Rogers, who it seems had engaged the French vessels. We all marched out, our Provincial pequits served as front, rear, and flank guards to the regulars. I went with my pequit in the advance guard. Just as we had joined the party already out, the fire ceased; and we halted and set out sentry, for we suspected the enemy had a large party on the land somewhere near us. In a few minutes a regular officer brought us the joyful news that the French great reddow,[23] their brig, and sloop had struck to us; we then marched down to the point of land where the cannon was, and saw the vessels all laying there under English colours.

We have not lost a man in this affair, although the action

---

23. *Serjeant Holden's Journal* says, "one rideau, one topsail schooner, and a sloop"

was very sharp and no battery for the cannon to play behind. *Monsieurs* has no vessel now on the lake except a row galley and battoes. We have killed a field officer of theirs who was on board, and have taken their commodore and about twenty men prisoners. These prisoners inform us that we killed 180 of their men that day. We opened our batteries beside the wounded. They are very short of provision and ammunition, and can git no relief, now we have got their fleet; for we cut of all communication between them and St. Johns. In our marching into camp we met our commodore and a large party of sailors going down to man our new fleet. In the evening some whale boats was carried across to cut off the enemy's retreat; and this night some of the brig's cannon was carry across to put into the French vessels.

Tuesday, 26th August, 1760.[24] This morning we have news by an express from General Murray, who writes that he has been joined by two regiments from England and by the garrison of Louisbourg, and that he intends the first fair wind to sail and invest Montreal, and desires us not to think hard if he reaps the glory of taking Montreal, and that he has provisions enough for all three of the armies. We likewise hear that General Amherst was three days ago within thirty miles of Montreal, and we have heard cannon fired several times at a distance that way. General Murray was encamped at a place called Sir Ells,[25] and the express was nine days a coming here; so by all circumstances I believe Montreal actually invested by General Murray. We are making up a party of the best men for the woods to go with Major Rogers; where they are destined I cannot yet tell. This afternoon a party of the provincials was ordered on board the French prizes; Captain Hart went out of our battalion and three of my men. Just at night we opened a new battery down by the lower end of the island.

Wednesday, 27th.[26] Last night nothing worth notice hap-

---

24. See Notes at end of *Diary*.
25. Perhaps Sorel.
26. See Notes at end of *Diary*

pened. This morning we had smart firing on both sides. The enemy have played their cannon brisker today than they have done any time before, but done no execution of any valve. A soldier of mine going with a dollar in his hand to the sutlers and a nine pound shot strake his hand, which only grazed the skin, but lost his dollar, and one of ye Hamshire men wounded, which is all they have done, as I hear. About 3 o'clock p. m. we was alarmed by a sudden explosion.[27] At first we thought that the enemy had opened a large battery, but we was soon informed that a number of our shells and some powder at the 12 gun battery took fire by some accident unknown; about thirty shells burst by this means, and three men killed outright and several others wounded. The enemy have kept a very smart fire all day, but done us no damage worth notice. All this we take as their last words.

Thursday, 28th August, 1760, Md. This morning we found that the enemy had deserted and left ye island. Immediately the grenadiers and light infantry went over and took possession of that fortress. I hear that the French commander has left orders that no provincial, ranger, or Indian be allowed to go on the island; which orders I think is going to be followed, for several of our officers endeavouring to go across, having got liberty of the Brigadier, were prevented by the regulars, which is looked upon a very high affair, when we have done most part of the fatigue during the siege, and our men have been more exposed than they, must now be denied the liberty to go and see what they have fought for.

This day I have the care of a hundred men in order to draw the cannon out of our batteries down to wharf and git them on board the vessels, in order to follow the enemy, who ran away to Saint Johns; we have got all of them down except one hoit and all the shot and shells and platforms; and this day our brig and sloop passed by the island, having cut away the French boom that lay across. I hope soon to be able to give an account

---

27. See *Sergeant Holden's Journal* of the same date, 2 Proceedings, vol. 4.

of Saint Johns. There is some general officers that are very brief about today to see the batteries and island that was poorly all the while the siege lasted.

Friday, 29th August. This morning lay in my tent till eight o'clock, being very much fatigued last night with my day's work. I happened to hear of a general going to New England. I immediately wrote a letter to my partner at home, and sent it in one inclosed to Esquire Goldthwait, who told me that if I sent so he would enclose it in his and so send it home, which is the surest way I have to send. In the afternoon had all my things pact up in order to imbarque for St. Johns. I hear General Amherst is got nigh to Montreal, and we shall soon be there, if the enemy don't hinder us.

Saturday, 30th August. 1760. This morning about daybreak I got up to git my baggage on board in order to imbarque for St. Johns, and struck our tents half an hour after revallies beating, and marched down to ye battoes, and set of about 10 o'clock a. m., and passed by the French island we have taken. There was their grand dival and row galley, and our small reddows and prows went with us; we carry none of our heavy artillery nor any of our 13 inch mortars, only the field pieces and royals and some hoits.

When we were got about half way down, some of our leading boats discovered some enemy on the shore. Immediately the light infantry rowed right to shore and landed against them, but they fled and got clear. When we turned a point of land near St. Johns, we espied a great smoke at a great distance and one not so large pretty nigh us, which proves to be St. Johns, which the enemy have abandoned, after setting fire to the fort and buildings;[28] the other is thought to be Shamble,[29] six miles further down the river. We landed and formed without any opposition. This place look pleasanter than ye island. Just before night we

---

28. See *Sergeant Holden's Journal* of the same date, 2 Proceedings, vol. 4.
29. Probably Fort Chambelle, mentioned by Sergeant Holden, *Ibid*. See also his *Journal* under date of September 7, *Ibid*.

were ordered to pitch all our tents, and all to lay on our arms with our ammunition all on, being now in our enemy's country amongst them where they live. This evening the rangers brought in three prisoners, who informs that they have had a battle eight days since with General Amherst, but in whose favour it turned could not tell. Major Rogers has lost two of his men today and one officer wounded, and the enemy are gone to Montreal; thus Heaven apparently fights for us, and therefore it is our duty to acknowledge its the hand of Divine Providence, and not done by any force of ours or arm of flesh.

Sunday, 31st August. This morning its lowry and rainy, but we are all at work and throwing up entrenchments and forming lines; we have a battery every convenient distance along the lines which, when finished, I don't think 10,000 men could force. We have got sixteen prisoners[30] this morning. Just now orders came for us to leave off entrenching, as the army is going to march very quick. I then went to see the recruits, where I was well entertained; but what I most prize is, I there found a letter from my brother Jenks, which was to me as cold water to a thirsty soul in this howling and enemy's country. Today one of our sloops came down from Isle-aux-Noix, and the row galley taken there and several other boats. We got the chief of the artillery on shore. By the best information I can git we took about sixty pieces of cannon on the island and some mortars, a great number of shot and shells, and 500 barrels of powder and 100 barrels of pork and 200 of flour, and eighty head of cattle, and other warlike stores. So we may see what is to be depended on about the French not having any ammunition or provisions. Had the enemy behaved like men, they could a stood out a month longer, but it plainly appears they are intimidated and Heaven is against them.

Monday, the 1st of September, 1760. This morning we struck our tents at a quarter of an hour after revallies beating in order to imbarque for Shamble. We did not let off till 3 o'clock p. m.; we took up all that time in gitting the artillery and camp equi-

---

30. Holden says seventeen. 2 Proceedings, vol. 4.

page on board. We then put off and went down, and pretty bad falls about a mile long; we got to the place where Rogers took his prisoners last spring, called St. Thesis, where we stopped and encamped close by the fort, having come about six miles from St. Johns without any molestation from the enemy. There is a small village of the French here; and their women and children are here, but the men are gone.

Tuesday, 2nd September. 1760. This morning we are entrenching. Colonel Ingersoll's and Colonel Whitcomb's regiments are come up; they could not git over the fall last night. I went to view the fort,[31] which was a very pretty piece of work as any of the French works I have yet seen, but *Monsieurs* have set fire to it since Rogers left it. I hear that ten of our men drove a hundred French before them and took five prisoners and killed one; it plainly appears they are struck with a panic. Just now we are ordered to leave off entrenching till further orders, for tis supposed we are going to march further. Today, I am ordered to take the pequit at night.

Wednesday, 3rd September. 1760. Last night I lay out with the pequit to keep them alert, now we are in an enemy's country. I lay down under the breast work to git a little sleep. I could not help thinking what lodging I have exchanged for this, which is not half so good or convenient as we generally provide for our swine at home; however, I rested a little. Who would not be a gentleman soldier to lay thus abroad and venture their lives, and when they are at home to be slighted by the generality of mankind. Our rangers keep bringing in the best of the inhabitants, as they take their choice of them; they also inform us the ladys are very kind in the neighbourhood, which seems we shall fare better when we git into the thick settled parts of the country.

By all I can learn the Indians are all left the French, and will not fight at all, and the inhabitants seem inclined to come in and give up their arms and submit to the Crown of Great Britain. We are preparing a party to go and take Shamble, which is about six miles below us on this river.

31. See *Sergeant Holden's Journal* under date of September 2, *Ibid.*

Thursday, 4th September. Last night I had my tent pitched and fixed so that I lay quite well. This morning about revallies beating the party going to Shamble set off, consisting of about 1,000 men and several pieces of cannon and royals, the whole under the command of Colonel Derby. We are at work at compleating our breastworks, which is almost compleated. The French about here are busy in giting in their harvest, and some of our men are helping them; so we are very good neighbours at present.

Major Rogers says he heard cannon and platoons firing yesterday for an hour or two very brisk and smart, so we may expect soon to know the fate of Canada, or our army; and to-day some of our officers being out to see the village, heard a constant firing of cannon toward Montreal, so would fain hope General Murray has got the better of the French, which if he has, we shall soon, I hope, be moving homeward, for it begins to be cold nights, and our oznabrig tabernacles is but poor shelter for this cold climate.

Friday, 5th September. 1760. Last evening we had the agreeable news of the surrender of the fort at Shamble prisoners of war. There was about sixty French regulars in garrison there. Our people took some of the inhabitants,—women and children,— and placed them before their royal, and so fired over their heads, which answered instead of fachines batteries. After firing two or three shells, they hoisted English colours and submitted, but wanted the honours of war, which Colonel Derby would not comply with, threatening them that if they delayed any longer he would put all to ye sword.

We also have news that General Murray has had a field battle with the enemy three days ago, near Montreal, and has given *Monsieurs* a worse dressing than they have yet had in America, and there is an express come from General Amherst, who was got below all the falls, and has good water now all the way to Montreal; so we are waiting impatiently for news from these armies. About eighty of the French was brought in to camp last night from Shamble. This morning we heard a heavy piece of cannon fired a different way from those we have commonly heard, which is supposed to be the morning gun fired at General Amherst's army. We also learn that Monsieur Levy came over to Laparee[32] with a battalion of regulars, and orders to take the army we had driving before us, and to assemble the Canadians a this side the river, and give us battle; but on the approach of the other army he was ordered back, and the rest we had before us to join against General Murray, who is able now to give a good account of them, if we are not misinformed.

O, how apparently does Divine Providence interpose in our favour! Although I believe if he had come it would a have been to their own cost. God be praised, we are in a condition to receive them. Our men are animated and in high spirits, and fine lines thrown up and redoubts with cannon in front; and above all, I trust God on our side; therefore we fear them not. Although an host encamp around us, we will not fear.

Saturday, 6th September.[33] 1760. Last evening some of the militia officers of the French came in, and a party of rangers belonging to General Murray. The French came to submit to the British septere, as all have now on the south side of the river St. Lawrence. We have orders to prepare all things to be in readiness to march, I suppose to join General Murry. I hear this morning that Generals Amherst and Murry joins armies today. I am in hopes to see English colours flying on Montreal yet, for expect soon to march there. Today I have been out about a mile out of camp to git some blackberrys, and got as many as I could or dare eat. I saw some of the French women, and they are dressed much as those brought from Nova-Scotia. They have some very pretty children as ever I saw anywhere in my life. I cannot find in my heart that I could kill such innocents, although they have done it many a time on our frontiers. The country men come in daily with their wagons to carry our provisions and camp equipage to Shamble. This I look on as a forced obedience to us.

---

32. Probably La Prairie.
33. Birthday of my father's first son, Samuel. Note by William Jenks.

Sunday, 7th September. 1760. This morning have news of General Amherst landing on the island of Montreal. We had an express from him last night. There is about a hundred of the French wagons come in this morning to carry our baggage and provisions to Montreal. It looks quite strange to see these Canadians helping our army along to destroy the only place of refuge the miserable creatures have left in their country, winch must according to human reason soon fall into our hands.[34] We have got horses to draw our artillery which consists of about twenty as fine brass pieces as ever was brought into the field. There is sixty of the ablest of the invalids put out to garrison Shamble, and the rest we leave here on an island right opposite of our now encampment, under care of Major Emery of the Hamshire troops.

The provincials begin to be very sickly. Two of our battalion died yesterday, and several officers and soldiers are very sick in our regiment. I desire to bless God I am enabled to go forward with the army, and have not missed one tour of duty yet. This afternoon we marched off for Montreal, and got as far as Shamble, and halted a while. The fort look quite beautiful outside. I dared not go in because it was contrary to orders. There is a fine church just below the fort, the first I have seen in this country. There is great numbers of the inhabitants come taking their oaths of ———, and they are very helpful in carrying our stores, artillery, and baggage. There is near a hundred wagons of them, and the finest horses for draught that I ever saw in my life anywhere.

Monday, 8th. Last evening we set out from Shamble, and marched on through a fine, pleasant country, thick of inhabitants; some of them looked very easy and cheerful, others lamenting the fate of their country. Our army marched in as civil a manner to the inhabitants as if they had been in our own country. We kept on our march till near midnight in the dark, and waded over two rivers and got to an old shed. It rained very hard, and

---

34. See *Sergeant Holden's Journal* of the same date, 2 Proceedings, vol. 4.

we put in here, and I set up all night, for had not room to lay down and got no rest, being wet and very tired. This morning we set out again before sunrise, and it was extreme bad walking occasioned by the rain last night. Our baggage is not come up. I could git no refreshment of no kind, although never more wanted, I being very ill and weak by a continual flux following this several days.

We marched on very fast and waded over another river, and kept on without any sort of sustenance of any kind, until about noon, when we arrived to a village opposite Montreal, I went into a French house determined to git some refreshment or stay till the wagons come up. I got some sower milk, and drank very hearty of it, and then the master of the house came in and asked if we would eat any soup, which I told him we would. They then set before us a fine dish of it; and some pigeons stewed heads and all on, I here made a fine feast. Had not I met with this nourishment, I could not a held out to march half a mile further. I then set out for the regiment, who had got about two miles start. We have marched about fourteen miles to day through a fine country for land but not for improvements. We have passed by a great many crosses on the way. Just as I joined the regiment I saw Colonel Vaverland[35] put off to go over to General Amherst in a whale boat who called to shore and told us that the city had surrendered this morning, and that we had done fighting. It seems General Amherst had three skirmishes with the enemy yesterday and beat them out of their entrenchments. Had they held out a little longer all three of the armies would a laid siege to them, but I desire to bless God we have all Canada now under our command without any more blood shed.[36]

Tuesday, 9th September. 1760. Last night we set up our tents, and I lay very comfortable. Have got such refreshment as made me feel much better. I have joined with Captain Bailey, who tents with me. This morning I got up about an hour by sun,

---

35. General Sir William Haviland.
36. See *Sergeant Holden's Journal* of the same date, 2 Proceedings, vol. 4.

and went to view the city and country. Could see General Amherst's camp about two miles above the city. This city makes a very beautiful appearance and very fine buildings and beautiful improvements. They look so at a distance. The river is about two miles across, and we right opposite the city. I then took a walk after breakfast, with several general officers of our battalion down along the river about four miles.

We went below General Murray's encampment, which is about a mile below the city. Could see great part of the fleet coming up the river. We went below one frigate. This river lies about N. N. E. and S. S. W. and the city lies along by the water's edge and a large mountain on the back. There is no sort of fruit in none of these towns but thorns. They have fine land, but live miserable to my view. This moment one of Captain Bailey's men was found almost dead. Before they could call the doctor he died. He had not complained before, but had eat very freely of pork and cabbage, which killed him. This afternoon Lieutenant Richardson arrived with an express to General Haverland, and brought me three letters, one from my wife, one from brother Sergeant, and one from Esquire Goldthwait with the agreeable news of their being in health, &c.

Wednesday, 10th September. Last night I got me a quart of milk and boiled it for my supper; then went to cabin and lay very comfortable till morning, when we had orders to strike our tents, in order to march for Crown Point, which was accordingly done, but we did not march till noon, when all the provincials marched off under command of Brigadier General Ruggles. All the regulars stays behind. It was extreme hot, and we marched very fast. I thought I could not hold out, but through good Providence I was enabled to stand it till we came to encamp.

Thursday, 11th September. Last night I lay without any tent, or anything to cover me with, except a few bushes; and it rained very hard in the night, and we were as wet as water could make us. I slept but little. In the morning marched off for Chamble through very bad way. I got a little milk on the way. We arrived about noon, and halted here. I found that a Rhode Island officer had taken a tent from my men; I made application to the field officers for redress, but could get none. I then made a regular complaint to the Brigadier for the tent, and likewise for satisfaction of him and another officer of same regiment. Immediately the tent was returned, though with regret, and what other satisfaction I am to have I know not yet.

Friday, 12th September, 1760. Last night lay on the ground without any tent; a great dew and very cold in the night; however past the night pretty comfortably. I have been in to view the fort, which is very neat and beautifully built, though not strong. I hear one of my men are dead that I left at St. Therese, Benjamin Wentworth; he died the 11th instant. The ladys come very thick to market, some with one commodity, and some with other; however I cannot fancy them at no rate. They bring chiefly squashes and turnips and some cabbage and carrots. I went with a number of gentlemen to view the church. We got the sexton and leave to go in; which was very curious to see their images and other instruments of worship. Returning, went into a French house and got some bread and milk, which they took no pay for. This part of the country is very pleasant and delightsome. I could fancy to live here had I my partner and friends here. I went in the afternoon to the sutlers, where I saw mankind in their proper hue, when they give a loose to their appetites. To see men, yea such as is styled gentle, git drunk, and then they are stout and must go to fighting.

Saturday, 13th September. 1760. Last night was pretty cold. I lay but poorly, and I am in a poor state of health, which don't agree so well together. This morning I went out to git some breakfast. Returned; could git none, which still added to my affliction. This morning our boats arrived. I had some refreshment. About 2 o'clock p. m. marched of for St. Therese; arrived by sunset, and encamped on the ground we formerly had done. Got some tea for supper. I'd no stomach to eat.

Sunday, 14th Sept., 1760. Last night I lay very comfortable, and slept well. About daybreak struck our tents to imbarque on board battoes for St. Johns. Our men break out very fast with the small pox. I am greatly afraid it will spread in the army, although all the care we have taken to prevent it. We set off about 8 o'clock a. m., wind ahead; arrived at St. Johns about noon. Here I got some refreshment, set off again about 3 o'clock p. m. for Isle aux Noix, the wind blowing hard against us, and rough water.

Monday, 15th Sept., 1760. Last night got to Isle aux Noix about 8 o'clock. I lay on board the boat. About daybreak I went in to the fort to see after the sick I left behind. Found them all alive. English is very ill; but took all the sick with me. This fort I will not attempt to describe for desire it may be erased out of memory for ever, for its not fit for any person to live in, or even to behold. After we had drawn provisions for four days to carry us to Crown Point, set of about 9 o'clock a. m., the weather rainy and wind ahead. However, we are pressing forward for Crown Point, in hopes to live better and cheaper; passed by a floating battery built on two battoes by the French. We put forward until about sunset, when we went ashore opposite Isle a Mott, having come about thirty miles to day. I am something better than I have been this several days. We are cooking all our provisions in order to keep forward without any stop.

Tuesday, 16th Sept., 1760. Last night I lay very comfortably. We set off as soon as we could discover any appearance of day. The wind is now favourable at last; we made as much sail as we could, and to keep in order, which was in three colums, two battoes a breast. The wind freshened up; we run at a great rate, the weather pretty cold and clear. We kept forward till about 11 o'clock at night, when we halted on the east shore about five miles from Crown Point, having run by computation about ninety miles today.

Wednesday, 17th Sept., 1760. Last night I lay very well on board the battoe. We set off this morning about daybreak, and was obliged to keep in sight of the shore, it being very foggy and cold withal.

We arrived about 7 o'clock in the morning, and landed and got the sick into the hospital; went up and was kindly received by the officers we left behind here. I got a good breakfast, better than I have had since we imbarqed from here. I found Mr Goldthwait well, who received me gladly, and informed me he had a line from home, dated 2nd Sept., with news of all being in health.

Thursday, 18th. Today have been about to see what has been done since we have been gone. It looks as if I had got most home again, having come further since I left Montreal than it is to go home from here. Today Esquire Goldthwait is paying off some men part of their wages. I wrote three letters to send home, one for my girl, one for brother John, and one for brother Nathan, &c. Directed them to brother Jenks, at Medford. I hear now that Allen Newhall is going home.

Friday, 19th Sept., 1760. Last night was very cold. I lay but poorly. This morning Ensign Newhall undertook to make us a cabin to lodge both together in. This day I wrote several letters more to send home, and had a man's things prized by Lieutenant Knolton, Lieutenant Foster, Ensign Hankerson. They valued them at 7/6 L. M. He died at St. Therese. I have been out to walk, in order to git clear of the smell of the camps. I went into the hospital to see the sick, which was a very affecting sight, being about forty poor creatures.

Saturday, 20th Sept. 1760. Last night it was reported that the Hamshire[37] and Rhode Island regiments intended to desert. Immediately a guard of one captain, one subaltern, and sixty sergeants of the Massachusetts, and some regulars, to prevent their escape was paraded. They was kept on watch all night. Those brave fellows did not attempt to desert, but expect they will soon do it if they are so inclined, and fine character for soldiers. This morning Mr Newhall set off for Lynn by the way of Albany. At evening we came to the former custom of drinking to wives and sweethearts, and so concluded ye day.

---

37. Sergeant Holden refers to this episode under date of the 19th 2 Proceedings, vol. 4.

Sunday, 21st, 1760. Today am off duty. I spent most of the day at Lieutenant Burrell's house; it rained for the most part of the day. No sign of Sunday, except the flags being hoisted. Our chaplains having given us one sermon and prayed two or three evenings, which is all we have for about 20£ L. M., paid by the province per month to chaplains for preaching. A very ill use I think is made of that money; and 1/8d cut out of every dollar paid to the soldiers. Who would not fight for such a court?

Monday, 22nd Sept., 1760. This morning I have a hundred men under my care to work in the trench. Carry stones. I am in a poor state of health, and were I at home I should keep house. Today about eighty battoes set out for St. Johns to bring General Amherst and some of his troops that are coming this way. I have two or three men I am afraid have deserted, as I cannot find them. This day rainy in the forenoon, but pleasant in the afterpart of the day.

Tuesday, Sept. 23rd. This day am off duty, and I am determined not to go on again till I am better in health, for a great many officers in camp have refused that were more able than I am at present. However feel something better this morning than I did yesterday, and am in hopes to git well so as not to miss any tour of duty when it's my turn. Today I walked about five or six miles, in order to keep out of the smell of ye camp.

Wednesday, 24th Sept., 1760. This morning I lay in bed till eight o'clock, being not for duty, and not so bright as I could wish. The most that is going forward in camp is confining, and holding court martials. Today its showery. Just before night Lieutenant Richardson arrived here from Isle Noix with several of my men with him. Today Jacob Hasey of my company was taken ill with ye small pox. I hear all the artillery is just got here. some of the Royal Scotch arrived here last night from Laparee[38] on their way to Halifax.

Thursday, 25th Sept. This day lowry and rainy. I am off duty.

---

38. La Prairie.

In the morning the *Ligoneir* and *Grand Dival*[39] arrived from Isle Noix, and most part of the artillery and several companies of regulars. I and Captain Hart have bought us a horse[40] that was taken prisoner at Isle Noir, for to carry our packs through to No. 4. I have a cow some of my men brought me from Isle Noix; they give me her milk till we move from hence. Today Wm. Densmore of my company was carried to ye hospital, being ill with ye small pox.

Friday, 26th Sept. 1760. Today am off duty. Joseph Tucker of my company is carried to the hospital, being ill with the small pox. This is ye fourth I have sick with the small pox, and am afraid it will not be all, for one or two more complain. The men in camp begin to die very fast, and its very sickly; there is about 1,200 men of the provincials now returned unfit for duty, and great many more taken sick almost every day. This evening L. R. W. orders fifth a St ————.

Saturday, 27th Sept. 1760. This day is pretty pleasant for the season. I went with Captain Hart to find our horse, which we feared had got lost. After travelling about two or three miles, found him. Today Corporal Bradford of my company came from Ticondaroga, and brings news of Lieutenant Pope being sick, and that Thos Hoole of my company is dead; but the time when he died he cannot tell. Just before night arrived a regiment of Highlanders from Montreal on their way to their winter quarters, which is to be at Halifax, as I hear.

Sunday, 28th Sept. 1760. This day is very rainy and stormy. I spent most of the day in my tent. In the afternoon went down to ye landing to see the Highland Regiment and the Royal Scotch Regiment imbarque for Ticondaroga, and they are to make the best of their way to winter quarters. Our camps be now very sickly; there is not above a third part of the men now in camp that are fit for duty, and there dies more or less every day.

---

39. Sergeant Holden gives the name *Grand Deoble*. 2 Proceedings, vol. 4.
40. See Notes end of *Diary*

Monday, 29th Sept. This day very rainy and cold. I am off duty, and spent most part of the day in tent, for it was exceeding bad walking out, being nothing but mud and water, and very stormy. Joshua Chever has come into our mess. Nathaniel Henderson is come up the lake sick with a flux. Seven men died last night in the provincials, and they will most all die if this weather holds, and they fare no better. I spent most part of the afternoon in Lieutenant Burrell's house, as he has a fine fire place.

Tuesday, 30th Sept. 1760. Last night Timothy Townsend of my company died in hospital, and this morning was buried. I have care of eighty men to git the cannon out of the *Ligoneir*, and haul up the battoes and boards, that was drove and hove on the shore last night in the storm. About 2 o'clock was dismissed. I returned to camp and made report to the Brigadier of my day's work. It now comes on rainy and stormy, and I fear, will be bad again tonight. About 4 o'clock p. m. a gentleman brought me a number of letters, wherein I found found for me, two from my spouse, one from brother Nathan, and one from brother John, all dated in August, with the agreeable news of their being in health, and a small piece from brother Jenks with news, &c., which is as cold waters to a thirsty land. After perusing them I went to cabin; we lodge well a nights, and that's all.

Wednesday, the 1st of October, 1760. This day I am off duty; the weather wet and lowry. The most part of the day we are obliged to set in the cabins with our feet wrapt in our blankets to keep them warm; and here we sett talking and disputing of matters in love and matrimony and other diversion to pass away such tedious weather, and to bring our campaign to an end, as all we have now to do is only fatigue and nothing to be got nor nothing more to be fought for in America; so I don't think any ways out of character to wish an end to our fatigues, for no honour is to be got at fatiguing.

Thursday, 2nd October, 1760. Today its something more pleasant than has been for these several days, although it looks angry and lowry yet. I have been out to look for our horse and cow, which were missing; the latter is found, but the former I fear is lost or stole. I have had several walks with Captain Hart and Ensign Newhall, to find our horse, but they were all fruitless. Almost all the artillery is got on shore and drawn up on the bank, which I believe will be useless in this country for ye future.

Friday, 3 October, 1760. The weather is quite pleasant and agreeable. I have been out to walk to find our horse, and found him. Returned I heard that Jacob Hasey of my company is dead of the small pox, and one more not like to live. Today General Johnson arrived here from Montreal, on his way home. General Whitmore's regiment is arrived, and they are to garrison this place this winter.

Saturday, 4th October, 1760. Today am off duty. The weather quite pleasant and warm. I took great satisfaction in walking round the encampment and fort to see the works. Several vessels came up the lake. Colonel Haviland is arrived, and a lord that commands Whitmore's regiment I am in hopes that we shall have good weather now, so that the fort may be got forward before cold weather, that we may git forward to our province before winter.

Sunday, 5th October, 1760. This is a very fine day; I am apt to think its a weather breeder. I spent most of the day in walking to take the air and helping Captain Harris, who has been sick above a fortnight, and today has got out to ride a little in order to git strength. After sunset we had a sermon preached on the parade by one of our chaplains from *Psalms* 63-3. This is the only one I have heard from our chaplains. He stood eight minutes by the watch.

Monday, 6th October, 1760. Yesterday three of my men deserted, *viz.*, Wm. Critchett, Benjamin Hallowell, and Michal Conoly, and Ebenezer Osgood and Wm. Dinsmore is dead. My company begins to grow small by death and desertion. I have been out this morning, and there is vast numbers of pigeons flying and geese. Today Joseph Hasey and Juno Conore arrived here from Isle Noix in a very bad state of health. I fear Hasey will not recover. This day spent in visiting.

Tuesday, 7th October, 1760. Today I am off duty. Fine pleasant weather. I went out to walk as usual in order to git a better air than we have in camp, which is almost infectious; such numbers of sick and dead men all ways in camp. I hear that the Rhode Island regiment has got the spotted fever amongst them, which is as bad in an army as the plague, as the regular doctor says. Great numbers desert every night.

Wednesday, 8th October. 1760. Today I have care of a party to work in the fort. At noon Joseph Hasey of my company died. He is the seventh man I have lost in six weeks past, and I fear he is not the last, for have several dangerously sick now. Today the prize row galley came up the lake with men that are discharged, as I hear, as did ye *Grand Dioble*.[41] Today the sick are mustered, in order to send some home for New England.

Thursday, 9th October. Today am off duty. I wrote several letters home, one to my wife, one to brother Jenks, as I hear several of my men are to be sent home as invalids. Last night I heard a number of wolves on the other side the lake. Today two of Colonel Thos' men were brought in, having deserted, to take the event of their folly.

Friday, 10 October, 1760. This day Ezra Pratt and Nathan Winn of my company set off for New England, having got their dismission, and Wm Pratt went to help the sick home. Today I received a letter from Point Shirley with the confirmation of good news. Ensign Newhall of my company is quite ill. I have taken a great satisfaction today in walking out without the camp to take the air. I hear General Amherst is expected here soon.

Saturday, 11th October. Today am off duty. The weather quite agreeable and pleasant, which is a great favour to the sick that

---

41. The *Dival* of *25 September.*

set of yesterday in particular and to the whole army in general. In the afternoon I heard that the putrid fever is brook out at the old fort, and all men are forbid going into it on any account. The evening I went and spent in Captain Bayly's tent, where we concluded by drinking to wives.

Sunday, 12th October, 1760. Today morning great numbers of brants was seen flying over the camp. The weather quite pleasant and agreeable. I walked out to gain a good air. Returned and read over all my letters. Ensign Newhall remains very ill. No regard to sacred time is paid here except a flags flying on ye fort, although this moment I hear we are to have a sermon, so I must dress to go to meeting, a rarity up here.

Monday, 13th October, 1760. Today am off duty. It looks like a storm; I fear a long one. I have taken several walks about to divert myself. Last evening I spent very agreeably with Esquire Goldthwait, who informed me of Mrs. Hoole's death. I am almost impatiently wishing the arrival of General Amherst, for I understand that all ye invalids will be sent home on his arrival.

Tuesday, 14th October, 1760. Today it is very rainy. There is no men on fatigue. The weather is so bad I have kept in my tent almost the day in disputing and other diversions to pass away such dull weather, as its very uncomfortable in camp. I hear a number of letters is come from New England, but cannot find any for me. I hope soon to live without this desire of letters.

Wednesday, 15th October, 1760. This morning I hear General Amherst is arrived, which I find true. Last evening was in very agreeable company. Today is cleared up and is fine weather. I am off duty. I spent the day in walking with several gentlemen whose company and conversation was quite agreeable. At evening I had some things prized that belonged to one of my soldiers that is dead, and I assisted other gentlemen on ye like occasion.

Thursday, 16th October, 1760. I hear that all the invalids are to be sent home immediately, which rejoices me much, and that we all are to follow in about a fortnight, so hope by God's blessing soon to enjoy my friends again in New England. Today I have been settling about my soldiers things that are dead. I have lost eight this campaign, but am in great hopes that I shall lose no more, as it now begins to be more healthy in camp.

Friday, 17th October. 1760. Today I have care of 112 men to work on fort. I had a smart dispute with the chief engineer. Today I saw Mr Baldwin from New England. I have had a very pleasant tour of duty today. I don't expect to have above two or three at furthest more this campaign. I hear there is great numbers of letters on the way; may I have the pleasure of receiving some.

Saturday, 18th October, 1760. Today am off duty. I spent the day writing and walking out round the camp to pass away the time, although I confess that time is the most precious of all things when a person has the enjoyment of his friends company and conversation; although I have the society of social gentlemen, yet that is not so satisfactory here as elsewhere.

Sunday, 19th October, 1760. This day is very stormy and cold. I have wrote several letters home and intend them to be the last this campaign without some extraordinary happens. I spent most all of the day in Captain Bailey's tent reading Milton. Ye evening I spent very agreeably with Esquire Goldthwait, who tells me he soon intends for New England.

Monday, 20th Oct, 1760. Today am off duty. The weather clear, but now begins to be cold. I have been a walk to take the air out of camp. I hear that the invalids are to be reviewed tomorrow by Doctor Monro.[42] No news from home since 23rd Sept. I hear also that the rangers are to be dismissed directly.

Tuesday, 21st October, 1760. Today the weather cloudy and cold; likely for snow. I am off duty and have been to see the sick reviewed by Dr. Monro, who I think is endued with much more patience than I should have; although they are my countrymen, yet great numbers of them are a scandal to ye profession of a soldier.

---

42. Sergeant Holden gives his name "Mun Row." 2 Proceedings, vol. 4.

Wednesday, 22nd October, 1760. Last night it snowed , for this morning the ground looks white, which makes me think of home to git a better house to lodge in than this, which is made of oznabrigs, a very poor habitation for the inclemency of the season. Ensign Newhall has Dr. Monro's approbation to go home. I hope soon to follow, for am tired with this campaign.

Thursday, 23rd October. 1760. Today am off duty. It's a very cold frosty morning, and the invalids are preparing to pass the lake to go home by No. 4,[43] the whole under command of Major Gerrish. I believe the party consists of 500, some so bad that I think they will never reach New England. There two or three broke out with the small pox in camp, and it keeps breaking out every full and change of the moon and not above one in three that has it lives.

Friday, 24th October, 1760. Today I have care of a party to work in the fort. I marched them into the fort and stayed a while, but found myself so ill that I could not stand it. I gave charge of the party to two subalterns that was with me and returned to camp. I fear I am going to have a fit of sickness, for am very bad seized with a cold. Today Ensign Newhall set out for home.

Saturday, 25th October, 1760. This morning, blessed be God, I find myself much better. I hope it will go off without a settled fever, which I much feared yesterday. I have returned myself sick, the only time I have been returned so this campaign. I am not very zealous now for duty time. I think we ought to be dismissed to git home before winter.

Sunday, 26th October, 1760. This day I am some better, but not so well as to be fit for duty. Esquire Goldthwait I hear has received instructions from home to [stay] till the camp breaks up, so am like to have his company a while longer. I can hear no news at all from home. It seems they have forgot me.

Monday, 27th October, 1760. This day we have built us a chim-

---

43. See note, 2 Proceedings, vol. 4.

ney to our tent, for we can no longer stand to live without a fire. Today General Amherst set off for Albany, and now I fear we shall be kept till ye last of November, for ye command is left to Haverland, and I know he delights to fatigue ye provincials.

Tuesday, 28th October, 1760. Today am much better of my cold. The weather now looks winter like, and it is constantly snowing on the mountains to the N.W. of us. I spend most of my time in gossiping from one neighbour to another to pass away the tedious hours till we can be set at liberty, &c.

Wednesday, 29th October, 1760. This is a pleasant, although a frosty morning. Our lads has been bringing a house for them to cook in. Can see the snow on the mountains. Looks as if it were three or four feet deep. I believe we shall soon have a share of snow here, for it has got to be a nigh neighbour.

Thursday, 30th October, 1760. Today pretty pleasant for the season. Colonel Thomas is arrived from Isle Noir, after demolishing all the works and fortifications on that almost infernal island. I pray it may never have any inhabitants on there any more forever, without its owls and satyrs or dragons of the deserts, but be blotted out of memory to all ages.

Friday, 31st October, 1760. Today its very pleasant weather, and the commanding officer keeps all the troops on fatigue, so eager are they to git all they possibly can out of us before they dismiss us. I think this parallel with ye devils rage, when he knew his time was short to plague mankind in; so I know their time is short like their masters. Today Esquire Goldthwait set off for Albany.

Saturday, 1st November, 1760. Last evening I saw Phineas Douglas, and he tells me his brother Joseph is gone home lame, and that his friends was all well lately. Today I have care of hundred men to work in the fort; the weather blustering and cold. I kept with the party about half ye day, and the other officers the rest. At evening it rained pretty much.

Sunday, 2nd Nov, 1760. This morning the weather quite clear and pleasant. I understand that we shall tarry till ye 20th instant, without we should git the barracks done before, and that we shall all be gone off by then whether they are done or not. Today I spent in my tent in reading and writing. No sign at all of Sunday now, for the flag is not hoisted at all.

Monday, 3rd November, 1760. Today the weather pleasant for the season; can see the tops of the mountains all covered with snow all round. I believe we are in a warm climate compared with those mountains. I have been all round the fort twice to see how the barrack goes on. I am in hopes they will be done by ye 10th or 12th of this month; so hope to have our freedom again in short time.

Tuesday, 4th November, 1760. Today am off duty; the weather pleasant for the season. Today Colonel Hawk and a party with him set out for No 4; they are to make a bridge over Otter Creek. I hear Major Gerrish got through to No 4 with the loss of but one or two of his party. The party of eighty sent by Major Hobble to Albany, I hear seventy of them are dead and another small party sent that way since, I hear eighteen of them are gone the way of all flesh. So frail a creature is man!

Wednesday, 5th November, 1760, Powder Plot. This day all the carpenters that can work on the barracks was ordered to assist those already on that work; and the masons will have done their barrack fit for the carpenters in two days more. I have been round the fort to see the works, and they go on quite briskly, for the provincials are of the mind that we shall be discharged as soon as the barracks are covered; so by that rule we shall march for home by the 10th or 12th instant.

Thursday, 6th November, 1760. Last evening the provincials, as it was Pope Night, kept firing all over the camps. Although all possible care was taken to detect them and suppress the fire, yet they kept a constant firing and squibbing in different parts of the encampments till bedtime. This day I am off duty; the weather quite warm for the season. Have had several walks round the fort to see the works, and they will be so far compleated as to admit of our dismission in about a week at furthest.

Friday, 7th November, 1760. Today I am on duty at drawing timber into the fort. I had a task which I finished before noon; this is the only task I have had on the works this campaign. In the afternoon I spent my time very agreeably in walking out with several gentlemen to git a better air than can be enjoyed in camp. Last night two of Captain Butterfield's men died suddenly.

Saturday, 8th November, 1760. This morning rainy and lowry; looks quite like for bad weather, which has kept off for a great while. However, the working party kept at work till night. Today the brig was sent to Ticondaroga, to be bawled up for to winter. The camp ladys now, like the swallows, are seeking a more convenient climate to winter in, for they are packing off.

Sunday, 9th November. 1760. Today exceeding stormy, having rained and snowed all night. I lay a bed till ten o'clock. In the afternoon returned all my arms into the ship stores, as its orders for the first and second battalion, to return all their arms in. I hope now soon to be on my march for home, for certainly they don't intend us for any more fighting. Just at night it cleared up, but too late for the working party to turn out.

Monday, 10th Nov, 1760. Today the weather quite pleasant, considering the climate and season. Today Rufus Hayward of my company was carried to the hospital sick with the small pox; I fear it will go hard with him. Today I gave warrants to some of my serjeants to clear them from the melitious officers at home, for I think to good to be hauled out by them.

Tuseday, 11th November, 1760. Today am off duty. The weather cold and churlish. Last night John Connore of my company died in the hospital; he is the tenth man I have lost, and I fear that is not all. We continue working on the fort and barracks to compleat them, so that the troops that winter here may be comfortable.

Wednesday, ye 12th Nov, 1760. Today a large party of invalids was sent home by No. 4, under the care of Colonel Whitcomb; and another party that are not able to go by No. 4, is going by Albany under the care of Colonel Saltonstall, so that we shall not have any sick left in camp I hope when these are gone.

Thursday, 13th November, 1760. Today I have care of hundred men in drawing up the cannon brought from ye Island Noir, and drew up thirty-three before the working parties left off. Today Colonel Saltonstall set out with his party of sick for Albany. The weather is very cold, and looks now like snow; its the coldest day we have had this fall.

Friday, 14th November, 1760. Last night it snowed best part of the night, and this morning the snow is about six inches deep on a level, and extreme cold and windy. Yet our good friends the regulars turned out the provincials on fatigue sooner than usual, and kept their own men off of the works. Today Captain Hart and myself had our horse shod, and frowed to carry our packs to No. 4.

Saturday, 15th November, 1760. Last night was an extreme cold one; however I lay comfortably, considering I had no covering for a house but an oznabrig tabernacle. Today there is no drum beat for the works, and we have orders to make a return of all invalids able and unable for march, and I believe that we shall soon be on our march for the pumpkin country. I almost dread our passage to No. 4; its about a hundred miles and now its bad travelling. Today Captain Bayley was carried to the hospital, being ill with the small pox, and and Putnam is ill of ye same.

Sunday, 16th Nov., 1760. Today Captain Page of our battalion was sent off with a party of sixty well men to No. 4. Yesterday a stage on the barrack gave way, by which means three men fell from the roof that were shingling, and hurt themselves so much that their lives are despaired of. Today a party of provincials was sent to Ticondaroga for provisions. After we have worked on the fort till ye cold drove us off, now we have provisions to bring here for all the garrison, under ye pretence of bringing it for us to carry us to No. 4. I perceive that its Sunday today, for ye flag is flying. I hear this morning that several of the regulars' cows are dead, froze to death last night; but I had rather think some of our rogues helped them because they are almost outrageous at being kept here in camp at this season. I heard that Colonel Haverland, going round the fort, fell down and broke his leg. Poor man! I am sorry it was his leg. Today orders came for all the tools to [be] returned in, and all the artificers to be paid off tomorrow.

Monday, 17th November, 1760. Today a party was sent up to Ticondaroga with our baker to bake bread to carry us to No 4, our oven here being fell in and rendered useless. In the afternoon we had orders to march to Ticondaroga, and take eight days' provisions to carry us to No. 4. The weather is so bad that the carpenters cannot work, or we should tarry three days longer.

Tuesday, 18th November, 1760. This morning about daybreak we struck our tents and delivered them in, and march off about 8 o'clock a. m. I am rejoiced to be on a march again. We arrived at Ticondaroga about 3 o'clock p. m., and were till 10 o'clock at night gitting over the lake. The weather tedious cold. I have a bad pain in my right knee that I can hardly march with ye regiment.

Wednesday, 19th Nov, 1760. This morning we tarry here waiting for our bread to be baked. The weather extreme cold. I lay very comfortably by a large fire without any hut or tent, and now it looks homish. as the man said by his barn, although we are but just setting out. My knee so lame, I fear I shall have a bad time through ye woods, but desire to put my trust in Him that can do all things according to his pleasure, and go as well and far as I can. Set off about 10 o'clock, and marched till about 3 o'clock and camped.

Thursday, 20th November., 1760. Last night lay very well by a large fire; the weather extreme cold, and the way exceeding bad. We have come about fourteen miles. We marched off this morning about sunrise, and march on through extreme bad way about fifteen miles, and passed by a man left on the road burnt by falling in the fire. He was left with two others to take care of, who, when the poor creature fell into a sleep, took all the provisions and marched of and left him, first covering him over with hemlock boughs, and reported that he was dead, and they had buried him. These villains were whipt one 500 lashes, ye other 250 for their inhumanity, by order of a court martial at No 4.

Friday, 21st Nov, 1760. Last night lay by a fire; it snowed some in the night. Set off this morning by day, and marched on in exceeding bad way and came to Otter Creek, and camped just by a wolf killed by some of our men and laid by the way.

Saturday, 22nd November, 1760. Set of early, and past Otter Creek, and kept on over the height of land. Met Colonel Whitcomb and several horses going for some sick.

Sunday, 23rd Nov., 1760. Set off early through vast mountains, and went over some reached almost to the clouds, and got into the road hard by ye Hamshire troops.

Monday, 24th November., 1760. Set off about 4 o'clock. Rained steady all day. Have sixteen mile to No 4.

Tuesday, 25th Nov, 1760. Continued at No 4. Mustered my men and sent them off. Today two provincial was whipt for ———.[44]

Wednesday, 26 November, 1760. I waited here last night for Captain Hart, &c. Set off about 7 o'clock a. m. Have now none to take care off but myself, as all my company are dismissed and gone home before me.

---

44. *Sergeant Holden's Journal* supplies the blank under the same date. "Two men that was confined for burying a man alive in No 4 woods received their punishment, one received 500 lashes, the other 100." Though perhaps there is some confusion of dates, and his reference is to the incident above under date of November 20. 2 Proceedings, vol.4.

Notes

Three pages in the handwriting of Rev. William Jenks, D.D., son of the Diarist.

Smollett, vol. 5, p. 276, says General Amherst "detached Colonel Haviland, with a body of troops from Crown Point, to take possession of the Isle aux Noix, in the Lake Champlain, and from thence penetrate the shortest way to the bank of the River St Lawrence." He had before directed General Murray to advance from Quebec to Montreal, and now proceeded "with the main body of the army, amounting to about 10,000 men, including Indians," from Albany to Lake Ontario and down the St. Lawrence. Colonel Sewall observes that the junction of the forces about Montreal was, in his opinion, by no means unforeseen or unintentional, for on the march Colonel Haviland's corps was occasionally hastened and retarded; though Smollett says expressly, "they had no intelligence of the motions of each other."

"On the 6th day of September General Amherst's troops were landed on the island of Montreal," and after marching so lay all night on their arms before the city. Next day a letter was sent by the Marquis de Vaudreuil demanding a capitulation, which was granted. "General Murray, with the troops from Quebec, had by this time landed on the island; and Colonel Haviland, with the body under his command, had just arrived on the south side of the river opposite to Montreal,— circumstances," adds Smollett, "equally favourable and surprising."

Colonel Sewall observes that General Haviland had sent the baggage, tents, &c., up the Sorel after they were remanded back; so that the provincial troops on their return were exposed, as in this journal is related, to the cold and rain at night; that as orders had arrived forbidding any of Colonel Haviland's troops to visit the city, Brigadier Ruggles was greatly dissatisfied, and hurried on his men in such manner that, being compelled to lodge in the open air, exposed to the heavy rain, they fell sick; and from being a healthy army, with but very few unable to do duty, they returned a weakly, diseased body, with hardly a third of them serviceable, and "began to die away like rotten sheep."

Smollett terms the conquest of Canada "the most important of any the British arms ever achieved," and says, "The zeal and conduct of Brigadier General Gage, the undaunted spirit and enterprising genius of General Murray, the diligence and activity of Colonel Haviland, happily co-operated in promoting this great event." For he observes it must be allowed General Amherst "was extremely fortunate in having subordinate commanders who perfectly corresponded with his ideas, and a body of troops whom no labours could discourage, whom no dangers could dismay."

General Amherst's whole conduct was irreproachable, and Sir Wm. Johnson had influence over the Indians to restrain them from every atrocity, (p. 281, &c.)

Bath, *Mar. 29,* 1811

Then follow 126 blank pages and the seven pages on which are these entries in pencil, as if someone had intended to use the book for a diary or journal, and then gave up the idea.

Saturday, September. I re-hemmed Mr Batta three handkerchief, one of our boarders.

Friday.

Thursday.

Wednesday.

Tuesday.

Monday.

Sunday.

(A number of pages of miscellaneous memoranda follow.)

1766, *February 12th.* The river was open, and the first boat went down then; it was B. Hall's.

February 20th. Died the Widow Tyler, and was carried to Boston to be buried.

March 29. At half after two o'clock in the morning was born my son Samuel, of a Saturday.

Sunday, 30 March. Died Mr. Kidder, very suddenly; was well at ten a. m., and dead by the time the first bell rung for the afternoon service.

Sunday, 6 April. Died Mrs. Bradshaw, wife of Deacon Jonah Bradshaw, of a lingering disease, having been deprived of her reason for a long time.

(A memorandum of things from *Jan. 1, 1766.*)

Wednesday, ye 8th January. Was married Henry Fowle to Mary Patten.

Wednesday, 15th. Then Mr. Hezeh Blanchard took out Draper's newspaper for himself and me; he paid 12/6 old ten, and I 12/6, being ye ½.

Wednesday, 22nd January. Was married John Wade and Betty Pool.

February 6, Thursday. Was married Mr Charles Pelham and Molley Tyler. Paid Critchett one dollar for one share in a horse. Paid 2/ to another for a share in do. Captain Hart gave a quart brandy for one do. in do. Sept. 25, 1760.
Lent Benjamin Hallowell one dollar, Sept 25th, 1760.

Tuseday, 26th August, 1760. Then Corporal Ephraim Rhoads was broke and reduced to do duty of a private by a court martial. Done at camp before Isle aux Noix.
Bought three gallons rum and 9 lb. sugar, one bottle wine.
Ensign Newhall bought 15 lb. sugar and one bottle wine.

Ens[n] Newhall Dr.

Augt., 1760		Yorke currency
7th	To cash lent him	0 – 5

Crown Point, 23[d] July.

Lent L[t] Richardson 20 ℔ sug[r] @ 1/4	1 – 6 – 8
do 6 ℔ chocolate @ 4/–	1 – 4
do 6 ℔ coffe @ 2/6 —	0 – 15
do 1 cheese, wt 16 gr, @ 1/8	1 – 9 – 6
Lent Cap[t] Hart 4 ℔ coffee.	
Borrowd of do. 20 ℔ sug[r] & 6 ℔ coffee	
	Ballanced.

[A pen mark is run through this entry.]

Lent Mr. Hobby 2 ℔ cheese.
Cr. to L[t] Richardson to 25 ℔ soap.

Augt. 1760
27th Ezra Pratt to 12[r] vinegar.

Crown Point, 23[d] July, 1760. Bought of M[r] Neagle, setler.	Yorke currency.
one cheese, w[t] 16½ @ 1/8	£1 – 7 – 6
& 3 ℔ tobacco @ 2/	0 – 6
1 pr shoes 15/	0 – 15
1 pr buck ells 2/	0 – 2
25th 50 ℔ chocolate @ 3/3	8 – 2 – 6
1 pr pumps 15/–	0 – 15
to 158 ℔ sugar @ 1/3[d]	9 – 17 – 6
81½ ℔ cheese @ 1/8	6 – 5 – 10
27th 1 pr shoes 15/	0 – 15
1 ℔ soap 1/6	0 – 1 – 6
	28 – 7 – 10

On the inside of the cover—
Cadaraque or Frontenack
Le Galletta or, Le Gallo
Camp Crown Point,
November ye Sixteenth, 1760.

The Journal of
Lemuel Lyon

Preface

Having been, for several years, engaged in the establishment of a museum in Poughkeepsie, I have, by extensive travel and research, and by the kindness of many of my fellow-citizens in Dutchess county and elsewhere, obtained numerous objects, not only curious in themselves, but valuable as materials for history. Among these are two manuscript journals, kept by common soldiers, each during a single campaign, and written at periods seventeen years apart.

One of these soldiers served in a campaign of the conflict known as the French and Indian War, which commenced a hundred years ago. Believing that a faithful transcript of his journal, given *verbatim et literatim*, as recorded by the actor himself, might have an interest for American readers, as exhibiting the everyday life of a common soldier in a war which led to the founding of our republic, I have yielded to the solicitations of friends, and the dictates of my own judgement and feelings, and in the following pages present to the public faithful a faithful copy of his diary.

Perceiving that much of the intrinsic value of this journal would consist in a proper understanding of the historical facts to which allusions are made in it, I prevailed upon Mr. Lossing, the well-known author of the *Pictorial Field-Book of the Revolution* to illustrate and elucidate this diary by explanatory notes. His name is a sufficient guarantee for their accuracy and general usefulness; and I flatter myself that this little volume will not only amuse, but edify, and that the useful objects aimed at in its publication will be fully attained. With this hope, it is submitted to my fellow-citizens.

Abraham Tomlinson
Poughkeepsie Museum
December, 1854

Introduction

The conflict known in America as the French and Indian War, and in Europe as the Seven Years' War, originated in disputes between the French and English colonists, in the New World, concerning territorial limits. For a century the colonies of the two nations had been gradually expanding and increasing in importance. The English, more than a million in number, occupied the seaboard from the Penobscot to the St. Mary's, a thousand miles in extent; all eastward of the great ranges of the Alleganies, and far northward toward the St. Lawrence. The French, not more than a hundred thousand strong, made settlements along the St. Lawrence, the shores of the great lakes, on the Mississippi and its tributaries, and upon the borders of the gulf of Mexico. They early founded Detroit, Kaskaskia, Vincennes, and New Orleans.

The English planted agricultural colonies—the French were chiefly engaged in traffic with the Indians. This trade, and the operations of the Jesuit missionaries, who were usually the self-denying pioneers of commerce in its penetration of the wilderness, gave the French great influence over the tribes of a vast extent of country lying in the rear of the English settlements.

The ancient quarrel between the two nations, originating far back in the feudal ages, and kept alive by subsequent collisions, burned vigorously in the bosoms of the respective colonists in America, where it was continually fed by frequent hostilities on frontier ground. They had ever regarded each other with extreme jealousy, for the prize before them was supreme rule in the New World. The trading-posts and missionary-stations of the French, in the far Northwest, and in the bosom of the dark wilderness, several hundred miles distant from the most remote settlements on the English frontier, attracted very little attention until they formed a part of more extensive operations.

But when, after the capture of Louisburg, by the English, in 1745, the French adopted vigorous measures for opposing the extension of British power in America; when they built strong vessels at the foot of Lake Ontario—made treaties of friendship with powerful Indian tribes—strengthened their fort at the mouth of the Niagara river—and erected a cordon of fortifications, more than sixty in number, between Montreal and New Orleans,—the English were aroused to immediate and effective action in defence of the territorial limits given them in their ancient charters. By virtue of these, they claimed dominion westward to the Pacific ocean, south of the latitude of the north shore of Lake Erie; while the French claimed a title to all the territory watered by the Mississippi and its tributaries, under the more plausible plea that they had made the first explorations and settlements in that region. The claims of the real owner—the Indian—were lost sight of in the discussion; and it was a significant question asked by an Indian messenger of the agent of the English Ohio Company: "Where is the Indian's land? The English claim it all on one side of the river, and the French on the other: where does the Indian's land lie?"

The territorial question was brought to an issue when, in 1753, a company of English traders and settlers commenced exploring the head-waters of the Ohio. The French opposed their operations by force. George Washington was sent by the Virginia authorities to remonstrate with the French. It was of no avail. The English determined to oppose force to force and in the vicinity of the now flourishing city of Pittsburg, in western Pennsylvania, the "French and Indian War" began. Provincial troops were raised, and armies came from England. Extensive campaigns were planned, and attempts were made to expel the

French from Lake Champlain and the southern shore of Lake Ontario. Finally, in 1758, three armies were in motion at one time against French posts remote from each other—Louisburg, in the extreme east; Ticonderoga, on Lake Champlain; and Fort Du Quesne, where Pittsburg now stands. General Sir James Abercrombie commanded the expedition against Ticonderoga, accompanied by young Lord Howe as his lieutenant. The French were under the command of the marquis Montcalm, who was killed at Quebec the following year. The English and provincial troops rendezvoused at the head of Lake George, went down that sheet of water, attacked Ticonderoga, and were repulsed with great loss. It was this portion of that campaign in which the soldier served who kept the Journal given in the succeeding pages. It is a graphic outline picture, in few and simple words, of the daily life of a common soldier at that time.

During the campaign of 1759, Quebec was captured by the army under Wolfe; Lord Amherst, more successful than Abercrombie, drove the French from Lake Champlain ; Sir William Johnson captured Fort Niagara; and all Canada was in virtual possession of the English, except Montreal. That fell early in the Autumn of 1760; and the struggle for supremacy in America, between the French and English, was ended for ever.

PART OF THE ORIGINAL JOURNAL

123

The Ruins of Fort Ticonderoga

Military Journal for 1758

April 5 1758. I Lemuel Lyon of Woodstock inlisted under Captain David Holms of Woodstock in New England For this present Cannody Expordition[1]—I received of Captain Holms £2.0s.,0d.

May 30. Received £3.-l6-0.

June, 2nd. We arrived at Colonel Maysons at 12 o'clock and marched from there to Landard[2] Abits and Sergent Stone treated us there then we marched to Mansfield to Deacon Eldridgs about four o'clock then we marched to Bolton to Landard Trils, and we gave 7d a night for horse keeping.

Wednesday 7th. We had carts to press,[3]—then we marched off from there to Landard Strengs in Harford and from there to Landard Geds and had raw pork for dinner—then we marched to Landard Crews and the chief[4] lodges there—My mess lodged at a private house one Daniel Catlins.

Thursday 8th. Marched off and arrived at Landard Gessels and there we went to breakfast and then we marched from there to

---

1. Canada expedition.
2. Landlord. The proprietor of an inn or tavern was universally called landlord. The title is still very prevalent.
3. To take carts for the military service. Under martial law, any private property may be used for the public good. A just government always pays a fair price for the same.
4. Probably General Lyman, who was the commander-in-chief of the Connecticut forces at that time.

our stores in Litchfield:[5] to Squire Sheldings and then to Landard Buels and lodged there and our captain was sent for to a man in another company that had fits.

Friday 9th. Then marched from there and we had new teams pressed there and we arrived at Landard Hollobuts in Goshen from there to Widow Leggets in Cornwell[6], and from there to Coles in Cainan[7] and lodged there.

Saturday 10th. Marched to Lawrences and from thence to Landard Bushes in Sheffield seven mile and went to dinner thence marched and arrived at one Garnt Burges and lodged there and our ensign went to prayer with us.

Sunday 11th. Marched into the Paterroon Lands[8] to Landard Lovejoys and went to dinner—had a hard shower then marched into Cantihook[9] to one Hayer Cams the stone house and lodged there and thence to Cantihook Town to one Bushes and slept there.

Monday 12th. At Cantihook.

Tuesday 13th. Marched and arrived at the half way house in Albany and bated, and then into Green Bush[10] by sundown and lodged their in Ranslay's barn.

Wednesday 14th. Still at Albany and their I first shifted my clothes and washed them—then we had six rounds of powder and ball and had orders from Colonel Whiting to go to Senakada[11]—this day Asel Carpenter came to Albany.

Thursday 15th. We went over the river early to receive our rations in provision and in money and we marched two miles and

---

5. In Litchfield County, Connecticut.

6. Cornwall.

7. Canaan.

8. Livingston's manor, in Columbia county. The estates of Livingston, Van Rensselaer, and others, who received grants of land from government, on certain conditions, in order to encourage immigration and agriculture, were called Patroon Lands, and the proprietors were entitled Patroons, or patrons.

9. Kinderhook.

10. Now East Albany, on the east side of the Hudson river.

11. Schenectady.

stopped and refreshed ourselves there half an hour and Lieutenant Smith came up and we received our Abilitan money.[12]

Friday 16th. We had prayers in our company at three o'clock then all marched of but fourteen and they stayed here to guard Lieutenant Smith and the money and yesterday Mr. Holmes set of for home and I give five pence for carrying my letter; we stayed here til 5 o'clock this afternoon and we heard nothing from Lieut. Smith and we had no provisions so we marched for Scanacata[13] and we got in at sundown well and there was a larrom[14] this night.

Saturday 17th. Still at Schenacata[15] and we moved into our barracks and Barnabas Evings was taken poor with a working in the body, Ben Denny was taken very poor.

Sunday 18th. I was first called upon guard with fifteen more. My turn came first at 11 o'clock— this afternoon 3 o'clock Lieutenant Smith come up with our Abilitan money.

Monday 19th. Still at Schenacata and there was a regiment of province men[16] come up to Schenacata and this night twenty-five of our men went over the river west one mile to guard wagon horses—this day a short training one regiment.

Tuesday 20th. Their marched of three hundred of the Bay Forces[17] for Fort Edward[18] and I received my Abilitan in full £1.8s.0d.

---

12. Billeting-money that is, money to pay for lodgings at private houses. When soldiers are quartered at private houses, it is said that such ones are billeted at such a house, &c.

13. Schenectady.

14. Alarum, or alarm.

15. Schenectady.

16. Provincial troops, or American soldiers. The English troops were called regulars.

17. Massachusetts Bay troops. The Massachusetts colony was called Massachusetts Bay until after the War for Independence.

18. Fort Edward was situated upon the east bank of the Hudson, about fifty miles north of Albany. The fort was built by General Lyman, of Connecticut, in 1755, while that officer was encamped there with about six thousand troops, awaiting the arrival of General William Johnson, the commander-in-chief of the expedition against the French at Ticonderoga and Crown Point. A portion of the site of the fort is now (1854) occupied by the flourishing village of Fort Edward. Some of the embankments are yet visible near the river. It was near this fort that Jane M'Crea was killed and scalped, in 1777.

Wednesday 21st. Still here and we were embodied for prayers in the morning and then trained a little. Corporal Carpenter was taken poor.

Thursday 22nd. Had orders to march to the half moon[19] and Captain Lenese's company too and at seven o'clock we marched and arrived at Tess-ceune[20] and lodged there at Landard Abraham Grotes.

Friday 23rd. Marched in the rain and very greasy travelling it was and we arrived at Teburth and from thence to the place called Lowdins Ferry[21] to Landard Fungdors and from thence to the Half Moon and lodged there.

Saturday 24th. I received a letter from John at the Half Moon and from thence we marched and arrived at Still Water[22] and lodged there and Barnabas Evings was poor.

Sunday 25th. We got two battoes[23] to carry our packs up to Salatogue[24] and we went a foot and eight of our men were drawn out to stay at Salatogue—Captain Lewis shot at an Indian and killed him and set in the battoe—from Salatogue we marched on to Fort Miller[25] and lodged there.

---

19. Near Waterford, on the west side of the Hudson river, thirteen miles north from Albany.

20. Niskayuna, a short distance from Waterford, and remarkable as a settlement of Shaking Quakers.

21. On the Mohawk, about five miles above Cohoes Falls. It was the chief crossing-place for troops on their way north from Albany. There the right wing of the American army, under Arnold, was encamped, while General Schuyler was casting up entrenchments at Cohoes Falls, a few weeks before the Saratoga battles, in 1777.

22. Stillwater is on the west bank of the Hudson, in Saratoga county, twenty -four miles north from Albany. The battle of Bemis's heights was fought near there, in 1777, and is sometimes known as the battle of Stillwater. Opposite the mouth of the Hoosick river, at Stillwater, was a stockade, called Fort Winslow.

23. A batteau is a kind of scow or flat-boat, used on shallow streams like the Hudson above Waterford.

24. Saratoga. This settlement was near the mouth of the Fish Creek, on the south side. The village of Schuylerville is just across the stream, on the north side. On the plain, in front of the village of Schuylerville, was a regular quadrangular fortification, with bastions, called Foil Hardy. It was erected in 1756, and named in honour of the governor of New York at that time. (continued on next page)

Monday 26th. Rainy and wet I come up the river in a battoe to Fort Edward to the encampment there we drew a pound of powder and ten bullets a piece and eight days' provision in order for to march to the Lake[26.]—Barnabas Evings was very poor with fever nago[27] and was forced to stay behind and David Bishop with him—we lodged in bush tents and very wet it was.

Tuesday 27th. Marched all of Colonel Phiches[28] regiment that were here with three teams to carry the officers—we arrived at the Half Way Brook[29] and there a great percel stationed for a while and from thence we marched to Lake George and went over upon the hill east and their encamped— one with myself went upon guard this night.

Wednesday 28th. We cleared our ground and pitched our tents—I sent two letters home.

Thursday 29th. Still here General Limont[30] and Colonel Phiches regiments come up to the lake this day—I washed my cloths one more regiment come up.

---

25. On the west side of the Hudson, six or eight miles below Fort Edward. The river is there broken by swift rapids. During this campaign, Major (afterwards General) Putnam was here surprised by a party of Indians, and boldly descended the rapids in a canoe, and escaped. It was a feat they never dared to attempt, and they felt certain that he was under the protection of the Great Spirit. Here a stream called Bloody Run enters the Hudson. It is so named because a party of soldiers from the garrison, in 1759, went there to fish, were surprised by the Indians, and nine were killed and scalped.
26. Lake George.
27. Fever-and-ague.
28. Fitch's.
29. Later called Snook's creek. It enters the Hudson three miles below Fort Edward.
30. General Phineas Lyman, who built Fort Edward. He was a native of Durham, Connecticut, where he was born in 1716. He completed his education at Yale college, and afterward became an eminent lawyer. He was appointed commander-in-chief of the Connecticut forces in 1755, and in the expedition to Lake George deserved all the honour awarded to General Johnson, who was jealous of Lyman's abilities as a soldier. Lyman did his duty nobly, and was but little noticed. Johnson was unfit for his station, but being a nephew of Sir Peter Warren, then a popular English admiral, he received the honour of knighthood, and the sum of twenty thousand dollars, for his services in that campaign! General Lyman served with distinction until the close of the campaign in 1760, and in 1762 commanded the American forces sent against Havana. He was in England about eleven years, and, after his return, went with his family to the Mississippi, where he died in 1788.

Friday 30th. This day there was a very unhappy mishap fell out in the province forces and that was one —— shot one — — partly through the body but did not kill him the man which was shot lived at Bridgewater—today they drew out nine men to go in battoes up the lake.

Saturday July 1st. Colonel Worster[31] and his regiment came up today and three of our sick men one of them brought news that one man shot another by accident at Schenacata and an hour after he died—today our chapling[32] came up and one of Major Rogers[33] men came in that had been gone seven days and expected to be gone but two he was so beat out that he could not tell what had become of the other—This night I went upon a battoe and guarded Colonel Phiches tub of butter.

---

31. Colonel David Wooster, of Connecticut, the eminent general of the Revolution, who was killed at Ridgefield, while engaged in the pursuit of Tryon, after the burning of Danbury, in the spring of 1777. He was born in Stratford, Connecticut, in March, 1710, graduated at Yale college in 1738, and soon afterward received the appointment of captain of a vessel of the coast-guard. He was in the expedition against Louisburg in 1745. He afterward went to England, where he was a favourite at the court of George II., and received the appointment of captain in the regular service, under Sir William Pepperell. He was promoted to a colonelcy in 1755, and rose to the rank of brigadier before the close of the French and Indian war. He was one of the most active men in getting up the expedition against Ticonderoga, in 1775, which resulted in the capture of that fortress, and also Crown Point, by Colonel Ethan Allen and Benedict Arnold. Wooster was appointed one of the first brigadiers of the continental army, in 1775, and third in rank. He was also appointed the first major-general of the militia of his state, when, organized for the War for Independence; and in that capacity he was employed, with Arnold, Silliman,-and others, in repelling British invasion in 1777. He lost his life in that service. His remains were buried at Danbury; and in 1854 a monument was erected over his grave by his grateful countrymen, at the expense of his native state.
32. Chaplain.
33. Commander of a corps of rangers, who performed signal services during the greater part of the French and Indian war. He was the son of an Irishman, an early settler of Dunbarton, in New Hampshire. He was appointed to his command in 1755, and was a thorough scout. In 1759, he was sent by General Amherst to destroy the Indian village of St. Francis. In that expedition he suffered great hardships, but was successful. He served in the Cherokee war in 1761, and in 1766 was appointed governor of Michilimacinae, where he was accused of treason, and sent to Montreal in irons. He was acquitted, went to England, and, after suffering imprisonment for debt, returned to America, where he remained until the Revolution broke out. He took up arms for the king, and in 1777 went to England, where he died. His *Journal of the French and Indian War* is a valuable work.

Sunday 2. In the forenoon I went to meeting and heard Mr. Eals his text was in the *5th Chapter of James* 16th verse a good sermon—I wrote a letter and sent home and in the afternoon to meeting again.

Monday 3rd. Yesterday Major Putnom's S Company came up and this morning Major Putnom[34] come up and the Connecticut regiment were embodied for to learn how to form your front to the right and left for General Abbacromba[35] and his *aid de Camp* to view.

Tuesday 4. This day I cut my hat and received my ammunition and provision for four days and made ready for to go on.

Wednesday 5th. This day the army by sunrise got ready for to march and marched of by water, and arrived at the Saberday point[36] and stayed their til midnight then marched again to the first narrows and landed there and went down.

---

34. Israel Putnam, afterward the Revolutionary general. He was born in Salem, Massachusetts, in January, 1718. He was a vigorous lad, and in 1739 we find him cultivating land in Pomfret, Connecticut, the scene of his remarkable adventure in a wolf's den, so familiar to every reader. He was appointed to the command of some of the first troops raised in Connecticut for the French and Indian war in 1755, and was an active officer during the entire period of that conflict, especially while in command of a corps of rangers. He was ploughing in his field when the news of the skirmishes at Lexington and Concord reached him. He immediately started for Boston, and, at the head of Connecticut troops, was active in the battle of Bunker Hill. He was one of the first four major-generals of the continental army appointed by Congress in June, 1775, and he was constantly on duty in important movements until 1779, when a partial paralysis of one side of his body disabled him for military service. He lived in retirement after the war, and died at Brooklyn, Windham county, Connecticut, on the 29th of May, 1790, at the age of seventy-two years.

35. General James Abercrombie, the commander-in-chief of the campaign. He was descended from an ancient Scotch family, and, because of signal services on the continent, was promoted to the rank of major-general, the military art having been his profession since boyhood. He was superseded by Lord Amherst, after his defeat at Ticonderoga, and returned to England in the spring of 1759.

36. Sabbath-day Point. This is a fertile little promontory, jutting out into Lake George from the western shore, a few miles from the little village of Hague, and surrounded by the most picturesque scenery imaginable. It was so named, at this time, because it was early on Sunday morning that Abercrombie and his army left this place and proceeded down the lake. There a small provincial force had a desperate fight with a party of French and Indians, in (continued on next page)

Thursday 6th. 12 o'clock at night we marched off again[37] and landed at the first narrows and then we marched on to the falls[38] within two miles of the fort and there we was attacked by the enemy[39] and the engagement held one hour and we killed and took upwards of two and fifty, and of Captain Holmes' company we had three men wounded—Sergent Cada, Sergent Armsba and Ensign Robbins—and at sundown the French come out again five thousand strong and our men came back again to the landing place and lodged there.

Friday 7th. Major Rogers went down to the mills and drove them of there from and killed and took upwards of 150 and at

1756, and defeated them. Abercrombie's army went down the lake in batteaux and whale-boats, and reached the Point just at dark. Captain (afterward General) Stark relates that he supped with the young Lord Howe that evening, at the Point, and that the nobleman made many anxious inquiries about the strength of Ticonderoga, the country to be traversed, &c., and, by his serious demeanour, evinced a presentiment of his sad fate. He was killed in a skirmish with a French scout two days afterward. His body was conveyed to Albany, in charge of Captain (afterward General) Philip Schuyler, and buried there. He was a brother of the admiral and general of that name, who commanded the British naval and land forces in America in 1776.
37. "The order of march," says Major Rogers, "exhibited a splendid military show." There were sixteen thousand well-armed troops. Lord Howe, in a large boat, led the van of the flotilla, accompanied by a guard of rangers and expert boatmen. The regular troops occupied the centre, and the provincials the wings. The sky was clear and starry, and not a breeze ruffled the dark waters as they slept quietly in the shadows of the mountains. Their oars were muffled, and, so silently did they move on, that not a scout upon the hills observed them; and the first intimation that the outposts of the enemy received of their approach was the full blaze of their scarlet uniforms, when, soon after sunrise, they landed and pushed on toward Ticonderoga.
38. Rapids in the stream which forms the outlet of Lake George into Lake Champlain. Here are now extensive saw and grist mills. The distance from the foot of Lake George to Fort Ticonderoga is about four miles.
39. The English lacked suitable guides, and became bewildered in the dense forest that covered the land. Lord Howe was second in command, and led the van, preceded by Major Putnam and a scout of one hundred men, to reconnoitre. The French set fire to their own outpost, and retreated. Howe and Putnam dashed on through the woods, and in a few minutes fell in with the French advanced guard, who were also bewildered, and were trying to find their way to the fort. A smart skirmish ensued, and, at the first fire, Lord Howe, another officer, and several privates, were killed. The French were repulsed, with a loss of about three hundred killed, and one hundred and forty made prisoners. The English battalions were so much broken, confused, and fatigued, that Abercrombie ordered them back to the landing-place, where they bivouacked for the night.

sundown the last of the army marched down to the mills and Major Putnom made a bridge over by the landing place—this night we lodged by the mills.

Saturday 8th. Then marched back two or three regiments to the landing place to guard and help get up artillery—and we worked all the forenoon on loading the battoes and at noon we set out down to the mills with the artillery and we got near the mills and we had orders to leave the artillery[40] there and go back and get our arms—and we went down to the mills of our regiment two hundred were ordered to go over on the point to keep the French from landing there and we stayed while next morning sun two hours high—and when we came in all our army and artillery was gone back and the mills fired and we marched back to the landing place and had to secure matter of 200 barrels of flour—and we heard the French were a coming upon us and we stove them all and come of us as soon as we could— and about 10 o'clock we set sail and and by sundown we arrived at Lake George[41]—according to all accounts the engagement began about 10 clock and held ten hours steady and we lost three thousand regulars.

---

40. This was Abercrombie's fatal mistake. He sent an engineer to reconnoitre the fort and outworks. The engineer reported the latter to be so weak, in an unfinished state, as to be easily carried, without artillery, by the force of English bayonets. The difficulties in the way of heavy cannons, in that dense forest, were very formidable; and Abercrombie was willing to rely upon sword and bayonet, on the strength of his engineer's report. That functionary was mistaken; and when the English approached the French lines, they found an embankment of earth and stones, eight feet in height, strongly guarded by abatis, or felled trees, with their tops outward. The English made a furious attack, cut pathways through these prostrate trees, and mounted the parapet. They were instantly slain, and thus scores of Britons were sacrificed, by discharges of heavy cannons. When two thousand men had fallen, Abercrombie sounded a retreat, and the whole British army made its way to the landing-place at the foot of Lake George, with a loss of twenty-five hundred muskets. They went up the lake to Fort William Henry, and the wounded were sent to Fort Edward and to Albany. At his own solicitation, Colonel Bradstreet was sent to attack the French Fort Frontenac, where Kingston now stands, at the foot of Lake Ontario; and General Stanwix proceeded to erect a fort toward the head-waters of the Mohawk, where the village of Rome now flourishes.

41. The head of the lake was especially designated as "Lake George." There was the dilapidated fort William Henry, built by Sir William Johnson, in the autumn of 1755; and, about half a mile south-east from it, Fort George was afterward erected. The ruins of its citadel may yet (1854) be seen.

Monday 10th. Still at Lake George in our old encampment—two cannon and two mortar pieces all of them brass come into Lake George today.

Tuesday 11th. I washed my clothes today had tea for breakfast.

Wednesday 12th. Today I was called upon guard. Stephen Lyon went to Fort Edward.

Thursday 13th. Today washed my clothes.

Friday 14th. Nothing remarkable.

Saturday 15th. Nothing remarkable called out to work.

Sunday 16th. Went to meeting to hear Mr. Pommerai [42] and his text was in the *16th Chapter of Isaiah* the 9th verse—in the afternoon went to hear Mr. Eals and his text was in *4th Chapter of Amos* and the 12th verse—Sung the 45 psalm the last time sung the 44th psalm—this day Colonel Dotay's regiment marched off.

Monday 17th. This day Sergent Joseph Mathers had a new shirt put on of seventy stripes[43]— I washed and at night was called upon the picket guard—Barny went down to the Half-way Brook[44] and back again to guard artillery.

Tuesday 18th. One Samuel Jonson died very suddenly he belonged to Captain Latimer's company of new cannon—Nehemiah Blackmore was whipt ten stripes for firing his gun.

Wednesday 19th. This day to work upon the hospital getting timber to it—I went upon the island[45] to stay there a week.

---

42. Pomeroy.
43. Flogging was facetiously termed "putting on a new shirt."
44. This was the outlet of three little lakes, situated about half way between the head of Lake George and the bend of the Hudson at Sandy Hill. They are the headwaters of Clear river, the west branch of Wood creek, which empties into Lake Champlain at Whitehall.
45. This was Diamond Island, directly in front of Dunham's Bay, not far from the village of Caldwell. It was so called because of the number and beauty of quartz-crystals found upon it. Burgoyne made it a depot of military stores when on his way from Canada, by the way of Lake Champlain, in 1777. It was the scene of a sharp conflict between the little garrison and a party of Americans under Colonel Brown, on the 25th of September, 1777, while Gates and Burgoyne were confronted at Saratoga. Brown was repulsed.

Thursday 20th. Still at work Colonel Worster set out to go down to Albany and a number of men with him—this morning ten men were a going to the Half Way Brook to guard the post and the Indians waylaid them and killed nine of them and one got in safe—and they rallied out from the brook 100 and went back to see what was the matter and they laid wait for them and they fired upon the front first and killed two captains and two lieutenants on the spot—and our men were surprised and run back all but a few— and they stood a little while and lost seventeen men—the engagement began sun two hours high about an hour after Lieutenant Smith and 200 of our men went down to help guard the teams down to Fort Edward.

Friday 21st. This day at night Lieutenant Smith came back and very poor he was—the rest of the guard returned well.

Saturday 22nd. This day Colonel Partrages[46] regiment were resolved to have their full allowance or go off and they got it[47] —a small shower— and at night our post came in and our men that stayed behind came up—I received a letter from home.

Sunday 23rd. Went to meeting and the text was in the 3rd chapter of *John* and the 16 verse and in the afternoon the text was in the 6 chapter of *Micah* 6 and 7 verses—this day wet and hard showers.

Monday 24th. This day a week ago Ensign Robins died at Albany—this day Henry Morris came up to Lake George with two wagon loads of rum and sold it right off.

Tuesday 25th. Captain Holmes and five of our men went down to the Half Way Brook to be stationed there til further orders— at 9 o'clock one James Makmehoon[48] was hanged upon the gallows upon the top of the Rockka noose[49] —our post came in and I was released from the hospital work.

---

46. Partridge's.
47. They were volunteers.
48. M'Mahon?
49. This locality can not be identified.

Wednesday 26th. Major Putnom had orders to list 400 rangers and listed some today.

Thursday 27th. This day the captains of the companies drew out nine men of a company for rangers.

Friday 28th. There was about forty teams and wagons a coming up about half way between Fort Edward and Half Way Brook and a scout of French and Indians waylaid them and killed every ox and destroyed all their stores everything[50] —and about midnight our camps were alarmed of it and Major Putnom rallied about a 1000 men and went after them.

Saturday 29th. This day Rogers went upon the track with his rangers[51] and sent back for all the picket guard and they went— and this day I was very poor and took a portion of fizik.

Sunday 30th. This morning by break of day some of Major Putnom's men that he left with the battoes spied some more a coming down the lake—and they come and told and Limon rallied up about 2000 men and went up the lake—I was poor and went to meeting Mr. Ingarson[52] preached and his text was in *Psalms* the 83 and the 14 and 15 and the afternoon the text was in *Deuteronomy* 32 and 29 verse.

Mon. 31st. Nine of our New England men were put under guard for making a false larrom about the battoes coming down upon us and also one regular that Rogers took that deserted last year to the French from us.

Tuesday August 1st. There was about 700 men went down to the Half Way Brook to be stationed there—and eight of our company and Captain Holmes came back.

Wednesday 2. Today General Limon came in off of a scout and the men that went with him and Rogers and Putnom went of a

---

50. Rogers, in his *Journal*, speaks of this occurrence. He says it was on the 27th, and that one hundred and sixteen men were killed, of whom sixteen were rangers.
51. He went out with seven hundred men, to intercept the marauding party, but they escaped.
52. Ingersoll.

scout with fourteen or fifteen hundred for ten days[53] —this day Craft died and was buried—Stephen Lyon come off scout.

Thurs. 3rd. Two of our men went out a fishing for two days but had poor luck.

Friday 4th. We had orders to march to Fort Edward and, I washed up my clothes.

Sat. 5th. This morning about half our regiment marched forward to build breast works along upon the road in some bad places—we arrived at Fort Edward at 9 clock and we built two breast works.

Sunday 6th. We drew three days' provision and this afternoon the rest of our regiment came down and the teams that went up the day before—we received our pacet[54] of letters from home.

Monday 7th. Captain and all that were able to go were ordered to guard down to Fort Miller and back again.

Tues. 8th. In the morning we were drew out for work and worked the forenoon then we were ordered to fix every man in the regiments to make ready to go out to help Major Putnom and we met them a coming in about sundown—and we helped them a long as far as we could that night and lay out that night—and three of the wounded men died there and Ben Deny for one.[55]

---

53. Rogers says that, on his return from his attempt to intercept the marauding party, he was met by an express, with orders to march toward the head of Lake Champlain, at South and East bays, to prevent the French marching upon Fort Edward. There he was by Major Putnam and Captain Dalyell or D'Ell.
54. Packet.
55. A severe engagement took place on Clear river, the west branch of Wood creek, about a mile north-west from Fort Anne village (then the site of a picketed blockhouse, called Fort Anne), between a party of rangers and provincials under Rogers, Putnam, and Captain Dalyell, or D'Ell, and about an equal number of French and Indians under Molang, a famous partisan leader. The English troops were marching when attacked: Putnam was in front, with the provincials; Rogers was in the rear, with his rangers; and D'Ell in the centre, with the regulars. Molang attacked them in front, and a powerful Indian rushed forward and made Putnam a prisoner. The provincials were thrown into great confusion, but were rallied by Lieutenant Durkee, who was one of the victims of the Wyoming massacre twenty years afterward. D'Ell, with Gage's light infantry, behaved very (continued on next page)

Wed. 9th. We got in about 8 o'clock and, buried the dead and the wounded were dressed and carried over on the island[56] —Powers came up with a load of settlers[57] stores and treated us well.

Thur. 10th. I was called out to work upon the block house this day—our post went of home with our letters.

Friday 11th. We went up to guard teams to Half Way Brook and to build a breast work thirty-six Ox teams and six wagons.

Sat. 12th. Colonel Phichi[58] had a letter from Major Putnom at Tiantiroge[59] he is taken prisoner.[60]

Sun. 13th. Day the chief of our men upon duty and the rest went to meeting the afternoon the text was in the 2nd of *Timothy* the 1st chapter and 10 verse.

Mon. 14. I had nothing to do I wrote a letter to John.

Tues. 15. I was upon picit[61] guard and wet and stormy it was—one of the regulars whipt for sleeping upon guard.

Wednesday 16. The rangers discovered a scout of French and

---

gallantly, and the rangers finally put the enemy to flight. The latter lost about two hundred men. Colonel Prevost, then in command at Fort Edward, sent out three hundred men, with refreshments for the party, and all arrived at Fort Edward on the 9th. This was the relief-party mentioned in the text, under date of the 8th.

56. This is an island in the Hudson, opposite Fort Edward, and known as Rogers's island.

57. Sutler's.

58. Fitch.

59. Ticonderoga.

60. The Indian who seized Putnam tied him to a tree, and for a time he was exposed to the cross-fire of the combatants. His garments were riddled by bullets, but, strange to say, not one touched his person. He was carried away in the retreat, his wrists tightly bound with cords. The Indians rejoiced over the capture of their great enemy, and he was doomed to the torture. In the deep forest he was stripped naked, bound to a sapling, wood was piled high around him, the death-songs of the savages were chanted, and the torch was applied. Just then a heavy shower of rain almost extinguished the flames. They were again bursting forth with fiercer intensity, when a French officer, informed of what was going on, darted through the crowd of yelling savages, and released the prisoner. He was delivered to Montcalm at Ticonderoga, then sent to Montreal, and, after being treated kindly, was exchanged for a prisoner taken by Colonel Bradstreet at Frontenac.

61. Picket.

come in to Fort Edward and all that were able were ready at a minuets warning—today I sent a letter to John Lyon.

Thursday 17th. W, p, thirty-one stripes still and nothing to do the lieutenants fixed up their tents.

Friday 18th. Six of our men were ordered to go over to work upon the block house over the river—I was really tired at night.

Saturday 19th. I washed my clothes—Colonel Fitch at Salatogue.

Sunday 20th. We were almost all out upon duty to work at the highways and in the afternoon a very hard shower which set our tents all afloat.

Monday 21st. I went down to Fort Mizerey[62] and I heard of John Day's death at Salatogue—this day Morris came up and we lived well.

Tuesday 22nd. I went up the river to look for a horse— Steven and I was called upon picit guard.

Wednesday 23rd. I went out to look oxen and was treated well—one man's gun went of and cut of his finger—we drove out the two men out of the block house kept the great cattle.

Thursday, 24th. I was called out to guard up teams and to work on the road and had a gill of rum for it—Zachariah Catlin died at Fort Edward.

Friday 25th. I was called upon the quarter guard and we heard the great guns that were fired at the Lake[63]—they shot at a mark and our provincials beat them and it made them very mad.

Saturday 26. David Lyon and Barnes set out to go to Albany sick—this day they held a regimental court marshal upon three deserters of Captain Mather's company—one William Cannody

---

62. Fort Misery was a breastwork at the mouth of Moses's kill, or creek, a short distance from Fort Miller, on the east side of the Hudson.
63. At Fort George, at the head of Lake George.

and William Clemanon were judged to have 1000 lashes and to-day received 200 and 50 stripes a piece the other was forgiven.

Sunday 27. I was out upon the works at the great block house—we were out of provision we drew for seven days and but four gone so the regulars shot pigeons and our men did so too.

Monday 28th. Every private in our company was out upon duty that was able and about 4 o'clock we came in and the orders were that every man should make ready to fire three valleys[64] —and first they fired the cannon at the fort one after the other round the fort which is twenty-one then the small arms and so three rounds a piece and then made a great fire on the parade and played round it and one gill of rum a man allowed for the frolic and a barrel of beer for a company[65] —a very wet night.

Tuesday 29th. Very wet in the morning then cleared of cold I went upon duty and sent a letter home.

Friday September ye 1st. Our duty was to help get out the cannon out of the bottom of the river that was dropped in by the means of going to near the end of the brig[66] and sunk the scows and drowned one ox very cold work—A woman, whipt seventy stripes and drummed out of camp.

Saturday 2nd. I was called upon the picit guard today—last night I went down to Fort Misketor[67] and Smith Ainsworth treated us well.

Sunday 3rd. I was out upon the escort and every man upon some duty—I went to meeting part of the forenoon and the text was in *Acts* 24 and 25—Charles Ripla was put in ensign.

Monday 4th, Our post set of home—I went down to Fort

---

64. Volleys.
65. It was the king's birthday. The firing of twenty-one heavy guns formed a royal salute.
66. Bridge.
67. Fort Musquito was a breastwork cast up at the mouth of Snooks' creek.

Misketor to guard teams and the post and the Lobster's[68] and our men hopped and rassled[69] together to see which would beat and our men beat.

Tuesday 5th. Still and nothing strange.

Wednesday 6th. Most all of our men upon duty I was to work a making a road to go up to the great block house.

Thursday 7th. All our men out upon works guarding teams a great number of them nigh 100 and when we came back their was a scout come in to Fort Edward that went out from the lake—they discovered nothing.

Friday 8th. This day Sergent Erls went out to Fort An[70] after the con-nu[71] and Lieutenant Larnard and Ephraim Ellinghood Knap and John Richason and Jeb Brooks and Hezekiah Carpenter the six of our company forty in all went along—I went to work at the high way and had half a pint of rum for it.

Saturday 9th. I was warned a quarter guard and I changed with Moses Peak and went upon the escort and got in by 12 a clock—I was warned out to work but did not do much—Sergent Erls come in with his con-nu and the general was much pleased with it.

Sunday 10. I was upon guard but went to meeting a part of

---

68. This was a nickname for the regular troops, who were dressed in scarlet uniforms.

69. Wrestled.

70. Fort Anne was erected in 1757, a year before the occurrences here narrated took place. It was a strong blockhouse of logs, with portholes for cannon and loopholes for musketry, and surrounded by a picket of pine-saplings. When the writer visited the spot in 1848, he dug up the part of one of the pickets yet remaining in the earth, and, on splitting it, it emitted the pleasant odour of a fresh pine-log, though ninety years had elapsed since it was placed there. This fort was near the bank of Wood creek, about eleven miles from the head of Lake Champlain, at the village of Whitehall. It was in the line of Burgoyne's march toward the Hudson, in 1777; and near it quite a severe skirmish took place between Colonel Long, of Schuyler's army, and a British detachment under Colonel Hill, on the 8th of July, the day after Ticonderoga was abandoned to the enemy. Victory was almost within the grasp of Colonel Long, when his ammunition failed, and he was compelled to retreat.

71. Canoe.

the forenoon and the text was in the 24 of *Acts* and 25 verse and the afternoon the text was in *James* the 6th and 12 verse.

Monday 11. I took four days' provision and Josh Barrit and one ranger with me and we went out near Fort An and we spied a fire and some person—and we come back and made our report to the general and he blamed us some and said we should have a new pilot and go again—Jo Downer put under guard.

Tuesday 12th. I was freed from duty and we went and split out some plank to do up our tent.

Wednesday 13th. To work in the fort a wheeling gravel all day—four regulars whipt in fort some for gaming and one for being absent after being warned upon guard.

Thursday 14th. I was warned on escort down to Mizzery[72] and flanked all the day—Tuesday 12 at night there was two bonfires and two barrels of rum allowed for the rejoicing of Broadstreet's taking Catarocrway.[73]

Friday 15th. Day I was to work over upon the island and worked hard a shovelling dirt &c—Ephraim Ellinghood taken poorly.

Saturday 16th. Day I went to cutting fassheens[74] and stented four a piece in half a day and twelve stakes.

Sunday 17th. All our men upon works Mr. Pomri[75] preached one sermon and his text in *James* Chapter 5th and 12 verse—Stephen Child had a post to Albany and set out this day one regular come in that was a fishing at Half Way Brook.

Monday 18th. I was to work over to the block house and took my farewell of working there and all our sick were drawn up and some discharged.

---

72. Fort Misery.

73. The Indian name of the site of Fort Frontenac (where Kingston, Upper Canada, now stands), taken by Colonel Bradstreet, was Cataraqua. That was also the Indian name for Lake Ontario.

74. Fascines bundles of sticks, mixed with earth, and used for filling ditches in the construction of forts.

75. Pomeroy.

Tuesday 19th. Four of our company had a final discharge from the campaign and set of home—Seth Bassit Jonathan Corbin John Peak and Silas Hoges.

Wednesday 20th. Still here the main of us and nothing remarkable only almost all our Woodstock men came up and with great joy we received them and much more the things that were sent us—I received a letter from Ben Lyon.

Thursday 21st. Nothing remarkable this day.

Friday 22nd. Our Woodstock Old melisha[76] set out home and Lieutenant Smith and Corporal Peak and William Mercy and Samuel Leavins had a pass to Albany and went with them along down and many more that did not belong to our company.

Saturday 23rd. Our post came up and I received a letter from home.

Sunday 24th. Mr. Pomri preached one sermon in the middle of the day so that the work men might have some opportunity to hear some his text was in *Ezekiel* the 37 Chapter and 36 verse—I was to work upon the island and I heard part of the sermon.[77]

Monday 25. Nothing remarkable only Stephen Lyon got hurt Samuel Morris and Chub went down along to Albany.

Tuesday 26th. One scout went out for three days—this day a great number of teams came down from the lake.

Wednesday 27th. The Thompson men that came up to see us set out for New England and Sergent Cromba had a pass to Albany and went down along.

Thursday 28th. Nothing remarkable only the scout came in that went out for three days.

Friday 29th. Nothing remarkable only very long orders &c.

---

76. Militia.

77. The channel between Rogers's island, on which the great block-house was built, and Fort Edward, does not exceed two hundred feet in width.

Saturday 30th. Nothing remarkable only the crissing[78] of the Royal block house—and the whole of our regiment that were able went over to work and had a good frolic to drink—the men in general worked well at the entrenching round the block house the trench three foot deep.

Sunday October ye 1st. Nothing remarkable but something very strange—and that is the camps were so still and no work going forward nor no prayers nor no sermon and a gill of rum into the bargain—this we had from the generals our month promised to us yesterday—Mr. Pomri went down to Seratoga to see his son that was sick and to day he come back &c.

Monday ye 2nd. All the regiment that were able to work went over to the Block House besides what was upon guard and they were divided into four parties and they that got done first was to have the best fat sheep one sheep to each party—I was upon the grass guard and at night I found it very tedious lying out for it stormed exceeding hard all night.

Tuesday ye 3rd. Our mess being all of duty we made us up two straw bunks for four of us to lay in and as it happened we did it in a good time for it was a very cold night.

Wednesday ye 4th. Being very cold Corporal Sanger and Eliezer Child had a pass down to Albany and likewise a small scout went for number four and we made our chimney—Serjant Kimbal was broke and turned into the ranks.

Thursday 5th. General Ambross[79] arrived at Fort Edward about 12 o'clock and immediately he went of to the lake nothing more remarkable today.

Friday 6th. Henry Lyon and Ephraim Ellinghood poorly and cleared from duty—three men whipt about three hundred lashes apiece and one woman two and fifty lashes on bare rump.

Saturday 7th. Our picket went up toward the Half Way Brook

---

78. Christening.
79. General Amherst.

to meet General Ambross and about 3 o'clock he arrived at Fort Edward and at 2 o'clock the picket went down with him again and his wagon and six horses.

Sunday 8. In the forenoon all our men upon works in the afternoon we were allowed to attend meeting and Mr Pomri preached one sermon and his text was in *Ezekiel* 36 and 37 verse—our family this day had a great rarity for dinner and that was a bild pudding.

Monday 9. Nothing remarkable among us this day.

Tuesday 10. I was upon guard and a very stormy day and night it was orders came out strict that all fires should be put out by 8 of the clock in the morning and not to have no more til 6 at night and they that don't obey the orders are to have their chimney tore down and not to have no other during this campaign—Colonel Fitch lost a barrel of wine.

Wednesday 11th. Still warm and wet some of our regiment discharged home but none of our company.

Thursday 12. A very clear cold morning all our men upon works and upon guard that were able—Colonel Hart's regiment of the Hampshire march down to Fort Edward in order for home.

Friday 13th. All our men upon works again today three discharged *vis*—Richard Jordin Stephen Lyon and John Howlet— at night 300 of the Bay men came down sick and two of them that carried their packs died in the night.

Saturday 14th. All warned out upon works but the stormy weather defected them in it—the regulars which came down from the lake with us have orders to march next Friday down along in order for their winter quarters at Hallefax[80] —this night the sentry which stood at the south of the store house spied a man a getting of flour and he hailed him three times but he would not stop and the sentry fired but did not hit him and in his hurry he left his tom me hawk[81] and one shoe.

---

80. Halifax, Nova Scotia.
81. Tomahawk.

Sunday ye 15. Very cold all upon works and guard by sunrise this evening their came in a great number of teams and Samuel Peak brought the melancholy news of Stephen Childs being killed and skulpt[82] and another captivated—I was out upon the grass guard.

Monday 16th. All upon works and all the teams set off for the lake—twelve men taken from the quarter guard to guard teams—this evening there came in a great number of wagons an hundred or more.

Tuesday 17th. Being very pleasant in the morning then showery and wet all the rest of the day til 10 o'clock at night— about 12 o'clock at night the teams came in with the artillery—this day a number of our men went down to Fort Miller in battoes to carry the sick and captain's bag went down and the men stayed out.

Wednesday 18th. Being cold the teams set out for the lake— about forty of the king's wagons—this afternoon there was a Lobster[83] corporal married to a Road Island whore—our men came in from Fort Miller.

Thursday 19th. Our regiment was mustered by 9 o'clock in the morning and our brigade-major called over the role of each company and after that we had a drink of flip[84] for working over at the Royal block house—at one of the clock our men were all called to work—A court martial held at Captain Holmes' tent and Captain Holmes President and at the role of the picit guard there was one Isac Ellis whipt thirty stripes— was to had fifty—Colonel Henmans[85] men came in loaded with artillery stores.

Friday 20th. Cold still and our men all upon works— this afternoon Lieutenant Smith came up to us again from Green Bush, and Shubal Child came to his team.

---

82. Scalped.
83. British regular.
84. A mixture of beer and rum, warmed by thrusting a hot iron into it.
85. Hinman's.

Saturday ye 21st. Still cold— in the morning our men called out to work by sunrise or before and six of our company *viz.* David Bishop Ephraim Ellingwood Samuel Mercey Nathaniel Abbott David Jewet and Drake marched of with their packs— this night their came down a great number of teams from ye lake here loaded with cannon balls and bum shells—Likewise a number of sick came down.

Sunday 22. The teams set out for ye lake again—I was upon the quarter guard—a large number of sick set out for home and it yet held cold and at night it cleared of very clear and still but very freezing cold and a black frost.

Monday ye 23rd. I come of guard—Clerk Burrows began his month with Bess—at night three regiments of Province men came down from ye lake and lodged in the wood near the upper block house—some teams down from ye lake with artillery stores.

Tuesday 24th. A number of teams started for ye lake again—I received two letters from Captain Benjamin Lyon and one from Joshua—the post came up yesterday to Fort Edward—This day our drawing and we had good pork—Three regiments of Bay men moved down along which was Colonel Pribbels[86] Colonel Williams and Colonel Nichols.

Wednesday 25th. General Abbacromba arrived at Fort Edward near night and all our regiment there were off duty were ordered to be out upon the parade with their side arms on but the general forbid it—Colonel Partrages' regiment came down and some of the Lather caps and stayed here.

Thursday ye 26th. Stormy morning—snow pretty wet and raw cold—I went upon the picit last night and had one quart of rum for keeping sheep.

Friday 27th. Being lowry and wet one of our men discharged home and set off—Nathaniel Barnes a number of teams set out for the Brook and returned again before sundown.

---

86. Prebles.

Saturday 28th. Being still cold all our men turned out to work sunrise and that want enough and they sent for every weighter[87] and every one that belongs to the regiment— a number of teams set out down homeward and three of our company went with them *viz.* Sergeant Armsba, Jonathan Child and Pain Convis—this afternoon the orders came out that every setler[88] that belongs to the Provincials should quit this place by the first of November.

Sunday ye 29th. Rainy and wet—about 9 o'clock in the morning every man in the regiment that could go went to the falls[89] to help draw down the battoes and very muddy it was.

Monday ye 30th. Being very pleasant in the morning we were all turned out after battoes up to the falls and we went twice apiece.

Tuesday ye 31st. All our men turned out by the revallies[90] beating to go after battoes and General Provorce[91] was out amongst our tents to help turn us out and he said it was the last work we should do that was flung up today—I went upon the quarter guard at noon and they got down all the battoes.

Wednesday November ye 1st. Lowry and wet I come off guard— our men all upon works and three regiments of our Connecticuts came down about noon and Colonel Whitings had orders to go over to the Royal Block House and their to remain til further orders and the other two regiments set off home in battoes and two or three regiments of Lobsters—we had orders come out that we should have two days to clean up in and to set for home on Sunday—this day I wrote a letter and sent to John.

Thursday ye 2nd. Very cold—our men turned out to cutting fassheens and the orders were that it was the last day's work that we should do.

Friday ye 3rd. Very cold our men all turned out upon works

---

87. Waiter.
88. Sutler.
89. The "third fall," as it was called, in the Hudson, at Sandy Hill.
90. Reveille.
91. Provost.

notwithstanding yesterday's promise—our men had but poor encouragements to work and laid but little weight to what the general promised them for he said the first man that disobeyed his orders again should be shot to death whatsoever soldier or officer.

Saturday 4th. I was orderly after the general and our men all to work a drawing in cannon into the fort and our quarter guard was not relieved til afternoon and after that orders come out that we should strike our tents by 8 o'clock and be ready to march by 9—one Gimbals got his discharge from the regular service today.

Sunday ye 5th. Being very cold it began to rain so that we were detained but Colonel Whiting marched off—rainy all day long— we had orders to be ready to march at 7 o'clock in the morning.

Monday ye 6th. Cloudy still—at 8 o'clock we struck our tents and at 9 o'clock we marched off and about half after 12 we arrived at Fort Miller and made a little stop then marched again and arrived at Saratoga sun about one hour high and made no stop there but marched on about three mile and encamped in the woods.

Friday ye 10th. Very stormy and snow in the morning we drew two days' allowance of provisions but no money and about 2 o'clock we set out from Green Bush and arrived at Cantihook Town about ten o'clock at night—Thirteen of us and Lieutenant Larnard.

Saturday 11th. From thence we marched sun two hour's high and arrived at John Huggar Booms[92] and revived ourselves a little and bought some rum that belonged to Colonel Whiten's regiment and from thence to Love Joys and went to supper and from thence to Robberses and lodged there in the Paterroon lands.

Sunday 12th. Being still cold we set out at sunrise and arrived

92. Hogeboom's.

at Bushes in Sheffield and had a good breakfast and there was more with horses—and from thence to Larrances and revived ourselves there to Coles—and thence to Seggick in Cornwell and then to Wilcocks in Goshen and lodged there.

Monday 13th. Cold—I come up to Holleboate and sent my pack along from Goshen and then we marched and arrived at Litchfield and then to Herrintown to Wiers and from their to Strongs in Farmingtown and lodged there.

Tuesday 14th. Very cold and frosty—marched five mile through the meadows and went to breakfast and come to Mercies and stayed there and Captain Holmes came up.

Wednesday 15th. We marched and arrived at Chenys in Bolton and from thence we marched and arrived at Lees in Covantry[93] and lodged there—very rainy Stephen Lyon met us with the horses.

Thursday 16th. Being warm and pleasant we arrived at Woodstock.

---

93. Coventry.

Note

The soldiers had, necessarily, a great deal of leisure during permanent camp-duties, and contrived various ways to amuse themselves, and "kill time." In those days the common soldiers carried their powder in the horns of cows or oxen, and many amused themselves by ornamenting them by a skilful use of their knives. Below is a specimen of one of these ornamented horns, prepared during the campaign of 1758. Upon it is neatly cut the figure of a fortified building (a part of which is seen in the engraving), the owner's name, and a verse, as follows:

Elnathan Ives His Horn, Made at Lake George, September ye 22nd, Ad. 1758.

I, powder, With My Brother Baul
A Hero like do Conquer All.
Steel not this Horn For Fear of Shame
For on it is the Oners name.
The Roos is Red, the Grass is Green
The Days Are past Which I Have Seen.

Journal of a French Officer
at the Siege of Quebec

Edited by
Captain R. Gardiner

Memoirs of the Siege of Quebec Capital of all Canada and of the Retreat of Monsieur de Bourlemaque, From Carillon to the Isle Aux Noix in Lake Champlain.

From the Journal of a French Officer on Board the *Chezine* Frigate, taken by his Majesty's Ship *Rippon*.

Compared with the Accounts Transmitted Home by Major General Wolfe and Vice-Admiral Saunders;

With Occasional Remarks By Richard Gardiner, Esq; Captain of Marines in the *Rippon*.

In Joys of Conquest he res'gns his Breath,
And fill'd with England's Glory, smiles in Death,
Add. Campaign.

To the memory of Wolfe and Montcalm
Sunt lachryma rerum, et mentem mortalia tangunt

Preface

This scarce journal of the siege of Quebec is printed from a manuscript copy which was sent to me by Mr W. C. Lane, of Harvard University. The journal contains many details relating to the French camp which are not recorded by other writers of the period, and it is therefore of special value to students of Canadian history. The fact that it is reprinted for the first time by the nuns of the Franciscan convent, whose printing-press is situated upon the ground once owned by Abraham Martin, after whom the Plains were named, and upon a portion of the actual battlefield, will no doubt be highly appreciated by those who desire to possess a souvenir of the famous battle of the Plains.

A. G. Doughty
Quebec
Sept. 1900

To the Honourable George Hobart

Sir,

At the close of a successful campaign, or after the surrender of a fortified town or city, there is something singularly pleasing in hearing the account given by the enemy of the continual and constant apprehensions of the garrison within the walls, during the progress of a siege, and while it has been carrying on in form; how the inhabitants have been affected upon every nearer approach of an investing army; how they felt along each wounded line, and trembled at each widening breach; in hourly alarms, and like the watchful mistress of the web, though fierce in appearance, proud of the variety of her works, and threatening defiance to every invader, yet inwardly diffident of their strength, and flying to her retired hold on a more brisk and powerful assault than usual; how they formed on any motions actually made against them, or guarded and prepared against others expected to be made; what raised their hopes alternately, and what their fears; their consultations, and their resolutions: These are particulars more striking to the imagination than a perfect knowledge of our own designs, or a complete history of what passed in camp or trenches. The public prints in England are usually confined to the latter transactions only, and inform the reader what methods of attack were pursued on one side, but seldom what precautions were observed on the other, or whether we triumphed through superiority of courage and numbers, or through the neglect and inattention of the enemy;

in a word, that the English won a battle, and the French lost it; that we took a town, not how they defended it, makes up the detail of most of our public military descriptions: the knowledge of the former event is certainly the most material, but that of the latter is far from being unentertaining.

'Tis in this view I have presumed to lay the following sheets before you, as they may possibly contribute to amuse an idle hour in the country (if any of yours can with propriety be called such) and at the same time introduce to your recollection a man at a distance from you, who ever so remotely employed in the public service, has a heart still alive to the warm sensations of private friendships at home, and gratitude ever to think with pleasure on that in particular, which Mr. Hobart has honoured him with.

The Kingdom of France, perhaps was never more reduced in its naval power than at this æra of time before us; perhaps not in any one period of its history whatever. It was a standing complaint against the late Cardinal Fleury, that during his long ministry, the Marine Department was entirely neglected; and that in consequence of this inattention, at the breaking out of the last war, the French navy was not only not upon a respect-able footing, but was even held in contempt by the fleets of other nations, particularly by those of Spain and England, and was very unequal to support the Grand Monarque in the credit due to him as a maritime power; but the present low state and shattered condition of their marine is owing to a cause more glorious to our august sovereign, and his triumphant subjects to victory: Their ships are now diminished in their numbers, not from mismanagement in their Gallic State, but from British capture, from being subdued or destroyed from defeats repeated, conquest still following where e'er the flag of. England flew, with a most amazing rapidity, in all parts of the known world: in short, the French are at this instant but seldom seen upon the ocean, for this plain reason only, because they have been beat and burnt out of it by the English.

For some time past no line of battle ship has returned to

France, that upon enquiry has not been found to have got in by stealth; if reinforcements are to be sent abroad to any of their few remaining settlements, are we not presently informed that some man of war has slipt out in the night, and luckily has escaped the Channel cruisers, has run away in the dark, with her troops on board for the East or West Indies? Their ports are everywhere almost blocked up: their foreign trade not so much impaired as annihilated; their merchantmen all turned privateers, and so in due course of time becoming English prizes; our men of war hourly insulting their coasts, riding at anchor in their harbours, pursuing their scattered fleets from bay to bay, and river to river; spreading terror and confusion throughout every province in the kingdom, burning their towns and forts, cutting out their ships from under their guns, driving others against the rocks, and making the very shore of France conspire to the ruin of its own navy, and present destruction instead of refuge to the dispersed and flying squadrons of its sovereign.

Far be it from me to exaggerate the British power upon the watery element; but I believe that it is well known to be the true distressed state of the marine of France at this juncture, and his present Majesty, whose accession to the imperial crown of these his realms, so illustriously begins, and is so fair in prospect to add still greater honour to himself and glory to his people, has an undoubted right, if ever any British monarch had, or victorious fleets and armies can procure it, to oblige more nations than one to acknowledge his sovereignty on the ocean, and to strike to his royal flag in whatever seas or climates it may be met.

Whether this superiority over the grand disturber of Europe, in his naval strength, is owing to the great increase of riches and commerce in England of late years or whether the people in general may not have taken a more martial turn, and have been roused and animated by the continual insults and depredations of the common enemy, into a more glorious warmth and spirit of action, is not for me to determine; certain it is, that British courage may sleep for a, while; but though it slumbers, it is only for a time, and will most assuredly awake whenever called upon in earnest: whatever is the cause, the event is plain and obvious, and our pre-eminence at sea confessed by all the states and potentates around us.

And here it might not be improper to mention the distinguished valour and intrepidity of his Majesty's officers and men in both services, as being perhaps in some measure conducive to this whole acquisition; but an officer writes with an ill grace upon so partial a subject; however, thus much it is possible may be said without offence, that hitherto but few of them have been found wanting in their most strenuous endeavours to promote the attainment of it, nor many of those employed abroad, discovered to be much inferior to the French in capacity and resolution, and once indeed have been so happy as to be told from the throne, (a reward and recompense glorious beyond all others) that their behaviour had been such, as that the enemy for the future might learn "What troops they had to deal with" when they opposed his Majesty's arms in battle.

I have hinted this only in order, with your indulgence, to take notice of a remark too frequently made, and a very severe censure it is upon military gentlemen in general, that is, "That allowing them bravery, they still are deficient in their knowledge of the art of war, and by no means equal to the French in the latter respect, however superior they may be to them in the former:" the following shoots will, I hope, afford a noble, and I would willingly think a convincing proof to the contrary, and tend to root out a notion so long established, and so implicitly swallowed, to the disadvantage of our officers in the fleet and army; whether we consider the conduct of the important expedition before us, on the land or sea side of the question; whether we consider the great abilities, and thorough knowledge in his profession, required of a British admiral to steer his squadrons with safety in so intricate a navigation as that of the river of St. Laurence, and so little known to Englishmen; where all lights and informations were to be had, and must be had, from the enemy themselves, and directions of every sort were to be borrowed from French charts, French observations, and French pilots: Or whether we consider the comprehensive judgement, penetration, presence of mind, and martial science, to be expected from a leader of troops, such as to promise, or even give faint hopes of success in so remote, uncultivated, inhospitable a country as that of Canada; where rivers, woods, and mountains break off all communication; where the very face of nature is set against the invader, and is strong as the strongest barrier; where uncommon heats and cold are in alliance with, and fight for the adversary; where a field of action is to be made, and to be found, to try your strength upon, and to give even a chance for victory; and where, if by accident, an inconsiderable plain presents itself, wide enough for troops to enter upon action, entrenchments and redoubts forbid access: where the foe lies buried up to the teeth, each avenue shut, and every pass securely fortified: and this in a region where Britons having been known to fail before in their Attacks, had given fresh spirits to a vain glorious enemy, who vaunted their forts and lines to be impregnable, provoking, not fearing an assault, and laughing at the quixotism of a British landing.

However, if oppressed and loaded with such uncommon difficulties, the British officers still made their way to conquest, returned home in triumph, receiving the applause of their country, rejoicing their sovereign, and bringing fresh laurels to crown his aged brow, blooming even from the wilds of America; surely it is but common candour to believe, and allow, that men who thus succeeded, who thus triumphed, beyond all hope and opinion, surmounting obstacles judged to be insurmountable, and reaping such iron harvests of the field, could not be men very ignorant in their profession, or remarkably deficient in their knowledge of the art of war.

The navigation of the fleet was no less difficult and hazardous as, as will more particularly appear from a view of the South channel of the River St Laurence, even after our shipping had advanced securely above the very dangerous passage of the traverse at the end of the Isle of Orleans; the following observations which I have traced from a French chart found on board the *Chezine* will serve to illustrate this more clearly.

From the E.N.E. point of Orleans to the S.E. better than a mile, lie the Isles Aux Rots and Madame, between which and that of Orleans is situated the traverse at the opening of the two channels which lead up N. and S. of the Isle of Orleans, to Quebec.

The whole breadth of the River St. Laurence off the traverse from the north shore to the south, from Cape Torment to Bertier, is only three leagues, depth of water ten fathom; and the broadest part of the south channel, which our ships went up by the side of the isle of Orleans, opposite to St. John's, one league only; and the narrowest half a league.

The whole of this channel is exceeding dangerous, and the passage up so nice, that it might with some propriety be considered as the principal outwork of Quebec, and in ordinary attacks more to be depended upon, than the strongest fortifications or defences of the town.

In the winding part of the S. Channel, from Beaumont over to the village of St. Laurence, in the Isle of Orleans, there runs out a sand three quarters of a mile long, and the shore from side to side is barely two miles broad. This sand stretches up the channel from the E.N.E. to the W.S.W. along the New England shore for seven miles ahead, being one third of the navigation from the traverse to the points of Orleans and Levi, between which the English fleet afterwards anchored. The length of the Island of Orleans, from the E.N.E. point to the W.S.W. is about six French leagues, and the broadest parts about two.

From St. Bernabie, where the fleet first came to an anchor, up to the traverse, (a distance of thirty-eight leagues) there is a number of shoals, sands, and little islands interspersed; and here indeed the difficulty of navigation seems to commence; for the river of St. Laurence is pretty clear and open till the ships arrive off this cape, and the greatest danger to be dreaded is that of fogs, or the hard gales of wind which may drive a fleet on S. or N. shore; as was the case in the expedition against Quebec in the Queen's time, under the command of Sir Hovendon Walker, and General Hill, (A. D. 1711.) where the British squadron was run upon the Island of Eggs, which they could not weather. Eight transports were stranded with 884 men on board, and the whole, through the ignorance of the pilots and violence of the winds, in imminent danger of being lost.

The fogs were likewise very alarming to mariners, and very frequent in this river: so much so, that we ought to think ourselves extremely happy and much favoured by Providence, (which through the whole progress of the present war seems in a particular manner to have distinguished the justice of the British cause) that our naval officers were blessed with a clear serene sky and moderate weather to work their ships in, and to steer them from sand to sand and shoal to shoal, in the most difficult parts of the hazardous Channel, keeping their course direct, and sliding up to the very walls of the town without interruption or one fatal accident, without running on shore in one place, upon rocks in another, or even foul of their own ships; and guiding the helm with such exactitude and masterly skill, as if the guardian angel of the British realms had itself conducted this most fortunate armament, and from every isle or island, cape or point of land, which it was dangerous to approach, had timely warned the English admiral, proclaiming aloud: "Hither to shalt thou come, but no farther."

The following beautiful lines of Claudian, if ever they were applicable to any man, were so in a particular manner to Mr. Saunders on this occasion:

O! nimium dilecte Deo, qui militat æther,
Et conjurati veniunt ad classica venti.

Success in so perilous a navigation will, I hope, incline the yet unprejudiced part of the world to imagine, that the officers of our fleet are likewise not unacquainted in their several and respective departments, nor at all inferior to the enemy in seamanship, and what relates to the head as well as the heart of bold, active, and experienced commanders.

Such and so great were the difficulties attending this extraordinary expedition in the first instance only, and before the troops could be brought into action, or even landed to make an attempt, so that when the whole of the operations of this campaign are taken into consideration, it may well be esteemed, and I think, impartially, the most arduous undertaking, and the most important achievement that has taken place since the beginning of this war; an expedition big with as interesting events, as perhaps was ever designed by an able and penetrating minister or carried into execution by a gallant and enterprising general; so as to leave the scrutinizing world and lookers on of all nations in suspense which to admire most, the extensive genius of the one, or the matchless intrepidity of the other; the glorious offspring of which illustrious endeavours was the reduction of all Canada to his Majesty's obedience, and the chastising the overbearing insolence of a proud, wary, restless and perfidious enemy, whilst it pleased Providence to bless the King's cause, and crown his arms with such a rapidity of success, and such a torrent of brilliant victories, as must forever distinguish the military prowess and awakened spirit of England in all martial history throughout the world.

I should now, Sir, apologize for the tedious length of this. Will it be allowed in excuse that, warmed with the delightful prospect of the glory of our country, I have suffered the pen to wander, nor stopped its progress, while on a subject so transporting to a soldier and a Briton? In either of which lights should you think of me to advantage, my ambition is answered; for your approbation will always convey sufficient applause, and your friendship confer sufficient honour upon.

Sir,

Your most obliged and obedient humble servant
Richard Gardiner
From on board his Majesty's ship *Rippon*
Quiberon Bay
Feb. 18, 1761

The squadron under Sir Edward Hawke is now lying between the main land of France and the beautiful island of Belleisle: at a little distance from us to the E. S. E. is St. Gildas, a pleasant village, situated on an eminence which commands the Bay of Quiberon, Belleisle, the sea, the Cardinals, and several small islands; on the summit of the hill stands the celebrated convent of the Paraclete, founded by Abelard and Eloisa, and walled in with extensive gardens to the southward; the situation is very delightful to the eyes, and the village (as I am informed) is in summer time a place of great resort.

Journal of a French Officer

May 10, 20, 1759

On the 10th of May, 1759, Monsieur de Bougainville arrived at Quebec, from Old France, in the *Chezine*, Captain Duclos; soon after which we had an account of the arrival in the river of fifteen merchantmen, under the convoy of Monsieur Kanou; and on the 20th counted twenty-three sail in the[1] basin of Quebec. These vessels came in very good time, for the English fleet was soon after them, and on the night of, the 23rd, the fires on Point Levi gave us notice of its approach to the[2] Bee. These signals were confirmed by a courier, who brought intelligence, that fourteen ships were already come to an anchor at St. Bernabie[3].

Monsieur de Montcalm, who was then at Quebec, immediately dispatched an express to Monsieur de[4] Vaudreuil with this account, who instantly repaired to the garrison, and both generals made the

---

1. The basin before Quebec, from the south shore to the north, opposite to the village of Charlebourg, is about two miles and a half broad. This basin is formed by the two Channels of the River St Laurence (called the North and South Channel) which empty themselves into it, and unite before the town; after this confluence the river runs up above the town in one channel only, to the S.W. leading to Montreal &c. but the stream sets to the N.E. Quebec stands on a Point of land on the north shore, projecting towards the Basin and the Isle of Orleans.

2. The Bee, or Bie, is a small island in the River St Laurence, distant from Quebec and Point Levi (which is opposite to it) about forty-three French leagues.

3. St Bernabie is about three leagues lower down from the Bee, to the W. N. W.

4. Le Marquis de Vaudreuil, Grand Croix of the royal and military order of St Lewis, was Governor and Lieutenant- General for the French King, in Canada, and usually resided at Montreal.

necessary dispositions for a vigorous defence. Orders were given out for assembling the militia everywhere, and five battalions were sent for from Montreal[5]; a body of horse, consisting of 200 men, were raised, and the command given to Monsieur de la Roche Beaucour. The Beauport side of the coast was fortified all along from the river St. Charles to the falls of Montmorency; a bridge of boats was built over this river, and the *tête du pont* (or head of the bridge) defended by a hornwork: an entrenchment was thrown up in the prairie, (or meadow) of Monsieur Hiche, which was carried on from St. Rock to the bridge; the entrance of the river St. Charles was secured by a boom, and this boom defended by two hulks with cannon, which were run ashore a little within the chain; several *bateaux* (or boats) were put upon the stocks, some of which were to carry a twelve, and others a fourteen pounder: a kind of[6] floating battery was likewise begun upon, of twelve embrasures to carry cannon of twelve. eighteen, and twenty-four pounders, and ninety men, and the command given to Captain Duclos, of the *Chezine*, who was the inventor of it.

Batteries *en barbette* were erected on the Quay du Palais, and those on the ramparts, and in the Lower town, were repaired, completed, and considerably enlarged. Eight vessels were likewise fitted out as[7] fire-ships, which did no execution, owing

---

5. Montreal is a large fortified town, situated upon an island in the river St Laurence, about 180 miles higher up, and to the Southward of Quebec. It is called Montreal at present (or Mont Royal) from a very high mountain that overlooks the island; but formerly, and indeed originally, it bore the name of Ville Marie, or Mary's Town. The River of St Laurence, at Montreal, is about three miles broad, but it is not navigable beyond for rocks and cataracts. The Province of Canada, or New France, of which Quebec was considered as the capital, is situated about 70 and 105 long. W. and between 39 and 58. Lat. N. is according to the latest computations 1800 miles long, and 1260 broad; bounded by New Britain and British Canada on the North; by New Scotland, New England, and New York, on the East; and by unknown lands on the West.

6. *To the uncommon strength of the country, the enemy have, added for the defence of the river, a great number of floating batteries and boats.* Letter from Major General Wolfe.

7. Seven of these fire-ships were sent down from Quebec, at midnight, the 28th of June, upon our men of war and transports, but were all towed ashore by the boats of the squadron, without doing any mischief, notwithstanding the fleet was so numerous, and spread so great a part of the Channel : the next night General Monckton landed with his brigade, and took possession of Point Levi. Letter from Vice Admiral Saunders. *Sept. 5.*

to the ill-management of the officers who had the direction of them: fire-stages were likewise built, but met with as little success as the ships. A street was opened in the garden of the Bishop's palace, for the easier communication between the town and ramparts: the passage that leads to lower town was blocked up, and the walls of the houses pulled down, that were adjoining to it. The breaches in the city walls were all filled up, and such of them as could not be finished with masonry, for want of time, were secured by a palisade, from any sudden attack (or *coup de main*). The ships which were not likely to be wanted during the siege were ordered up the river, as far as Batiscan[8] and all the seamen taken out, but such as were absolutely necessary for working them; the rest were employed at the batteries; and all persons who could be of no service in the siege, such as ladies and others, were desired to withdraw from the city; this request being considered by most people as an order, was submitted to, but not without reluctance.

JUNE 26, 1759

About the middle of June, advice was received that the whole of the English fleet was arrived at the Bee. and the wind at north east continuing to favour them, we soon learnt that they had passed all the dangerous shoals and had ground, and without any accident were safe at an anchor along the Isle of Orleans. The traverse,[9] a channel so difficult to cross, if our pilots are to be

---

8. Batiscan lies about twenty leagues above the town; Admiral Holmes went up with his division ten or twelve leagues, in order to destroy them, but could get no farther.
9. The traverse lies at the E. or N. E. End of the Isle of Orleans, about twenty miles below Quebec, where the River St Laurence divides itself into two channels, one running on the North, and the other on the south side of Orleans. The breadth of the river, from shore to shore, from Cape Tormens to Bertier, is about nine miles, but the mouth of the South Channel, which our fleet passed at the traverse, is choked up with a number of rocks, and sands, and little islands. From the N. E. end of it, at the distance of four leagues to the S.W. are sands and rocks running up for twelve miles to the Isle Vertu, which is two leagues long; opposite to this is another island, guarded with a round sand, bigger and broader than it self considerably, being only a mile and a half long, called the Isle Rouge; the passage for the fleet, between these two islands, is a league and a half broad. (continued on next page)

credited, was cleared without any trouble by the English squadron, notwithstanding the buoys were all cut away, and many of the ships ran over it, even in the night. The fleet of the enemy consisted of 160 sail. We counted sixteen of the line (of which three mounted eighty guns) and eight frigates; the rest were transports of different sorts. Vice-Admiral Saunders commanded the men-of-war, and Major General Wolfe the troops destined to form the siege, and which might in the whole amount to about 8000 or 9000 effective men.

JUNE 30, 1759

The whole of our army was assembled at Beauport, the last day of June, consisting of five battalions of regular troops, from 700 to 800 a battalion, the troops of the colony, and near an equal number of savages; the rest were only militia, and made up in the whole about 14000 men.

From the Isle Rouge, proceeding on to the S.W. about four leagues, is situated the Isle au Lievre, the approach to which, on the north side, is prevented by a sand five miles long, and three quarters broad, with a rock in the middle of it; on the south side are three little rocks, and from the middle of this island to the S.W. End of it, runs a sand twelve miles long, and three broad, with three rocks in it. Opposite this sand, to the southward, are four rocks, and a sand with five more rocks a little higher up upon it; the passage for the shipping between these two sands, to the south of Lievre, is about a league broad, and on the north side of the island but half a one: This sand extends above fifteen miles from below Les Pelleciers up to Cape Camoras, and higher.

About seven miles farther up, a broad oval sand runs almost across the river, within three miles of Cape au Oye, on the opposite shore; the river is here about ten miles broad, seven of which are covered with this sand, to the westward of which is another sand and rock, and the Island of Au Coudre, the passage open to the fleet between them not being broader than one mile and a half.

From the Isle Au Coudre up to the traverse is one continual ad wide extended sand lying in the middle of the river, full of rocks, stretching thirty miles in length, and better than two leagues broad in some parts of it. The passage on each side for the squadron, in the narrowest part, is only a mile and a half, on the north side it is scarce a mile.

This sand with the little Isles Aux Rots, Madame, and the sands interspersed around them, lead the approach to the Island of Orleans, and the mouth of the South Channel to Quebec at the traverse; and from the traverse up to Quebec the navigation is already mentioned in the dedication.

From Point Levi all along the coast to the mountains of Our Lady, on the south shore, a distance of about 120 miles, are situated a number of towns and villages, and a greater still in proportion to the distance, on the Canada or north side.

The right of the camp was fixed near the decoy, and the left extended to the Falls of Montmorency. The church of Beauport was in the centre; on the left were encamped the battalion of Royal Roussillon, the Volunteers of Dubrel, the militia of Montreal, and all the savages, under the command of the Chevalier de Levy.

Mr. Dumas commanded the right wing of the army, which was composed of the militia of Quebec, and of the *Trois Rivieres*[10] (or Three Rivers) whilst the troops of the colony were divided between the left and right. Mr. de Senezergue, Brigadier General, commanded the centre of the camp, and had under his orders the battalions of La Sarre, Languedoc, Guyenne, and Bearn. The headquarters were fixed at the house of Mr. de Vienne, called *La Mistanguienne*. The garrison of the town was composed of the burghers and the seamen, in all about 2000. The troops and the burghers rolled together, and did duty with one another, and the seamen and their officers were employed at the batteries under the command of the officers of the artillery. The troops in the garrison were relieved every four days from the camp. A company of pioneers was likewise formed to carry on the necessary works during the siege, under the direction of the surveyor, or builder of the King's ships.

Mr. de Ramesay, Lieutenant de Roy, commanded in the town, and had under him Mr. le Chevalier le Berne, to whom the defence of the lower town was particularly entrusted.

JUNE 30, 1759

On the 30th of June, the enemy landed 3000 men at Point Levi, to oppose which body, a party of a hundred Savages only were detached from the camp, who skirmished[11] with them for a few hours, and then returned back, bringing with them about thirty scalps. Had a more considerable force been ordered out

---

10. The *Trois Rivieres* is a Government on the north shore, near half-way between Quebec and Montreal; the capital of this Government bears the same name, but is only an open straggling village.

11. "The advanced parties upon this occasion had two or three skirmishes with the Canadians and Indians, with little loss on either side." General Wolfe's letter.

upon this service, sufficient to have brought on a serious affair, and to have ended it to our advantage, it certainly had been more for the interest of our generals; this indeed was proposed, but as it did not tally with the plan of defence agreed on, it was rejected and dropped: whatever was the reason, the English did not fail to turn it to good account; and to avail themselves of our inactivity on this occasion, which furnished them with an opportunity to fortify themselves on this side, and to erect batteries which played briskly on the town, and soon reduced it to ashes.[12] They opened these batteries on the 12th of July in the night, which never ceased firing from that time to the 18th of September; a day famous for the surrender of Quebec.

July 8, 1759

The camp of Point Levi was scarcely fixed when[13] another was discovered of greater extent on the point of the Island of Orleans: but this last disappeared in a few days, and we observed a number of barges, (or flat-bottomed boats, full of soldiers) to enter the[14] North Channel, and draw up under the cannon of the two frigates, which two days before came to an anchor op-

---

12. *Batteries of cannon and mortars were erected with great dispatch on the Point of Levi, to bombard the town and magazines, and to injure the works and batteries. The effect of this artillery has been so great (though across the river) that the upper town is considerably damaged, and the lower town entirely destroyed.* Wolfe.

The breadth of the river from the English batteries to the lower town and citadel, was about three quarters of a mile: the batteries consisted of 12, 24, and 32 pounders with seven mortars. Brigadier Monckton, who commanded at Point Levi had fortified his camp with several redoubts, and a battery of two guns upon the Point itself. General Wolfe mentions an attempt of the enemy to destroy these works, who sent out a detachment of 1600 men for that purpose, but falling into confusion, they fired upon one another and went back again.

13. Colonel Carleton marched with a detachment to the Westernmost Point of the Isle of Orleans. It was absolutely necessary to possess these two points and fortify them, because from either the one or the other, the enemy might make it impossible for any ship to lye in the Basin of Quebec, or even within two miles of it. Wolfe.

14. "It being resolved to land on the North Shore, below the falls of Montmorency, I placed on the 8th instant (July) his Majesty's sloop the *Porcupine* and the Boscawen armed vessel, in the Channel between Orleans and the North Shore to cover the landing." Letter from Admiral Saunders.

174

posite to the church of the Guardian Angel[15]. At first it was a doubt in our camp, whether this motion of the enemy had any real object or design, and under this false persuasion, that nothing could be attempted on that side, no measures were taken, either to prevent or disconcert their operations, or to make them purchase their success at a dear rate.

July 9, 1759

General Wolfe observing no disposition on our side to dispute a landing made a[16] descent on the 9th of July in the morning, and in effect, met with no opposition, but from the savages[17]; these latter attacked a corps of 400 men, which they defeated; but this party being considerably reinforced, the Indians were obliged to give way in their turn, and were driven off; they sent however to the Chevalier de Levy for assistance, but he arrived too late. This was not the only instance, in which the slowness of our motions was a service to the enemy.

General Wolfe finding no farther resistance to be made, took possession of the heights to the left of the falls of Montmorency, and which command all the country of the right; there fired his own camp, and fortified it with entrenchments towards the wood; he erected likewise a strong battery, which enladed and raked the camp of the Chevalier de Levy, and would have reduced him to the necessity of quitting it, had he not thrown up traverses[18] to secure it from the cannon. Gen-

---

15. About three miles from the river and falls of Montmorency, lower down the North Channel.

16. *We passed the North Channel at night, and encamped near the enemy's left, the River Montmorency between us.* Wolfe.

17. *The next morning (after landing) Captain Dank's company of rangers, posted in a wood to cover some workmen, were attacked and defeated by a body of Indians, and had so many killed and wounded, as to be almost disabled for the rest of the campaign; the enemy also suffered in this affair and were in their turn driven off by the nearest troops.* Wolfe.

18. Banks of earth thrown perpendicularly across a line to intercept the enemy's shot, and to prevent its being raked. These traverses are some sometimes six or seven feet high, especially if the line is commanded by any eminence, and about 12 or 18 feet thick, so as to be cannon proof; a communication is preserved at one end of the traverse by leaving a passage five or six feet wide.

eral Wolfe being master of the shore side to the left of the falls of Montmorency, made no farther advances, the object he had in view was, to make an attack upon our camp[19]; but the opposite banks of the river where he was obliged to cross, were so high and steep, and the little safety there was in passing a ford he had but a slender knowledge of, together with the number of thick woods which covered the country round, presented such a variety of difficulties to him, as were not easily to be surmounted; however by drawing our attention another way, and obliging us to[20] divide our forces, he flattered himself, he should in the end accomplish his design.

JULY 18

With this view, he caused[21] two ships to pass above the town of Quebec. This movement did not much alarm us at first, but others soon after taking the same route, and this little fleet increasing every day, our generals began to be[22] uneasy, and thereupon detached 1200 men from the camp to keep the enemy in awe on that side, and to prevent their making a descent.

Notwithstanding this precaution, Mr. Wolfe contrived to[23] land some troops at the Point Aux Trembles, who[24] carried off

---

19. *I had hopes that possibly means might be found of passing the river above, so as to fight the Marquis De Montcalm upon terms of less disadvantage, than directly attacking his entrenchments. In reconnoitring the river Montmorency, we found it fordable at a place about three miles up, but the opposite bank was entrenched, and so steep and woody, that it was to no purpose to attempt a passage there.* Wolfe.

20. *However to divide the enemy's force, &c.* Wolfe.

21. *On the 17th, I ordered Captain Rous of the Sutherland to proceed with the first fair wind and night-tide above the town of Quebec, and to take with him his Majesty's ships Diana and Squirrel with two armed sloops, and two carts loaded with provisions, and on the 18th they all got up except the Diana, and gave General Wolfe an opportunity of reconnoitring above the town.* Saunders.

22. *I thought of attempting it (to land) at St Michael's about three miles above the town, but perceiving that the enemy were jealous of the design, were preparing against it, &c. it seemed so hazardous, that I thought it best to desist.* Wolfe.

23. I sent a detachment under the command of Colonel Carleton to land at the Point De Trempe to attack whatever he might find there, bring off some prisoners, and all the useful papers he could get.

24. *The colonel brought off some prisoners, and returned with little loss.* Wolfe.

some ladies, and conducted them on board the admiral's ship. His Excellency received his prisoners very graciously, entertained them for two days, and then sent them back, greatly charmed with his politeness, and the genteel treatment they had met with.

This little squadron moved still higher up, and came to an anchor at the Falls of Richelieu[25], and from thence detached 800 men in flat-bottomed boats, who landed at Des Chambeaux[26], and marched directly to a house, where the cloathing and camp equipage of many of our officers were laid up, and set it on fire. Here they spread into the country, and collected together a number of cattle, which they made a show of carrying off; but a body of twenty horses appearing unexpectedly, the English took fright, threw themselves into their boats with some precipitation, and returned on board their ships again.

All these transactions were attended with no events of consequence, and in no shape forwarded the main design of general Wolfe, who in the end took a[27] resolution to make an open and general attack upon our camp, and that in such manner as was most likely to finish the dispute between us. Accordingly the 31st of July was pitched upon as the day for this brilliant onset, and at nine o clock in the morning, four vessels got on their way, and advanced towards the Point De Lesse. This is a low point near the Falls of Montmorency, and running out a little into the sea, presenting when the tide is out a very good field for action; on the shore (which rose in a kind of amphitheatre)

---

25. At the Falls of Richelieu on the South Shore, nearly opposite to Des Chambeaux about twenty-four miles above the town of Quebec.

26. This landing at Des Chambeaux was not effected till after the action of the 31st of July. *Immediately after this check (July 31st) I sent Brigadier Murray above the town with 1200 men &c. He landed unexpectedly at De Chambaud, and burnt a magazine there, in which were some provisions, some ammunition, and all the spare stores, cloathing, arms and baggage of their army.* Wolfe.

27. *I now resolved to take the first opportunity which presented itself of attacking the enemy, &c.;* Wolfe.

Previous to this engagement of the 31st, the enemy had sent down on the 28th at midnight, a raft of fire-stages, of near a hundred radeaux; which succeeded no better than their fire-ships already mentioned. Saunders.

our generals had thrown up entrenchment flanked with two[28] redoubts, one of which mounted cannon. Two of the sail just now mentioned ran in within the Point, and two others went aground on purpose above it; a fifth, which appeared to us to be a man-of-war of[29] sixty guns, came very near the former, but did not run ashore, and all three began a very brisk fire upon our entrenchments, which lasted from eleven in the morning to seven o clock at night[30]. This fire was seconded by the batteries on the falls, which, notwithstanding the traverses, galled our men more than the discharge from the shipping.

Soon after the cannonading took place, about a[31] hundred boats put off from the Point de Levi and made for the Isle of Orleans; it was then past all doubt, that an assault was intended. The general was beat, and the whole of our troops marched out, and lined the[32] entrenchments from the centre of the camp to the left.

The fire of the English was very smart; but our Canadians, though it was the first time they had ever seen the face of an enemy, remained unterrified, and stood to their arms with a steadiness, that greatly pleased our generals, and merited their applause.

28. A redoubt is a work thrown up for the security of lines and entrenchments, consisting generally of three, four, or move sides, surrounded, with a bank and ditch, and mounting cannon; it is a temporary fortification, and mostly used for the defence of a camp, or some post of consequence.

29. *To cover (the troops on landing) I placed the Centurion in the Channel between the Isle of Orleans and the Falls (of Montmorency) and ran on shore at high water, two catts, which I armed for that purpose, against two small batteries and two redoubts, where our troops were to land.* Saunders. The fire of this ship was of great service, particularly in silencing in a great measure the battery of the enemy which commanded the ford at the falls, where the two brigades of General Murray and Townshend were to pass in order to attack the left of the French-army.

30. *A great quantity of artillery were placed upon the eminence, so as to batter and ensilade the left of their entrenchments.* Wolfe.

31. *The boats of the fleet were filled with grenadiers, and a part Brigadier Monckton's brigade from the Point of Levi.* Wolfe.

32. The entrenchments ran all along the shore from the river St Charles to the ford at Montmorency, and were defended by nine redoubts and ten batteries with a mortar near Beaufort; mounting in all thirty-three guns; the batteries were within less than a quarter of a mile of one another, that is, within musket shot; for the the point blank flight of a musket ball is generally computed at no more than 200 yards, yet a very little elevation of the musket will do good execution at a distance of 360. The floating battery of twelve guns was placed at the mouth of the River St Charles.

About five o clock in the afternoon, the[33] boats, which not without great difficulty had got the length of the Isle of Orleans, advanced towards the Point De Lesse, and there landed about 2000 men.

At that very instant appeared general Wolfe at the head of a column of 4000 men, which had passed the[34] ford at the Falls of Montmorency, and marched up to one of our redoubts, which he had abandoned for want of powder and ball; he gave orders to the[35] grenadiers to seize upon this redoubt, but they were dislodged very soon by the fire of our musketry, and obliged to retire in disorder, when the general, instead of rallying and bringing them back to the charge, ordered the[36] retreat to be beat.

The advantage which we had of the ground, and the good order he observed in our troops, probably inclined the English general to lay aside all thoughts of succeeding in this attack, and induced him to give up. Certain it is, that had he attempted to have forced our lines, his whole army would have run a risk of being[37] cut to pieces; for he must have carried the entrenchments by an escalade on three sides very difficult to be mounted, and that in the face of an array much[38] superior to his own.

33. With Brigadier Monckton's detachment from Point Levi.

34. The breadth of the ford at the Falls at Montmorency was about 150 yards; the Falls of Montmorency were 300 feet high.

35. Grenadiers were ordered to form themselves into four distinct bodies and to begin the attack, supported by Brigadier Monckton's corps, as soon as the troops (under Mr Townshend and Murray) had passed the ford, and were at hand to assist; but instead of forming themselves as they were directed, they ran on impetuously towards the enemy's entrenchments in the utmost disorder and confusion, without waiting for the corps which were to sustain them, and join in the attack, &c. *The grenadiers were checked, and obliged to shelter them selves in or about the redoubt, which the French abandoned upon their approach.* Wolfe. Not very likely for want of Powder and Ball.

36. *I saw the absolute necessity of calling them off, that they might form themselves behind Brigadier Monckton's corps. It was near night, a sudden storm came on, and the tide began to make, so that I thought it most advisable not to persevere in so difficult an attack.* Wolfe.

37. "If the attack had succeeded, our loss must certainly have been great." After which the general gives his reasons for this severe attack; "The desire to act in conformity to the King's intentions, induced me to make this trial. " and closes his account of it, with an opinion that does honour to the troops under his command, a confidence in them, and conviction that breathes the true martial spirit of that active and intrepid leader, "persuaded that a victorious army finds no difficulties." A position that not only deserves to be adopted (continued on next page)

We lost in the action fifty-seven men killed and wounded, and the enemy about[39] 300. The seamen that belonged to the two ships that were aground, after[40] setting fire to them, retired to their boats.

August

During the greatest part of the month of August, General Wolfe remained[41] inactive in his camp upon the Falls of Montmorency, and confined his operations to the burning and plundering of what houses there were in the country he was master of, waiting the arrival of the forces under Mr. Amherst, before be made any new attempts; however, that general did not appear, and in the mean while, the season of action was slipping away, and Mr. Wolfe saw with regret, that his prey was ready to fall out of his hands; this determined him at all events to make one trial more, and to possess himself of the eminence on which Quebec is built.

In consequence of this resolution, he reinforced the squadron

---

and embraced by every succeeding officer at the head of troops, but to be laid down and admitted as an axiom in military theory, and which the experience of all ages must forever confirm.

38. "The enemy were indeed posted on a commanding eminence, numerous in their entrenchments, and their fire hot." Wolfe.

39. Killed. officers eleven, and 171 men. Wounded, officers forty-six, and 604 of the men. Missing, rank and file seventeen. In all 849. Wolfe.

40. *To prevent the two catts from falling into the enemy's hands (they being then dry on shore) I gave orders to take the men out, and set them on fire, which was accordingly done.* Saunders.

41. General Wolfe and the admiral were far from being inactive all this month. *On the 5th of August, I sent twenty flat-bottomed boats up the river, to embark 1260 of the troops. I sent up Admiral Holmes, and directed him to use his best endeavours to get at and destroy the enemy's ships above the town, but the wind holding westerly, it was the 27th of August before they got up.* Saunders.

I sent Brigadier Murray above the town with 1200 men; directing him to assist Rear Admiral Holmes in the destruction of the French Ships (if they could be got at) in order to open a communication with General Amherst. Wolfe.

Before Admiral Durell got into the river, three frigates and seventeen sail with provisions, stores, and a few recruits, got up, and are those we are so anxious if possible to destroy. Saunders.

This was the little fleet under Monsieur Kanou that arrived from Old France the beginning of May, one of which was the *Chezine* as already mentioned.

already above the town[42] raised his own camp upon the Falls, and removed it to the Point De Levi. This alteration produced a change in our camp. Troops were drawn off from the left wing which was now no longer in danger of any attack, and a recruit was sent to the right composed of a battalion of Guyenne, and a detachment of the Montreal militia.

September 5th

Several days passed, and nothing material or of moment was observed to be in agitation; but on the 5th of September, several columns of the enemy were discovered marching upon the Heights of Point Levi, and taking the road that led to the Falls of Chaudiere[43], where they embarked on board the squadron.

This movement put it out of doubt, that the enemy had some design upon the[44] north shore, and meant to possess themselves of some post there; of which immediate notice was sent to Mr. de Bougainville, who commanded in that quarter, and in the mean time, a reinforcement of five companies of grenadiers, the volunteers, and the picquets were detached to his assistance.

The north shore is nowhere accessible, especially to an army, but at Cap Rouge, Sillery St. Michael, and Le Foullon, where a convenient, road was made, wide enough even for carriages.

Monsieur de Bougainville took his post with the whole of the troops under his command at Cap Rouge, as being a pass of the most consequence at this juncture; and contented himself with placing guards of 100 men each at every other post, and which would have been a strength sufficient against any attack, had the orders that were given out (of breaking up the

---

42. General Wolfe being resolved to quit the camp at Montmorency, and having taken off all the artillery, on the 3rd of September, the troops embarked thence and landed at Point Levi. Saunders.

43. Nearly opposite to Cape Rouge, which is about five miles above Quebec, and about nine above Sillery where the troops landed.

44. On the 7th, 8th, and 9th, a movement of the ships was made, in order to amuse "the enemy now posted along the north shore." (*viz.* Monsieur Bougainville's command.) Brigadier Townshend's letter.

roads every where) been put in execution, but the same fatality attended these, as did many other orders, that have been totally neglected.

General Wolfe, after marching and counter marching, a number of feints and false alarms in different quarters, came at last to a resolution to make an attempt in earnest at Le Foullon,[45] and on the 12th of September at night, he landed 150 of the[46] Highlanders between St. Michael and Le Foullon, who with a great deal of[47] difficulty and danger climbed up to the summit of the cape, which was immensely steep, and[48] fell upon the detachment that guarded that post of Fullon, and taking them in the rear: our soldiers thus surprised, scarcely entered into action, but abandoned their post and fled.

The English army having now no enemy in front to oppose them, scaled the path up the mountain without any difficulty, and soon gained the great road of St. Foy.

This landing was effected between the hours of three and four in the morning, but it was scarcely known in our camp at six; and the first reports then were, that about a dozen flat-bottomed boats had appeared off Le Foullon, and seemed to make a show of disembarking some people there; but very soon after, an express arrived with an account, that the whole of the English army had landed, and were advancing in good order along the road of St. Foy.

Immediately our troops quitted their camp, and filed off, leaving a guard of 1500 men only to defend it, and took post

---

45. Within a league of Cape Diamond. Cape Diamond is situated to the southward of the town, and runs out into the river at the distance of about a quarter of a mile from the citadel. There was a battery erected upon it called the Queen's Battery, but there were no guns mounted.

46. The Light Infantry.

47. *When General Wolfe, and the troops with him had landed, the difficulty of gaining the top of the hill is scarce credible; it was very steep in its ascent and high, and had no path where two could go abreast; but they were obliged to pull theirselves up by the stumps and boughs of trees that covered the declivity.* Saunders.

48. *After a little firing, the Light Infantry (under Colonel Howe) gained the top of the precipice, and dispersed the captain's post.* Townshend. (100 men detached by Monsieur de Bougainville from Cape Rouge to defend the ascent of Sillery.)

upon the[49] Heights of Abraham, waiting the arrival of the enemy, who were drawing up in order of battle near the house de Borgia, which covered their left; and from thence extended to the great road leading to the port of St. Louis.

General Wolfe, upon first coming up, had ordered a company of Highlanders to taker possession of the[50] house de Borgia; from which an attempt was made to dislodge them by our troops, and which brought on a brisk and obstinate attack; but all our efforts were to no purpose; as it was absolutely necessary to bring up cannon to drive them out.

The two armies did not long remain in view of each other, without coming to action; our troops shewed[51] great eagerness to engage, and intrepidity, but kept it up a very little time only; it was judged proper to take immediate advantage of this spirit; however, it had been more prudent to have waited the arrival of Monsieur de Bougainville, who was advancing with the flower of the army; but our generals thought they could do the business without him, and so marched up[52]; to the enemy. Our troops

---

49. The Heights of Abraham, where the French army drew up, are scarcely half a mile from the works of the town to the S.W.

50. *The houses, into which the Light Infantry were thrown, were well defended.* Townshend.

51. It is most certain that the army (French) formed in good order, and that their attack was very brisk and animated. Townshend.

52. It was seemingly but ill judged of the French generals to rush on to an attack, without waiting for the arrival of Monsieur de Bougainville, could they have prevented coming to action, especially if what is here advanced be true, that he had the picked men or flower of their troops with him; add to this, his situation was such, that, according to Mr. Townshend, the English army must of necessity have been put between two fires. (*Scarce was this effected, when M. de Bougainville with his corps from Cape Rouge, of 2000 men, appeared in our rear.* Townshend.)

By General Wolfe's letter of the 5th of September, when this landing was only in agitation, and seemed to be intended as the finishing stroke of the campaign, the English army amounted to no more than 4000 or 5000 effective men; ("after the Points of Levi and Orleans were left in a proper state of defence.") a very unequal match for the French in point of numbers, even in any situation, and much less so in the present one, and of which Brigadier Townshend seemed so very sensible, that when the command devolved upon him by the much lamented fall of General Wolfe, his first employment, even, after the victory obtained, and the rout of the enemy, was to secure his camp. (*I have been employed, from the day of action to that of the capitulation, in redoubling our camp beyond insult.* Townshend.)

'Tis probable, a contempt of our numbers, and (continued on next page)

gave the first fire, and those of the English the[53] second, and the affair was over; our right took to their heels, our centre ran away after them, and drew along the left, and so the battle was lost in less time than I am telling the story.

An attempt was made to rally the runaways, but without effect; all that could be done, was to collect a body of 800 or 900 men together, whom they drew up in ambuscade in a[54] copse of wood upon the right of the Hills of Abraham, and whose fire retarded in some measure the pursuit of the conquerors; some others, who had recovered from their fright, formed themselves into a few platoons, and made a stand, so that the action began to be renewed

---

a fancied security of success on that account, might betray the Marquis de Montcalm into this rash engagement, and which was very little consistent with his usual coolness and wisdom; for he seems in Mr. Wolfe's own opinion, (who certainly was no mean judge) to have been an able and experienced officer: *The obstacles we have met with, in the operations of the campaign, are much greater than we had reason to expect, or could foresee: not so from the number of the enemy, (though superior to us) as from the natural strength of the country, which the Marquis De Montcalm seems wisely to depend upon.* Wolfe. He never could have been lead into this attack by any extraordinary confidence he had in the troops of the colony and the savages, for he must know the Canadians too well to risk battle, because they were in spirits and their courage was up, as is insinuated here; but the advantage of the ground, be superior extent of his line, the sight of the English army before the town, vexation at finding himself out-generaled, his lines and batteries, his entrenched camp and formidable redoubts become of no use, surprise, desire or revenge, thirst of glory, honour of the French arms, auger or disappointment, might all concur to hurry him on to immediate action, and without waiting for any farther addition to his forces to fall upon the enemy drawn up before him.

Whatever was the inducement, the event plainly shewed it a very indiscreet onset, and such a one. us might have ended in the total destruction of the French army, without affording an opportunity for a second trial; for, had the town of Quebec been situated at a greater distance from the field of battle, they must all have inevitably been cut to pieces, or reduced to the melancholy necessity of laying down their arms. (*If the town had been further off, the whole French army must have been destroyed.* Saunders.)

53. Our troops reserved their fire till within forty yards, which was so well continued, that the enemy everywhere gave way." Townshend.

The enemy began the attack, our troops received their fire, and reserved their own till they were so near as to run in upon them, and push them with their bayonets; by which, in a very little time, the French gave way and fled to the town in the utmost disorder and with great loss; for our troops pursued them quite to the walls, and killed many of them upon the glacis of the ditch. Saunders.

54. "Part of the enemy made a second faint attack; part took to some thick copse wood, and seemed to make a stand." Townshend.

upon the declivity of the mountain in different parts; however, the fatal blow was struck, and the enemy triumphed.

We lost in this engagement between[55] 700 or 800 men killed and wounded. Monsieur de Montcalm died of his wounds the next morning; Monsieur de Senezergues was found dead upon the field of battle, and General[56] Wolfe survived his victory only four hours. Mr. Monckton, second in command, was wounded, but not dangerously.

At the close of this unhappy affair, Monsieur le Marquis de Vaudreuil assembled a council of war, to which the principal officers were summoned. At this council he declared his opinion, "That the troops should take their revenge the next morning, and endeavour to wipe off the stains they had contracted the foregoing fatal day": this proposal, which seemed to carry a true sense of honour with it, ought never to have been rejected by[57] those gentlemen who receive their sovereign's pay, in order to maintain the spirit of honour; but so, however, it happened, and the united voice of all the members gave as their sentiments. "That there was an absolute necessity for the army to retire to the river[58] of Jacques Cartiers, and the sooner it was done, the better, there being no time to lose." So the array broke up their camp that very evening, abandoning provisions, ammunition, baggage, and artillery, and marched all night to gain the Point Aux Trembles, which was appointed the rendezvous for the whole.

---

55. *Their loss (of the enemy) is computed to be about 1500 men, which fell chiefly upon the regulars.* Townshend.

56. On the side of the British were killed only nine officers; but one of these nine (a loss almost irreparable to the English Nation) was the gallant general himself, whose name can only be forgot, when Quebec can be no more remembered. One captain, six lieutenants, and one ensign fell likewise in the action, with 545 rank and file. Wounded, officers 53, serjeants 95, four drummers, 506 rank and file; in all 648.

57. The Marquis De Vaudreuil, the Governor and Lieutenant-General for the King in Canada, was not regularly in the army, upon the officers of which only this reflection seems to be intended.

58. Jacques Cartiers appears to have been a very strong post; Mr. Murray, in his account of the raising of the siege of Quebec, speaks of it in that light, "They (the enemy) left their camp standing, and have retired to their former asylum, Jacques Cartiers." It is situated about twenty miles above Quebec.

Before he marched off, Monsieur de Vaudreuil dispatched an express to Monsieur le Chavalier de Levy, to give him intelligence of the dreadful catastrophe our troops had met with, and to desire him to come and take the command of the army upon him, in the room of Monsieur de Montcalm, who was dying. The courier found, the Chevalier at Montreal, where he was just arrived, coming up a channel he had cut in the river of Cataracouy, to secure that part of the country, which was threatened with an invasion, from Sir William Johnson, the conqueror of Niagara.

Monsieur de Levy set out from Montreal, immediately upon the receipt of the letter, and arrived at Jacques Cartiers the 16th of September. After a few hours conference with the Marquis de Vaudreuil, it was agreed between them, to write to Monsieur de Ramsay, governor of the town of Quebec, to acquaint him:

That a resolution was taken to march to his relief: that after the next day, the whole army would be in motion; that a disposition was made to throw a considerable supply of provision into the town; and, in a word, to encourage him by all means to hold out to the last extremity.[59]

The courier on his arrival at Quebec found the capitulation already in train[60], and a treaty entered into and carrying on between Monsieur de Ramsay and the besieging general: one would have imagined that the Marquis de Vaudreuil's letter would have broke off, or at least suspended a while, the

---

59. *By deserters we learn that Monsieur De Levi is come down from Montreal; some say, he has brought two battalions with him, and that M. De Bougainville with 800 men and provisions was on his march, to fling himself into the town the 18th, the very morning it capitulated.* Townshend.

60. This was exactly the case at Guadaloupe, in the West Indies, the same year; Monsieur De Bompar, the French admiral, had actually landed a reinforcement of 2000 men, and a supply of arms, upon the island, the very day it surrendered to General Barrington; which disembarkation, had it taken place about twenty-four hours sooner, must inevitably have preserved the colony, and the English troops would have been obliged to have returned on board the transports again, being at this time so reduced in their numbers, from service and sickness, that it would have been impossible for the general to have opposed this new body, or to have acted offensively any longer upon the island with a probability of success.

issue of this negotiation: but whether the orders it contained, were not precise or explicit enough, or whether Monsieur de Ramsay had reasons of his own, which weighed more with him than his instructions from Monsieur de Vaudreuil, is an affair not very certainly known.

September 18th

The treaty however continued, and the capitulation signed on both sides the 18th of September, at the English camp before Quebec.

A Battle Fought on Snowshoes

by
Mary Cochrane Rogers
Great-Great-Granddaughter of
Major Robert Rogers

.

A Battle Fought on Snow Shoes

Lake George was frozen and the snow four feet deep in the woods, when on March 10, 1758, Colonel Haviland, commanding at Fort Edward, sent Major Rogers with one hundred and eighty men to reconnoitre the French position at Carillon, or Ticonderoga.

Rogers and his Rangers marched from Fort Edward in snow shoes to the Half-Way Brook, in the road leading to Lake George, and there encamped the first night.

On the 11th they proceeded as far as the First Narrows on Lake George and encamped that evening on the east side of the lake.

At sunrise of the 12th they marched from their encampment. When they had gone some three miles, the major saw a dog running across the lake. Thinking that the Indians might be lying in ambush, he sent a detachment to reconnoitre the island. None, however, could be seen.

To prevent the enemy from discovering his force, Rogers halted at Sabbath-Day Point, on the west side of the lake. From the hills he looked northward over the lake with his perspective glass, but could see no signs of French or Indians. As soon as it was dark the party advanced down the lake. Lieutenant Phillips and fifteen men, laying aside their snow shoes and putting on skates, glided down the lake, as an advanced guard. The main body, flanked on the left by Ensign Ross, marched under the west shore. It was a very dark night and the band of rugged foresters kept close together to prevent separation. In this manner they continued their silent march close to the mountains fringing the lake until within eight miles of the French advanced guards, when they were informed by Lieutenant Phillips, who had hastened back, that a fire had been discovered in the woods on the east shore.

The Rangers, after hiding their sleighs and packs in a thicket, marched to attack the enemy's encampment, but when they reached the place no fires were to be seen. They did not know that the French had discovered their advanced guard and, putting out their fire, had carried the intelligence to Ticonderoga. The Rangers then returned to their packs and there lay the remainder of the night without fire, so that no column of blue smoke would reveal their hiding place.

At sunrise of the 13th the Rangers left the lake and on snow shoes struck into the woods on the west side, keeping on the back of the mountains that overlooked the French advanced guards.

They halted at noon at a point nearly west of the mountain—that from that day was to bear the name of Rogers—and some two miles from the French lines. Little did they know what that tragic afternoon held in store for them. Here they refreshed themselves until 3 o'clock, that the day scout from the fort might return before they advanced, since the major intended at night to ambuscade some of the roads in order to trap the enemy in the morning.

Once more they began their toilsome march, one division headed by Major Rogers, the other by Captain Buckley; a rivulet at a small distance was on their left, and a steep mountain on their right. They kept well to the mountain, for the major thought that the enemy would travel on the ice of the rivulet since it was very bad travelling on snow shoes. When they had gone a mile and a half a scout from the front told Rogers that the enemy was approaching on the bed of the frozen stream,—ninety-six of them—chiefly savages. The Rangers, concealed by the bank of the rivulet, immediately laid an ambush, gave the first fire and killed above forty Indians whom they scalped on the spot. The rest retreated, followed by about one-half of the Rangers, who were exulting over their victory, only to be suddenly confronted by more than six hundred Canadians and Indians fresh from Fort Ticonderoga, under Durantaye and De Langry, French officers of reputation, who were fully prepared to meet four hundred Rangers, of whose movements they had been apprised both by the prisoner taken and by the deserter from Putnam's men. Rogers ordered a retreat, which he gained at the expense of fifty men killed; the remainder he rallied and drew up in good order. They fought with such intrepidity and bravery that they obliged the enemy "though seven to one in number," to retreat a second time, but Rogers had not sufficient numbers to follow up the advantage. The enemy then rallied and, recovering their ground, fought with great tenacity and determination, but were so warmly received that they were put to rout the third time. Finding the Rogers party so much inferior to themselves in number, the enemy again rallied and renewed the fight with vigour for some time. A body of two hundred Indians were now discovered going up the mountain on the right in order to gain the rear of the Rangers. Lieutenant Phillips with eighteen men gained the first possession and beat them back. Lieutenant Crafton with fifteen men stopped the French on the left from gaining the other part of the mountain. Two gentlemen volunteers hastened up and supported him with great bravery. The enemy now pushed so closely on the front that the combatants were often not twenty yards apart, and sometimes were mixed together. Lieutenant Phillips, surrounded by three hundred Indians, surrendered under promise of good quarter, but a few minutes later he and his whole party were tied to trees and hacked to death in a most barbarous manner, The savages maddened, it is said, by the sight of a scalp they found in the breast of a man's hunting frock, revenged themselves on their victims by holding up their scalps. The Rangers were now broken and put to flight, each man for himself, while the Indians, closely pursuing, took several prisoners.

My great-great-grandfather in his modest narrative does not mention his own hairbreadth escape. The Rangers, when put to flight, retreated in the best manner possible. Rogers was singled

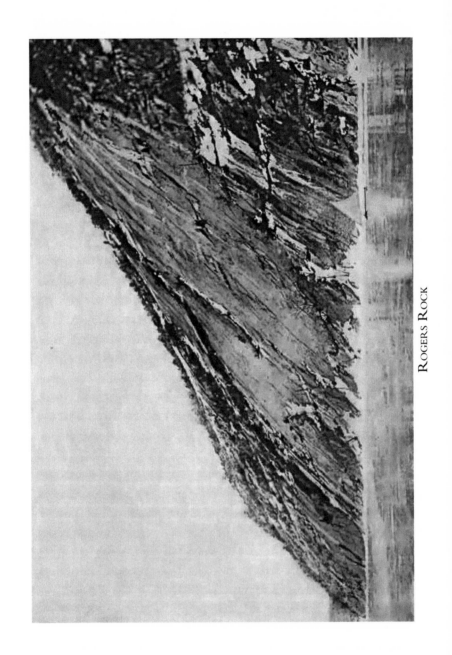

ROGERS ROCK

out by the French; the Indians, closely pursuing, ran him up the steep mountain then known as Bald Mountain, since Rogers Rock, to its face, and there on the brow of the precipice he threw away his knapsack and clothes together with his commission. There was but one chance for his life, and death was preferable to capture and torture by the savages.

Slowly the sun is setting over the mountain tops, gilding the lake below, as down the face of the precipitous rock for more than a thousand feet he slides in his snow shoes to the frozen lake below, and there, quickly changing his snow shoes for skates, glides over the vast white desert. Scarcely had he disappeared from sight when the foremost warrior reached the cliff sure of his prey—"No Roger!" There were his tracks! Other warriors came running up to the cliff sure of the prize—Rogers' scalp—for the enemy dreaded him, and with reason—and gazed upon his tracks.

Soon a rapidly receding form on the ice below attracted their notice, and the baffled savages, seeing that the famous Ranger had safely effected the perilous descent, gave up the chase fully persuaded that Rogers was under the protection of the Great Spirit. The Indians have a superstition, that the witches or evil spirits haunt this place, and seizing upon the spirits of bad Indians, on their way to the happy hunting grounds, slide down the precipitous cliff with them into the lake where they are drowned. *Atalapose* is their word for a sliding place.

During the one and one-half hours of battle the Rangers lost eight officers and more than one hundred privates killed on the spot. The enemy lost one hundred and fifty killed and some one hundred and fifty wounded, mostly Indians. Was Colonel Haviland so indifferent and short-sighted as to send Robert Rogers with his brave Rangers to meet this impossible situation at such a great loss of life, or was he influenced by improper motives? Evidently Rogers's suspicions were awakened, for the clause, "but my commander doubtless had his reasons, and is able to vindicate his own conduct," is italicized in his journal.

This is what Major General John Stark, the friend and companion of Rogers says, though not in the engagement, of Colonel Haviland's act:

> This officer was the same who sent him (Rogers) out in March, 1758, with a small force, when he knew a superior one lay in wait for him. He was one of those sort of men who manage to escape public censure, let them do what they will. He ought to have been cashiered for his conduct on that occasion. He was one of the many British officers who were meanly jealous of the daring achievements of their brave American comrades, but for whose intrepidity and arduous services, all the British armies, sent to America during the seven years' war would have effected little toward the conquest of Canada.
>
> *Memoir of General John Stark*, page 454.

Rogers was saved by a miracle and by his own daring. Thus ended his brave but unfortunate battle on snow shoes. General Montcalm in a letter dated less that a month after the encounter, says:

> Our Indians would give no quarter; they have brought back one hundred and forty-six scalps.

We cannot with certainty say what Rogers, at this time twenty-six years of age, might have done had he had four hundred strong—but there is every probability that he would have put the enemy to rout. When I visited this beautiful and romantic region, where one hundred and fifty years ago, and something more, the famous action took place, my mind passed in swift review through that notable afternoon when the Rangers fought one of their most desperate and unequal battles in the French and Indian War.

In fancy I saw this picturesque body of Rangers, clad in skin and gray duffel hunting frocks; each man well armed with firelock, hatchet, and scalping knife, a bullock's horn full of powder hanging under his right arm by a belt from the left shoulder, and a leathern or seal skin bag, buckled around his waist, hanging down in front full of bullets and smaller shot, the size of full grown peas, and in the bottom of my great-great-grandfather's powder horn a small compass, while the French officers were clad in bright uniforms and the Indians in true Indian fashion gaily decorated with war paint.

I seemed to hear this peaceful solitude made hideous with the yells of the savages. Behind this bank the Rangers lay in ambush for the Indians and killed and scalped about forty of them. Here they were confronted by more than six hundred Canadians and Indians well versed in forest warfare.

In this place the Rangers fought, "seven to one," from behind forest trees, for this theatre of action retains much of its original character preserved, improved and owned by Mr. David Williams. The Rogers Rock property includes the Slide and extends for more than a mile and a half along the shore of Lake George and some half of a mile back of Rogers Rock. For more than an hour and a half this unequal contest raged. The Rangers after a long toilsome march on snow shoes and having camped three nights, sleeping in hammocks of spruce boughs, the third and last night without fire and chilled—the French and Indians fresh from the Fort. The brave Rangers were fast falling everywhere, and the snow is crimsoned with their blood. They were the most hardy and resolute young men New Hampshire and other Colonies could produce, and their descendants are now filling their places in the world's niches well today.

Here is the trail Rogers followed up the steep mountain to the brow of the cliff, and there is the rock down which he made his miraculous escape. As the vision passes one cannot help saying, *all honour to those brave men who here fell March 13, 1758.*

An anecdote which my grandfather used to tell deserves to be mentioned. While Major Rogers was in garrison at Fort Edward in the winter of 1757-8, two British officers, half seas over, were one evening bemoaning their country's enormous debt. Rogers, coming in, and hearing the patriotic bewailing, cried:

"Give yourselves no more uneasiness about the matter, gentlemen, I will pay half of the debt and a friend of mine the remainder. We will clear the nation at once of her difficulties."

The officers treated the major and pronounced him the nation's benefactor. Hence the saying: *to pay one's debts as Rogers did that of the nation.*

A gentleman of the army, who was a volunteer on this party, and who with another fell into the hands of the French, wrote the following letter, some time after, to the officer commanding the regiment they belonged to at Fort Edward.

Carillon
March 28, 1758
Dear Sir,
As a flag of truce is daily expected here with an answer to *Monsieur* Vaudreuil, I sit down to write the moment I am able, in order to have a letter ready, as no doubt you and our friends at Fort Edward are anxious to be informed about Mr.—— and me, whom probably you have reckoned amongst the slain in our unfortunate *rencontre* of the 13th, concerning which at present I shall not be particular; only to do this justice to those who lost their lives there, and to those who have escaped, to assure you, Sir, that such dispositions were formed by the enemy (who discovered us long before), it was impossible for a party so weak as ours to hope for even a retreat. Towards the conclusion of the affair, it was cried from a rising ground on our right, to retire there; where, after scrambling with difficulty, as I was unaccustomed to snow-shoes, I found Captain Rogers, and told him that I saw to retire further was impossible, therefore earnestly begged we might collect all the men left, and make a stand there.

Mr.—— , who was with him, was of my opinion, and Captain Rogers also; who therefore desired me to maintain one side of the hill, whilst he defended the other. Our parties did not exceed above ten or twelve in each, and mine was shifting towards the mountain, leaving me unable to defend my post, or to labour with them up the hill. In the meantime, Captain Rogers with his party came to me, and said (as did those with him) that a large body of Indians had ascended to our right; he likewise added, what was true, that the combat was very unequal, that I must retire, and he would give Mr.—— and me a serjeant to conduct us through the mountain. No doubt prudence required us to accept his offer; but, besides one of my snow-shoes being untied, I knew myself unable to march as fast as was requisite to avoid becoming a sacrifice to an enemy we could no longer oppose; I therefore begged of him to proceed, and then leaned against a rock in the path, determined to submit to a fate I thought unavoidable.

Unfortunately for Mr.—— his snow-shoes were loosened likewise, which obliged him to determine with me, not to labour in a flight we were both unequal to. Every instant we expected the savages; but what induced them to quit this path, in which we actually saw them, we are ignorant of, unless they changed it for a shorter, to intercept those who had just left us. By their noise, and making a fire, we imagined they had got the rum in the Rangers' packs. This thought, with the approach of night, gave us the first hopes of retiring; and when the moon arose, we marched to the southward along the mountains about three hours, which brought us to ice, and gave us reason to hope our difficulties were almost past; but we knew not we had enemies yet to combat with, more cruel than the savages we had escaped.

We marched all night, and on the morning of the 14th found ourselves entirely unacquainted with the ice. Here we saw a man, who came towards us; he was the servant of Captain Rogers, with whom he had been often times all over the country, and, without the least hesitation whatsoever, he informed us we were upon South-Bay; that Wood-Creek was just before us; that he knew the way to Fort Anne extremely well, and would take us to Fort Edward the next day. Notwithstanding we were disappointed in our hopes of being upon Lake George, we thought ourselves fortunate in meeting such a guide, to whom we gave entire confidence, and which he in fact confirmed, by bringing us to a creek, where he showed the tracks of Indians, and the path he said they had taken to Fort Anne.

After struggling through the snow some hours, we were obliged to halt to make snow-shoes, as Mr.——— and the guide had left theirs at arriving upon the ice. Here we remained all night, without any blankets, no coat, and but a single waistcoat each, for I gave one of mine to Mr.———, who had laid aside his green jacket in the field, as I did likewise my furred cap, which became a mark to the enemy, and probably was the cause of a slight wound in my face; so that I had but a silk handkerchief on my head, and our fire could not be large, as we had nothing to cut wood with. Before morning we contrived, with forked sticks and strings of leather, a sort of snow-shoes, to prevent sinking entirely; and, on the 15th, followed our guide west all day, but he did not fulfil his promise; however the next day it was impossible to fail: but even then, the 16th, he was unsuccessful; yet still we were patient, because he seemed well acquainted with the way, for he gave every mountain a name, and showed us several places, where he said his master had either killed deer or encamped.

The ground, or rather the want of sunshine, made us incline to the southward, from whence by accident we saw ice, at several miles distance, to the south-east. I was very certain, that, after marching two days west of South Bay, Lake George could not lie south-east from us, and therefore concluded this to be the upper end of the bay we had left. For this reason, together with the assurances of our guide, I advised continuing our course to the west, which must shortly strike Fort Anne, or some other place that we knew. But Mr.——— wished to be upon ice at any rate;

he was unable to continue in the snow, for the difficulties of our march had overcome him. And really, Sir, was I to be minute in those we had experienced already and afterwards, they would almost be as tiresome to you to read, as they were to us to suffer.

Our snow-shoes breaking, and sinking to our middle every fifty paces, the scrambling up mountains, and across fallen timber, our nights without sleep or covering, and but little fire, gathered with great fatigue, our sustenance mostly water, and the bark and berries of trees; for all our provisions from the beginning was only a small Bologna sausage, and a little ginger, I happened to have, and which even now was very much decreased; so that I knew not how to oppose Mr.———'s entreaties; but as our guide still persisted Fort Anne was near, we concluded to search a little longer, and if we made no discovery to proceed next day towards the ice; but we sought in vain, as did our guide the next morning, though he returned, confidently asserting he had discovered fresh proofs, that the fort could not be far off. I confess I was still inclined to follow him, for I was almost certain the best we could hope from descending upon this ice to our left, was to throw ourselves into the hands of the French, and perhaps not be able to effect even that; but, from the circumstances I have mentioned, it was a point I must yield to, which I did with great reluctancy.

The whole day of the 17th we marched a dreadful road, between the mountains, with but one good snow-shoe each, the other of our own making being almost useless. The 18th brought us to the ice, which though we longed to arrive at, yet I still dreaded the consequence, and with reason, for the first sight informed us, it was the very place we had left five days before. Here I must own my resolution almost failed me; when fatigue, cold, hunger, and even the prospect of perishing in the woods attended us, I still had hopes, and still gave encouragement, but now I wanted it

Mrs Robert Rogers

myself; we had no resource but to throw ourselves into the enemy's hands, or perish. We had nothing to eat, our slender stock had been equally shared amongst us three, and we were not so fortunate as even to see either bird or beast to shoot at. When our first thoughts were a little calmed, we conceived hopes, that, if we appeared before the French fort, with a white flag, the commanding officer would relieve and return us to Fort Edward. This served to palliate our nearest approach to despair, and determined a resolution, where, in fact, we had no choice.

I knew Carillon had an extensive view up South Bay, therefore we concluded to halt during the evening, and march in the night, that we might approach it in the morning, besides the wind pierced us like a sword; but instead of its abating it increased, together with a freezing rain, that encrusted us entirely with ice, and obliged us to remain until morning, the 19th, when we fortunately got some juniper berries, which revived, gave us spirits, and I thought strength. We were both so firmly of that opinion, that we proposed taking the advantage of its being a dark snowy day, to approach Carillon, to pass it in the night, and get upon Lake George. With difficulty we persuaded the guide to be of our opinion, we promised large rewards in vain, until I assured him of provisions hid upon the lake; but we little considered how much nature was exhausted, and how unequal we were to the task; however, a few miles convinced us; we were soon midway up our legs in the new-fallen snow; it drove full in our faces, and was as dark as the fogs upon the banks of Newfoundland.

Our strength and our hopes sunk together, nay, even those of reaching Carillon were doubtful, but we must proceed or perish. As it cleared up a little, we laboured to see the fort, which at every turn we expected, until we came to where the ice was gone, and the water narrow. This did not agree with my idea of South Bay, but it was no time for reflection; we quitted the ice to the left, and after marching two miles, our guide assured us we ought to be on the other side of the water. This was a very distressing circumstance, yet we returned to the ice and passed to the right, where, after struggling through the snow, about four miles, and breaking in ever second step, as we had no snow-shoes, we were stopped by a large water-fall.

Here I was again astonished with appearances, but nothing now was to be thought of only reaching the fort before night; yet to pass this place seemed impracticable; however, I attempted to ford it a little higher, and had almost gained the opposite shore, where the depth of the water, which was up to my breast and the rapidity of the stream, hurried me off the slippery rocks, and plunged me entirely in the waters. I was obliged to quit my fusee, and with great difficulty escaped being carried down the fall. Mr.——, who followed me, and the guide, though they held by one another, suffered the same fate; but the hopes of soon reaching a fire made us think lightly of this: as night approached, we laboured excessively through the snow; we were certain the fort was not far from us, but our guide confessed, for the first time, that he was at a loss.

"Here we plainly observed that his brain was affected: he saw Indians all around him, and though we have since learned we had everything to fear from them, yet it was a danger we did not now attend to; nay, we shouted aloud several times to give information we were there; but we could neither hear nor see anybody to lead us right, or more likely to destroy us, and if we halted a minute we became pillars of ice; so that we resolved, as it froze so hard, to make a fire, although the danger was apparent. Accidentally we had one dry cartridge, and in trying with my pistol if it would flash a little of the powder, Mr.—— unfortunately held the cartridge too near, by which it took fire, blew up in our faces, almost blinded him, and gave excessive pain. This indeed promised to be the last stroke of fortune, as our hopes of a fire were now no more; but although we were not anxious about life, we knew it was more becoming to oppose than yield to this last misfortune.

We made a path round a tree, and there exercised all the night, though scarcely able to stand, or prevent each other from sleeping. Our guide, notwithstanding repeated cautions, straggled from us, where he sat down and died immediately. On the morning of the 20th, we saw the fort, which we approached with a white flag: the officers run violently towards us, and saved us from a danger we did not then apprehend; for we are informed, that if the Indians, who were close after them, had seized us first, it would not have been in the power of the French to have prevented our being hurried to their camp, and perhaps to Montreal the next day, or killed for not being able to march. *Mons.* Debecourt[1] and all his officers treat us with humanity and politeness, and are solicitous in our recovery, which returns slowly, as you may imagine, from all these difficulties; and though I have omitted many, yet I am afraid you will think me too prolix; but we wish, Sir, to persuade you of a truth, that nothing but the situation I have faithfully described could determine us in a resolution which appeared only one degree preferable to perishing in the woods.

I shall make no comments upon these distresses; the malicious perhaps will say, which is very true, we brought them upon ourselves; but let them not wantonly add, we deserved them because we were unsuccessful. They must allow we could not be led abroad, at such a season of snow and ice, for amusement, or by an idle curiosity. I gave you, Sir, my reasons for asking leave, which you were pleased to

---

1. Hebencourt.

approve, and I hope will defend them; and the fame would make me again, as a volunteer, experience the chance of war tomorrow, had I an opportunity. These are Mr.———'s sentiments as well as mine; and we both know you, Sir, too well, to harbour the least doubt of receiving justice with regard to our conduct in this affair, or our promotion in the regiment; the prospect of not joining that so soon as we flattered ourselves has depressed our spirits to the lowest degree, so that we earnestly beg you will be solicitous with the general to have us restored as soon as possible, or at least to prevent our being sent to France, and separated from you, perhaps, during the war.

I have but one thing more to add, which we learned here, and which perhaps you have already observed from what I have said, that we were upon no other ice than that of Lake George; but by the day overtaking us, the morning of the 14th, in the very place we had, in coming, marched during the night, we were entirely unacquainted with it, and obliged to put a confidence in this guide, whose head must have been astray from the beginning, or he could not so grossly have mistaken a place where he had so often been. This information but added to our distress, until we reflected that our not being entirely lost was the more wonderful. That we had parted from South Bay on the 14th, was a point with us beyond all doubt, and about which we never once hesitated, so that we acted entirely contrary to what we had established as a truth; for if, according to that, we had continued our course to the west, we must inevitably have perished; but the hand of Providence led us back contrary to our judgement; and though even then, and often afterwards, we thought it severe, yet in the end it saved us, and obliged us to rest satisfied that we construed many things unfortunate, which tended to our preservation. I am, &c.

Journals of Major Robert Rogers, p. 90-102. (London) 1765.

*By his Excellency John Earl of Loudoun, Lord Machline
and Tairenseen, &c.,&c.,&c.,one of the sixteen peers of
Scotland, Governor and Captain General of Virginia, and
Vice Admiral of the same, Colonel of the 13th Regiment
of Foot, Colonel in chief of the Royal American regiment.
Major General and Commander in Chief of all his Majesty's forces, raised or to be raised in North-America:*

Whereas I have this day thought proper to augment
the Rangers with five additional companies, that is,
four New England and one Indian company, to be
forthwith raised and employed in his Majesty's service; and whereas I have an entire confidence in your
skill and knowledge, of the men most fit for that
service; I do therefore by these presents appoint you
to raise such a number of non-commission officers
and private men as will be necessary to complete
the said five companies, upon the following establishment, *viz.* each company to consist of one captain, two lieutenants, one ensign, four sergeants and
hundred privates. The officers to have British pay,
that is, the same as an officer of the like rank in his
Majesty's regular forces; the sergeants 4s. New York
currency per day, and the private men 2s. 6d currency per day. And the better to enable you to make
this levy of men, you shall have one month's pay for
each of the said five companies advanced to you;
upon these conditions, that, out of the first warrants
that shall hereafter be granted for the subsistence of
these companies, shall be deducted the said month's
pay now advanced.

Your men to find their own arms, which must be
such as upon examination, shall be found fit, and be
approved of. They are likewise to provide themselves

with good warm clothing, which must be uniform in every company, and likewise with good warm blankets. And the company of Indians to be dressed in all respects in the true Indian fashion, and they are all to be subject to the rules and articles of war. You will forthwith acquaint the officers appointed to these companies, that they are immediately to set out on the recruiting service, and you will not fail to instruct them that they are not to enlist any man for a less term than one year, nor any but what are able-bodied, well acquainted with the woods, used to hunting, and every way qualified for the Ranging service. You are also to observe that the number of men requisite to complete the said five companies, are all to be at Fort Edward on or before the 15th day of March next ensuing, and those that shall come by way of Albany are to be mustered there by the officer commanding, as shall those who go strait to Fort Edward by the officer commanding there. Given under my hand, at New York, the 11th day of January, 1758.

Loudoun

By his Excellency's command

To Captain

Robert Rogers

In pursuance of the above instructions I immediately sent officers into the New England provinces, where, by the assistance of my friends, the requested augmentation of Rangers was quickly completed, the whole five companies being ready for service by the 4th of March.

Four of these companies were sent to Louisburg to join General Amherst, and one joined the corps under my command; and though I was at the whole expense of raising the five companies, I never got the least allowance for it, and one of the captains dying, to whom I had delivered a thousand dollars as advance pay for his company, which, agreeable to the instructions I received, had a right to do; yet was I obliged to account with the government for this money, and entirely lost every penny of it. It has already been mentioned, that the garrison at Fort Edward, was this winter under the command of Lieutenant Colonel Haviland. This gentleman, about the 28th of February, ordered out a scout under the direction of one Putnam, Captain of a company of one of the Connecticut provincial regiments, with some of my men, given out publicly at the same time, that, upon Putnam's return, I should be sent to the French forts with a strong party of 400 Rangers.

This was known not only to all the officers, but soldiers also, at Fort Edward before Putnam's departure.

While this party was out, a servant of Mr. Best, a sutler to the Rangers, was captivated by a flying party of the enemy from Ticonderoga; unfortunately too, one of Putnam's men had left him at Lake George, and deserted to the enemy. Upon Captain Putnam's return, we were informed he had ventured within eight miles of the French fort at Ticonderoga, and that a party he had sent to make discoveries had reported to him, that there were near 600 Indians not far from the enemy's quarters.

March 10, 1758. Soon after the said Captain Putnam's return, in consequence of positive orders from Colonel Haviland, I this day began a march from Fort Edward for the neighbourhood of Carillon, not with a party of 400 men, as at first given out, but of 180 men only, officers included, one captain, one lieutenant, and one ensign, and three volunteers, *viz*. Mess. Creed, Kent and Wrightson, one sergeant, and one private, all of the 27th Regiment; and a detachment from the four companies of Rangers, quartered on the island near Fort Edward, *viz*. Captain Buckley, Lieutenants Philips, Moore, Crafton, Campbell, and Pottinger; Ensigns Ross, Wait, McDonald, and White, and 162 private men. I acknowledge I entered upon this service, and viewed this small detachment of brave men march out, with no little concern and uneasiness of mind; for, as there was the greatest reason to suspect, that the French were, by the prisoner and deserter above mentioned, fully informed of the design of sending me out upon Putnam's return: what could I think to see my party, instead of being strengthened and augmented, reduced to less than one half the number at first proposed? I must confess it appeared to me (ignorant and unskilled as I then was in politics and the art of war) incomprehensible; but my commander doubtless had his reasons, and is able to vindicate his own conduct. We marched to the Half-Way Brook, in the road leading to Lake George, and there encamped the first night.

The 11th we proceeded as far as the first Narrows on Lake George, and encamped that evening on the east-side of the lake; and after dark, I sent a party three miles further down, to see if the enemy might be coming towards our forts, but they returned without discovering any. We were, however, on our guard, and kept parties walking on the lake all night, besides sentries at all necessary places on the land.

The 12th we marched from our encampment at sunrise, and having distanced it about three miles, I saw a dog running across the lake, whereupon I sent a detachment to reconnoitre the island, thinking the Indians might have laid in ambush there for us; but no such could be discovered; upon which I thought it expedient to put to shore and lay by till night, to prevent any party from descrying us on the lake, from hills, or otherwise. We halted at a place called Sabbath-day Point, on the west-side of the lake, and sent our parties to look down the lake with perspective glasses, which we had for that purpose, As soon as it was dark we proceeded down the lake. I sent Lieutenant Phillips with fifteen men, as an advanced guard, some of whom went before him on skates, while Ensign Ross flanked us on the left under the west-shore, near which we kept the main body, marching as close as possible, to prevent separation, it being a very dark night. In this manner we continued our march till within eight miles of the French advanced guards, when Lieutenant Phillips sent a man on skates back to me, to desire me to halt; upon which I ordered my men to squat down upon the ice. Mr. Phillips soon came to me himself, leaving his party to look out, and said, he imagined he had discovered a fire[2] on the east-shore, but was not certain; upon which I sent with him Ensign White, to make further discovery. In about an hour they returned, fully persuaded that a party of the enemy was encamped there. I then called in the advanced guard, and flanking party, and marched on to the west-shore, where, in a thicket, we hid our sleighs and packs, leaving a small guard with them, and with the remainder I marched to attack the enemy's encampment, if there was any; but when we came near the place, no fires were to be seen, which made us conclude that we had mistaken some bleach patches of snow, or pieces of rotten wood, for fire (which in the night, at a distances resembles it) whereupon we returned to our packs, and there lay the remainder of the night without fire.

The 13th, in the morning, I deliberated with the officers how to proceed, who were unanimously of opinion, that it was best to go by land in snow-shoes, lest the enemy should discover us on the lake; we accordingly continued our march on the west-side, keeping on the back of the mountains that overlooked the French advanced guards. At twelve of the clock we halted two miles west of those guards, and there refreshed ourselves till three, that the day-scout from the fort might be returned home before we advanced; intending at night to ambuscade some of their roads, in order to trepan them in the morning. We

---

2. A small party of the French, as we have since heard, had a fire here at this time: but, discovering my advanced party, extinguished their fire, and carried the news of our approach to the French fort.

then marched in two divisions, the one headed by Captain Buckley, the other by myself: Ensigns White and Wait had the rear-guard, the other officers were posted properly in each division, having a rivulet at a small distance on our left, and a steep mountain on our right. We kept close to the mountain, that the advanced guard might better observe the rivulet, on the ice of which I imagined they would travel it out, as the snow was four feet deep, and very bad travelling on snow-shoes.

In this manner we marched a mile and an half, when our advanced guard informed me of the enemy being in their view; and soon after, that they had ascertained their number to be ninety-six, chiefly Indians. We immediately laid down our packs, and prepared for battle, supposing these to be the whole number or main body of the enemy, who were marching on our left up the rivulet, upon the ice. I ordered Ensign McDonald to the command of the advanced guard, which, as we faced to the left made a flanking party to our right. We marched to within a few yards of the bank, which was higher than the ground we occupied; and observing the ground gradually to descend from the bank of the rivulet to the foot of the mountain, we extended our party along the bank, far enough to command the whole of the enemy's at once; we waited till their front was nearly opposite to our left wing, when I fired a gun, as a signal for a general discharge upon them, whereupon we gave them the first fire, which killed above forty Indians; the rest retreated, and were pursued by about one half of our people.

I now imagined the enemy totally defeated, and ordered Ensign McDonald to head the flying remains of them, that none might escape; but we soon found our mistake, and that the party we had attacked were only their advanced guard, their main body coming up, consisting of 600 more, Canadians and Indians; upon which I ordered our people to retreat to their own ground, which we gained at the expence of fifty men killed; the remainder I rallied, and drew up in pretty good order, where they fought with such intrepidity and bravery as obliged the enemy (though seven to one in number) to retreat a second time; but we, not being in a condition to pursue them, they rallied again, and recovered their ground, and warmly pushed us in front and both wings, while the mountain defended our rear; but they were so warmly received, that their flanking parties soon retreated to their main body with considerable loss. This threw the whole again into disorder, and they retreated a third time; but our number being now too far reduced to take advantage of their disorder, they rallied again, and made a fresh attack upon us.

About this time we discovered 200 Indians going up the mountain on our right, as we supposed, to get possession of the rising ground, and attack our rear; to prevent which I sent Lieutenant Phillips, with eighteen men, to gain the first possession, and beat them back; which he did, and being suspicious that the enemy would go round on our left, and take possession of the other part of the hill, I sent Lieutenant Crafton, with fifteen men, to prevent them there; and soon after desired two gentlemen, who were there, volunteers in the party,[3] with a few men, to go and support him, which they did with great bravery.

The enemy pushed us so close in front, that the parties were not more than twenty yards asunder in general, and sometimes intermixed with each other. The fire continued almost constant for an hour and a half from the beginning of the attack, in which time we lost eight of-

---

3. I had before this desired these gentlemen to retire, offering them a serjeant to conduct them; that as they were not used to snow-shoes, and were unacquainted with the woods, they would have no chance of escaping the enemy, in case we should be broke and put to flight, which I very much suspected. They at first seemed to accept the offer, and began to retire, but seeing us so closely beset, they undauntedly returned to our assistance. What befell them after our flight, may be seen by a letter from one of the gentlemen to the commanding officer, which I have inserted next to this account of our scout.

ficers, and more than 100 private men killed on the spot. We were at last obliged to break, and I with about twenty men ran up the hill to Phillips and Crafton, where we stopped and fired on the Indians who were eagerly pushing us, with numbers that we could not withstand. Lieutenant Phillips being surrounded by 300 Indians, was at this time capitulating for himself and party, on the other part of the hill. He spoke to me, and said if the enemy would give them good quarters, he thought it best to surrender, otherwise that he would fight while he had one man left to fire a gun.[4]

I now thought it most prudent to retreat, and bring off with me as many of my party as I possibly could, which I immediately did; the Indians, closely pursuing us at the same time, took several prisoners. We came to Lake George in the evening, where we found several wounded men, whom we took with us to the place where we had left our sleds, from whence I sent an express to Fort Edward, desiring Mr. Haviland to send a party to meet us, and assist us in bringing in the wounded; with the remainder I tarried there the whole night, without fire or blankets, and in the morning we proceeded up the lake, and met with Captain Stark at Hoop Island, six miles north from Fort William-Henry, and encamped there that night; the next day being the 15th, in the evening, we arrived at Fort Edward.

The number of the enemy was about 700, 600 of which were Indians. By the best accounts we could get, we killed 150 of them, and wounded as many more. I will not pretend to determine what we should have done had we been 400 or more strong; but this I am obliged to say of those brave men who attended me (most of whom are now no more) both officers and soldiers in their respective stations

---

4. This unfortunate officer, and his whole party, after they surrendered, upon the strongest assurances of good treatment from the enemy, were inhumanly tied up to trees, and hewn to pieces, in a most barbarous and shocking manner.

behaved with uncommon resolution and courage; nor do I know an instance during the whole action in which I can justly impeach the prudence or good conduct of any one of them.

The following is a list of the killed, missing, &c. The captain and lieutenant of His Majesty's regular troops, volunteers in this party, were taken prisoners; the ensign, another volunteer of the same corps, was killed, as were two volunteers, and a serjeant of the said corps, and one private.

Of Captain Rogers's Company

Lieutenant Moore	Killed.
Serjeant Parnell	Ditto.
Thirty-six privates	Ditto.

Of Captain Shepherd's Company

Two Serjeants
Sixteen privates

Of Captain James Rogers's Company

Ensign McDonald	Killed.

Of Captain John Starks's Company

Two Serjeants	Killed.
Fourteen privates	Ditto.

Of Captain Bulkley's Company

Captain Bulkley	Killed.
Lieutenant Pottinger	Ditto.
Ensign White	Ditto.
Forty-seven privates	K. and Miss.

Of Captain William Stark's Company

Ensign Ross	Killed.

Of Captain Brewer's Company

Lieutenant Campbell	Killed.

APPENDIX 1

The author found this muster-roll, with other valuable papers, in an old tea-chest in the attic of a colonial house at Littleton, Mass., now owned by a collateral descendant of Captain Bulkeley. In this house Major Robert Rogers and his officers once spent the night, while the privates were quartered in the church nearby. Captain Bulkeley served first in Phineas Osgood's company in their expedition to Nova Scotia, and later in Robert Rogers's Rangers. He was killed by the Indians near Rogers Rock, on Lake George, on March 13, 1758, and forty-seven of his men with him. This muster-roll of Captain Bulkeley's company, and other lists which I shall include in a larger work, are the only lists of Rogers's Rangers known to exist.

MUSTER ROLL OF CAPTAIN CHARLES BULKELEY'S COMPANY OF RANGERS 24TH JUNE TO 24TH AUGUST 1757 INCLUSIVE

Men's Names	Quality	Time of Entrance	Until When	Total No of Days
Chas. Bulkeley	Captain	June 24	Aug. 24	62
Jam. Rogers	Lieut.	June 24	Aug. 24	62
Thos. Cunningham	"	June 24	July 16	31
Henry Phillips	Ensign	" "	Aug. 7	45
" "	Lieut.	Aug. 8	" 24	17
Wm. Morris	Ensign	" "	" "	17
Oliver Bates	Serg't	June 24	" "	62
Jonas Warren	"	" "	" "	62

Name						
John Dinsmore	"	"	"	"	"	62
Alexander Robb	"	"	"	"	"	62
David Anthony	Priv.	"	"	"	"	"
Boaz Brown	"	"	"	"	"	"
Boston Burns	"	"	"	"	"	"
Benj. Bridge	"	"	"	"	"	"
Judah Bill	"	"	"	"	"	"
Robert Campbell	Priv.	June 24		Aug 24		62
Solomon Crosby	"	"	"	"	"	"
Daniel Conally	"	"	"	"	"	"
Philip Clim	"	"	"	"	"	"
Abram Clark	"	"	"	"	"	"
Samuel Clark	"	"	"	"	"	"
Samuel Cunningham	"	"	"	"	"	"
Samuel Crosby	"	"	"	"	"	"
Thos. Clish	"	"	"	"	"	"
James Coleman	"	"	"	"	"	"
Christopher Conally	"	"	"	"	"	"
Phineas Douglas	"	"	"	"	"	"
Hendrick Dawson	"	"	"	"	"	"
Samuel Douglass	"	"	"	"	"	"
Jonathan Danforth	"	"	"	"	"	"
Joshua Dutton	"	"	"	"	"	"
Jonathan Edmunds	"	"	"	"	"	"
Zachariah Fitch	"	"	"	"	"	"
Wm. Fitch	"	"	"	"	"	"
Matthias Farnsworth	"	"	"	"	"	"
Joseph Flagg	"	"	"	"	"	"
John Flagg	"	"	"	"	"	"
Samuel Gold	"	"	"	"	"	"
Jonathan Gates	"	"	"	"	"	"
" Hodgkins	"	"	"	"	"	"
Chas. Hans	"	"	"	"	"	"
Solomon Hartwell	"	"	"	"	"	"
Amaziah Hildreth	"	"	"	"	"	"
Daniel Hartwell	"	"	"	"	"	"

Name	Rank					
Francis	"	"	"	"	"	"
Thos. Hewit	"	"	"	"	"	"
John	"	"	"	"	"	"
Joseph Kidder	"	"	"	"	"	"
John Lessly	"	"	"	"	"	"
Francis Leighton	"	"	"	"	"	"
Nicholas Lin	"	"	"	"	"	"
Abel Lawrence	"	"	"	"	"	"
Wm. McGee	"	"	"	"	"	"
Abram Munroe	"	"	"	"	"	"
John Middleton	"	"	"	"	"	"
Robert McNee	"	"	"	"	"	"
Alexander McCally	"	"	"	"	"	"
John McKalley	"	"	"	"	"	"
Andrew Notgrass	"	"	"	"	"	"
James Nichols	"	"	"	"	"	"
Wm. Pool	"	"	"	"	"	"
John Phillips	"	"	"	"	"	"
Wm. Prentice	"	"	"	"	"	"
Jonah "	"	"	"	"	"	"
Patrick Rogers	Priv.	June 24		Aug 24		62
Nathan Robbins	"	"	"	"	"	"
Samuel Rice	"	"	"	"	"	"
Elezar Stearns	"	"	"	"	"	"
Benj. Spaulding	"	"	"	"	"	"
Aaron Smith	"	"	"	"	"	"
Philip Stewart	"	"	"	"	"	"
James Stuart	"	"	"	"	"	"
Hendrick Sixbury	"	"	"	"	"	"
Nathan Simonds	"	"	"	"	"	"
Wm. Smith	"	"	"	"	"	"
Alexander Scott	"	"	"	"	"	"
John Stuart	"	"	"	"	"	"
Isaac Southward	"	"	"	"	"	"
Wm. Taylor	"	"	"	"	"	"
John Trull	"	"	"	"	"	"

Nathan Taylor	"	" "	" "	"
David Vanderheyden	"	" "	" "	"
Solomon Wallace	"	" "	" "	"
David "	"	" "	" "	"
Elijah Willson	"	" "	" "	"
Wm. Willson	"	" "	" "	"
" Crosby	"	" "	Died Aug. 2	
" Glenny	"	" "	" " 10	
James "	"	" "	" " 13	
Ephraim Kellock	"	" "	" July 24	
Wm. McClellan	"	" "	" " 30	
Nathan Munroe	"	" "	" Aug. 5	
Peter Martin	"	" "	" July 18	
Richard Russell	"	" "	" July 25	

Thw following names of Rangers were found in an account book belonging to Captain Charles Bulkeley:

Wm. Annis	Elnathan Sherwin
Samuel Britton	David Willis
Eliab Bewer — Ensign	James White — Ensign
A. R. A. Cutter. Dr.	Jacob Emerson
Michael Conally	Ebenezer Kimball
Daniel Dwyer	Mr. Rolfs
Thomas Farmer	John Rossiers
Amasa Gilson	Robert Lottridges
George Shur	Graham & Comp
William Swan	Captain Burbank
William Stewart	Captain Sheperd
William Stark — Lieut.	Thos. & Benjamin Forseys
Abiel Smith	

Received of Captain Chas. Bulkeley three hundred Spanish mil'd dollars for inlisting recruits into His Majesty's Company of Rangers, commanded by said Charles Bulkeley at ten dollars each recruit and to appear with said recruit at Albany in ye Province of New York in sixty days from the above date, or to return the above said dollars to said Bulkeley on demand.

James Rogers

LIEUTENANT ROGERS RETURNED IN OCTOBER 1757
WITH THE FOLLOWING RECRUITS

Daniel Addleton	Daniel Murfey
Hugh Anderson	John Mater
Thomas Burnside	Morris Obrien
Benj. Brown	John Rogers
Nathan Chapman	John Sparrow
John Cahail	George Soper
Wm. Curtis	Benj. Scott
John Collins	Jer. Swan
John Craige	Oliver Spalding
Edward Costalow	Willm Scott (Petersburough)
Ebn. Cymbal	Ebenezar Sherwin
John Cumings	Samuel Stinson
Willm Devine	Wm. Stuard
Benj. Darling	John Spraguer
Matthew Dickey	Willm. Scott
Isaac Day (Harvard)	Abram Scott
Daniel Dickinson	Nathaniel Taylor
Jacob Emerson	Leonard Taylor
James Faulkiner	Jno. Thompson—enlisted Albany
Edward Logan	Daniel Ware
Chas. McCoy	

The names in italics are those of the captives

Taken in Major Rogers' fight, near Ticonderoga, March 13, 1758.

Joshua Convey, son of John; *Aaron Smith,* Jr., son of Aaron; *Andrew Lovejoy; Jacob Bacon; Phineas Wheeler,* son of Samuel; *Boaz Brown,* son of Thomas; *William Prentice,* son of John; *John Hunter, Jr.,* son of John; Joseph Blanchard aplt. for *David Wallis, John Stewart, William Willson, Robert Nae, Charles McBay;* Sarah Clark aplt. for *Samuel Clarke, Leonard Taylor, Wm. Wilson; Matthew Spencer,* son of Sarah, taken March; *Wm. Prentice,* 2nd time; *Charles McKay,* Peterboro', N. H., aplt. John McKay.

Major Robert Rogers 1731-1795

Robert Rogers was the son of James and Mary McFatridge Rogers. He was born in Methuen, Massachusetts, on November 7, 1731. Early in the spring of 1739 James Rogers, with his family, moved from Methuen, to the wilderness of the township now known as Dunbarton, New Hampshire. He named the rich green meadowland and upland, 2190 acres, where he settled, Munterloney, for a place where he had once lived in Ireland, a mountainous district in Counties Derry and Tyrone.

Robert thus speaks of the years passed here in Mountalona:

It would perhaps gratify the curious to have a particular account of my life, preceding the war; but though I could easily indulge them herein, without any dishonour to myself, yet I beg they will be content with my relating only such circumstances and occurrences as led me to a knowledge of many parts of the country, and tended in some measure to qualify me for the service I have since been employed in. Such, in particular, was the situation of the place in which I received my early education, a frontier town in the province of New Hampshire, where, I could hardly avoid obtaining some knowledge of the manners, customs, and language of the Indians, as many of them resided in the neighbourhood and daily conversed and dealt with the English.

Between the years 1743 and 1755 my manner of life was such as led me to a general acquaintance both with the British and French settlements in North America, and especially with the uncultivated desert, the mountains, valleys, rivers, lakes and several passes that lay between and contiguous to the said settlements. Nor did I content myself with the accounts received from Indians or the information of hunters but travelled over large tracts of the country myself, which tended not more to gratify my curiosity, than to inure me to hardships, and, without vanity, I may say, to qualify me for the very service I have since been employed in.

Rogers' Journals, Introduction. Dublin, 1769

Robert Rogers was six feet in height, a well-formed, fine looking man, with fine manners and magnetic presence. He was one of the most athletic men of his time, well known in all trials of strength or skill. General Stark used to say of him, that for presence of mind in time of danger, he was unsurpassed.

At the age of twenty-three years he organized and disciplined his Rangers. On the 6th of April, 1758, Captain Rogers was promoted to a Majority and had command of this famous corps.

His *Journals* of his Ranging service, present an interesting account of his severe and perilous warfare. It is very rare. A copy recently brought £25. Some of the principal causes of the war are exhibited with spirit and truth in his drama *Ponteach*. His *Concise Account of North America and* his *Concise Historical Account,* etc., are both rare books containing valuable information.

He died in London, on May 18, 1795.

I claim, and with a justifiable pride, that Robert Rogers, the famous partisan chief, was the greatest American in the French and Indian War.

Major Rogers was an author as well as a soldier. After the close of the Seven Years' War, he went to London and published four books, *viz.*:

Journals of Major Robert Rogers

Containing an account of the several excursions he made under the generals who commanded upon the continent of North America, during the late War. From which may be collected the most material circumstances of every campaign upon that continent, from the commencement to the conclusion of the War.

A Concise Account of North America

Containing a description of the several British colonies on that Continent; including the Islands of Newfoundland, Cape Breton, etc., As to their situation, extent, climate, soil produce, rise, government, religion, present boundaries, and the number of inhabitants supposed to be in each.

Also of the interior, or westerly part of the county upon the rivers St. Lawrence, the Mississippi; Christino, and the Great Lakes. To which is subjoined, an account of the several nations and tribes of Indians residing in those parts, as to their customs, manners, government, numbers etc. containing many useful and entertaining facts, never before treated of. By Major Robert Rogers

Ponteach or the Savages of America

A Tragedy

A Concise Historical Account of all the British Colonies in North-America,

Comprehending their rise, progress, and modern state: particularly of the Massachusetts-Bay, (The seat of the present Civil War,). Together with the other provinces of New-England. To which is annexed, *An Accurate Descriptive Table of the Several Countries.* Exhibiting, at one view, their respective boundaries, capes, dimensions, harbours, longitudes, bays, latitudes, rivers, divisions, or counties, various productions, chief towns, animals, &c, &c. interspersed with particulars relative to the different soils and climatest capital cities, &c, &c.

Archives Publiques du Canada. Correspondance Officielle
Série F.Vol. 303
Montréal, 18 *Avril*, 1758
Suit le bulletin. — *Détails des succès remportés par plusieurs partis de Canadiens et Sauvages durant l'hiver.*

Les Anglais ont eu tout l'hiver le projet de surprendre ou bombarder Carillon et s'y sont présenté plusieurs fois. Le Sr. d'Hebencourt, Capitaine au régiment de la Reine qui y a été établi commandant après la Campagne, et la garnison ont été très alerte, les courses des Anglais ont toujours été infructueuses et le Sieur d'Hebencourt instruit qu'ils avaient en campagne un parti de 200 hommes, profita le 13 mars de l'heureuse circonstance de 200 Iroquois ou Nepissingues du Sault St. Louis et du Lac des Deux Montagues arrivés la veille avec le Sr. Durantaye et plusieurs cadets de la Colonie, le Sieur de Langry Officer très intelligent, quelques lieutenans et sergens de nos bataillons que le zèle seul y fit marcher s'y joignirent. Le détachement Anglais composé des soldats d'élite et de 12 officiers, commandé par le Major Roger leur meilleur partisan a été totalement défait les sauvages ont rapporté 146 chevelures, peu de prisonniers, seulement quelques uns pour donner des lettres vivantes à leur père, expression dont les sauvages nomment les prisonniers. Le reste aura péri de misère dans les bois. Quelques uns, entr'eux deux officiers du Régiment de Blekins se sont rendus d'eux mêmes prisonniers à notre fort de Carillon au bout de cinq jours leur guide ayant expiré la veille.

Nous avons perdu à cette action huit sauvages et nous avons eu 17 blessés ainsi que deux cadets de la colonie et un canadien. On a couvert les morts avec grande cérémonie. On a fait des présens au nom du Roy aux families. Le Gouverneur général recompensera la bravoure de nos Iroquois par une promotion et dormant quelques haussecols et médailles à ceux qui se sont distingués, ils en seront plus animés à venger la perte qu 'ils ont fait.

Archives Publiques du Canada Correspondance Generale
Série B.Vol. 104, p. 133

A Montréal le 28 9bre 1759

Monseigneur

Il ne falloit rien moins, Monseigneur, que le succès du Détachement que j'avois confié au Sr de la Durantay pour faire renoncer nos ennemis à leurs préparatifs pour faire escalader en hiver Carillon. Les Srs la Durantay et de Richerville ayant été compris dans la promotion de 1757 en qualité d'enseignes en pied. J'ay placé aussy le Sr de la Chevrotière comme enseigne on second, j'ay prématuré les favorables dispositions de Sa Majesté à leur égard en les faisant participer aux 6000 1b qu'elle à accordée sur son état de 1757 aux Canadiens qui se sont le plus distingués. Je leur donnay d 'abord à chacun 200 1b. Vous verrés, Monseigneur, par une de mes lettres que je n'ay pas encore recû cette somme. Le Corps de nos officiers est en général penetré de l'attention dont Sa Majesté honore leurs services et des recompenses qu'elle est disposée à leur accorder. Je n'ay eu rien de plus pressé que de les en instruire. Le Sr Robert Roger qui étoit à la tête du Détachement que nos Cadets defirent, eut le secret de s'échaper lorsqu'il vit la perte évidente, il laissa sur le champ de bataille son habit et même l'ordre qu'il avoit de son Général, ce qui me donnoit tout lieu de croire qu'il y avoit peri d'autant mi eux qu'un sauvage m'assura qu'il l'avoit tué lui-même.

Je suis avec un trés profond respect, Monseigneur,

Votre trés humble et trés obeissant serviteur

Vaudreuil

APPENDIX 2: ANECDOTES

When Major Robert Rogers narrated his wonderful story to the officers in the Coffee House in London, he gave Munterloney as his home, which they supposed to be in Italy, and, knowing him to be an American, made the story still more improbable. Gathered in little groups about the tables, one night, these men were engaged in witty and pleasant discourse, when it was agreed that the person who should tell the greatest lie, or the most improbable story, should have his bill paid by the Company. After all the others had told their stories, Rogers was called upon. He said: "When a boy in Munterloney" he made birch and hazel brooms, which he carried on his back through the woods, guided by spotted trees, to Rumford, the nearest settlement, a distance of ten miles, and sold them. He told how his father, dressed in fur, was shot dead in the wilderness by a hunter, who mistook him for a bear.

He also related that his mother was followed several miles by a hunter who thought her track in the fresh, light snow, was that of a wolf. Rogers' bill was paid by the Company for it was agreed that the major had told the greatest lie, when, in fact, he had only told the truth. This incident was greatly appreciated by the major's family and admirers in America. Major Rogers went to England in 1765 and, while travelling in a mail-coach over Hounslow Heath, the coach was stopped by a highway robber, who presented a pistol at the window and demanded the passenger's money. The major played asleep, while the other passengers passed over their money. When it came his turn, he drowsily opened his cloak, as if about to comply. The robber lowered his pistol. At the psychological moment, the noted Indian fighter seized him by the collar, dragged him from his horse through the window of the coach, and held him prisoner while he ordered the terrified coachman to drive on to the authorities. There the major delivered him. The prisoner proved to be a celebrated offender for whose head a reward of £50 sterling had been offered. The famous Rogers received the bounty.

London, October 8
Tuesday last, about two o'clock, after Major Rogers had passed through Dartford, the *post-chaise* man who drove him, told him a highwayman hovered round the chaise. As soon as the fellow came to the major, he seized him by the hand and pulled him into the *chaise*. The highwayman answers the description in an advertisement of Sir John Fielding's. The major carried him to the mayor at Gravesend, and after an examination there, sent him to the Ratation-office, in Bow street.
New-Hampshire Gazette. January 24, 1772.

HIS REPUTATION AT HOME

From *The Veil Removed*, John Fellows, New York, 1843, pp. 20 and 21.

That no doubt may rest on the mind of the reader in regard to the authenticity of the statements of facts by Major Rogers in his journal, the following testimony of his title to credibility has been obtained from the distinguished gentlemen therein named, citizens of his native state, where his character would doubtless be duly estimated:

Concord, July 16, 1842

Dear Sir—

I have made some inquiry respecting Major R. Rogers, and among our oldest inhabitants I find but one opinion respecting his character, and that is fully expressed in the note enclosed to me, and transmitted herewith to you from Gov. Hill.

Mr. Hill has perhaps a better knowledge of Major Rogers' character, as an officer, than any other person here; he has been prompted by reasons which could not have operated on others.

Respectfully, your obedient servant,

Robert Davis

Mr. Charles Coffin

New York City

Concord

July 2, 1842

Gen. Robert Davis

My dear Sir—

I have this moment read Mr. Coffin's letter addressed to you, requesting information in relation to the character of the late Major. Robert Rogers. Having recently had occasion to make inquiries relative to his early history. I find nothing in the region of his birth that goes at all to discredit him. One of the last of his blood relations in this vicinity who personally remembered him, a lady, died about one year ago. From her mouth, through Mark Burnham, Esq., a native of the same town with Rogers, I derived the information that all the family were proud of his name, and were reluctant to associate it with a reputation that was not entirely unsullied. Maj. Rogers never resided in this state permanently after the commencement of the Revolutionary War: he was in the British service in Canada after the close of the old French War, partly in a military, and partly in a civil capacity.

The only child bearing his name was several years under my care as guardian: this circumstance, among others, has led me more particularly to mark the character of the celebrated warrior. I consider him to have been one of the most talented men of the country — perhaps the best partisan officer this country ever produced. I believe him to have been the author of that perfect mode of attack and defence which enabled a hundred of the rangers to do more service than thousands of the British regulars, especially in the winter service of the old war of 1756. Such safety to troops on fatigue amid the severest seasons of a severe climate was never secured — such certainty in the results, either on the advance or retreat, perhaps, was never realized by any other force than the rangers, under the perfect arrangement and discipline invented by Rogers. I consider him to have been as great a man in his peculiar sphere as Napoleon Bonaparte, and of moral courage and honesty coming nearly if not quite up to the mark of Andrew Jackson.

I am, respectfully, sir, your obedient servant,

Isaac Hill

LITERARY REVIEWS

Rogers' *Concise Account* (From *The Gentleman's Magazine* for December, 1765, Vol. 35, pages 584-5.)

This is an account very different from the compilations which are undertaken for booksellers, by persons wholly unacquainted with the subject, and who generally have neither sufficient diligence nor skill to regulate the multifarious materials which lie scattered before them, perhaps in an hundred volumes, nor even to reject, much less reconcile the inconsistencies and contradictions with which such materials always abound.

Major Rogers has travelled through great part of the country he has described, in the course of his duty as an officer in his majesty's army, and has received accounts of other parts immediately from the inhabitants, or from persons who had been carried prisoners thither, and afterwards released.

The work is concise and yet full; and the knowledge it contains is acquired with pleasure, and retained with ease, by the regularity of the method, and perspicuity of the stile.

The author gives an account of every province separately, and of its first discovery and settlement; he describes its situation as to latitude and longitude, and to the countries and seas by which it is bounded; its extent; its rivers; its climate; its commodities, buildings, and number of inhabitants: With a particular attention to such facts and circumstances as appeared most interesting in a political or commercial view.

In this work there is also an account of the interior part of America, a territory much larger than the whole continent of Europe, and hitherto almost wholly unknown.

This territory he has considered under three several divisions, marked out by three great rivers that rise near the centre of it, St. Lawrence, the Christino, and the Mississippi.

The river St. Lawrence he has traced, and is pretty well acquainted with the country adjacent to it, as far up as lake Superior; and with the country from the Green Bay westward, to the Mississippi at the Gulf of Mexico: He has also travelled the country adjacent to the Ohio, and its principal branches; and that between the Ohio and the lakes Erie and Meshigan, and the countries of the Southern Indians; and his situation gave him opportunities of gaining accounts of the other parts, more particular and authentic than any other.

He has subjoined such an account of the Indians, their customs and manners, as gives a just idea of the genius and policy of the people, and of the method in which they are to be treated by those who wish to preserve a safe and advantageous commerce with them. This is a very entertaining as well as useful part of the work, for which the major was particularly qualified, by a long and experimental acquaintance with their several tribes and nations, both in peace and war.

It is proposed to continue this *History* in a second volume, containing maps of the colonies and the interior country, in which the faults and deficiencies of those already extant will be corrected and supplied; by subscription; the price one guinea.

(Some extracts from this work shall be occasionally given in the future numbers of this miscellany.)

Journals of Major Robert Rogers: containing an account of the several excursions he made, under the generals who commanded on the continent of America, during the late war. From which may be collected the most material circumstances of every campaign on that continent, from the commencement to the conclusion of the war. From the specimen of the work now before us, it appears that the accounts of Major Rogers may be depended upon by the public; they are undoubtedly as authentic as they are important and necessary to those who would acquire a thorough understanding of the nature and progress of the late military operations in North America.

The author writes like an honest, a sensible, and a modest man; and has given, throughout his whole account, undoubted proofs that he is a brave and skillful officer. He headed, with much reputation, the provincial troops called rangers, during the whole course of what were called the French wars in America. — *Bibliotheca Americana Nova,* or catalogue of books relating to America, printed from 1700 to 1800, By O. Rich, London, 1832.

Quoted by John Fellows, in *The Veil Removed* (New York, 1843), p. 20.

Rogers' *Concise Account* (From the *Monthly Review* or *Literary Journal* : By several hands. London, January, 1776.)

A concise account of North America: containing a description of the several British colonies on that Continent, including the Islands of Newfoundland, Cape Breton, &c. as to their situation, extent, climate, soil, produce, rise, government, religion, present boundaries, and the number of inhabitants supposed to be in each: also of the interior, or westerly parts of the country, upon the Rivers St. Laurence, the Mississippi, Christino, and the Great Lakes. To which is subjoined, an account of the several nations and tribes of Indians residing in those parts, as to their customs, manners, government, numbers, &c. containing many useful and entertaining facts, never before treated of. By Major Robert Rogers. 8vo. 5s. bound. Millan.

Few of our readers, we apprehend, are unacquainted with the name, or ignorant of the exploits, of Major Rogers; who, with so much reputation, headed the provincial troops called Rangers, during the whole course of our late successful wars in America. To this brave, active, judicious officer, it is, that the public are obliged for the most satisfactory account we have ever yet been favoured with, of the interior parts of that immense continent which victory hath so lately added to the British empire. For, as to what Charlevoix, and other French writers, have related, experience hath shewn with what artful fallacy their accounts have been drawn up: — with the obvious design of concealing, from other nations, the true situation, and real circumstances of that country, of which we were, in many respects, totally ignorant, till the British lion, in revenge of repeated insults, tore away the veil, and opened to our view, the wide, extended, glorious prospect!

The present publication, however, as may be supposed, from the quantity and price above specified, contains but a part of the major's intended work; the remainder being proposed to be printed by subscription; and to be illustrated with maps of the several colonies, and of the interior country of North America. These we are assured, in the Author's advertisement, will be 'more correct, and easier to be understood, than any yet published.'

Our Author was, happily for his country, the better qualified not only for the task he hath now enjoined his pen, but also for the achievements in which his sword hath been employed, by the circumstance of his having received his—

> .... early education in a frontier town in the province of New Hampshire, where he could hardly avoid obtaining some knowledge of the manners, customs, and language of the Indians, as many of them resided in the neighbourhood, and daily conversed with the English.—Between the years 1743 and 1755, his manner of life[1] was such, as led him to a general acquaintance both with the British and French settlements in North America, and especially with the uncultivated desert, the mountains, valleys, rivers, lakes, and several passes that lay between and contiguous to the said settlements. Nor did he content himself with the accounts he received from the Indians, or the information of hunters, but travelled over large tracts of the country himself; which tended not more to gratify curiosity, than to inure him to hardship.

—And hardships[2] enough he was destined to endure!

The accounts here given of the British colonies are very brief. They seem to have been chiefly intended to form

---

1. What that manner of life was, the Author hath not more particularly intimated; but we do not suppose he was employed in any military capacity.

2. For a detail of our Author's adventures, after he obtained the command of those American light-armed infantry, called Rangers, see the *Journals of Major Rogers*, mentioned in our catalogue for this month: a work wrote, as he declares, 'not with silence and leisure, but in, deserts, on rocks and mountains, amidst the hurries, disorders, and noise of war, and under that depression of spirits, which is the natural consequence of exhausting fatigue.'

an introduction to the major's description of our late conquests in that part of the world; and which must, undoubtedly, be considered as the most valuable part of his work. Accordingly he himself observes, that—

.... it will not be expected, after volumes on volumes that have been published concerning the British colonies on the eastern shore of the American continent, that anything materially new can be related of them.... that I mean to attempt with regard to this is, to collect such facts and circumstances, as in a political and commercial view, appear to me to be most interesting; to reduce them to an easy and familiar method, and contract them within such narrow limits, that the whole may be seen as it were at once, and everything material be collected from a few pages, concerning seventeen provinces; a minute and circumstantial account of which would fill so many considerable volumes.

In doing this, where my own knowledge (acquired by travelling several times through most of them) did not serve me, I have endeavoured to make use of the most authentic materials, collected from others, and to set every fact and circumstance in a true and impartial light, without favour or prejudice to any particular part or party.

But the principal object I have had in view, and what I look upon to be the most interesting and deserving part of this work, is the account I have given of the interior parts of North America, which though concise, and vastly short of what I should be glad to exhibit, I flatter myself is as full and perfect as any at present to be come at. Certain I am, that no one man besides has travelled over and seen so much of this part of the country as I have done; and if my remarks and observations relative thereto are injudicious or wrongly placed, it is not owing to any want of attention to the subject, but merely to a want of skill. What is comprehended under the appellation of the interior country of America, is of itself a larger territory than all the continent of Europe, and is at present mostly a desert, uninhabited, except by savages: it cannot therefore be reasonably expected that any one man has it in his power to give a just and minute account of its several parts, but that he must pass over large tracts of country in very general terms, and in many things depend upon the reports of others, or proceed upon his own uncertain conjectures.

This wide-extended country may naturally enough be considered under three general divisions, occasioned by the three great rivers that take their rise near the centre of it, namely, St. Lawrence, the Christino, and the Mississippi. The first of these I have traced, and am pretty well acquainted with the country adjacent to it as far up as Lake Superior, and with the country from the Green Bay westward to the Mississippi, and from thence down to the mouth of the Mississippi at the gulf of Mexico. I have also travelled the country adjacent to the Ohio and its principal branches, and that between the Ohio and the Lakes Erie and Meshigan, and the countries of the southern Indians. But as to the country above Lake Superior, I have my intelligence chiefly from Indians, or from prisoners that have travelled with them into it. The same is the case as to the country at the head of the Mississippi, and that adjacent to the river Misauris. The Christino I have taken wholly from the Indians: and though the accounts they have given me of these countries are large, and in some particulars very inviting, yet I shall shall do little more than mention their names, till I have better authority to go upon.

In the account I have subjoined of the Indians, their customs, manners, &c. I have purposely omitted many things related by others who have wrote on that subject; some, because they are false, and others, because they are trite and trifling; and have only mentioned such as I thought most distinguishing and absolutely necessary to give a just idea of the genius and policy of that people, and of the method in which they are to be treated, in order to our having any safe and advantageous commerce with them. And, without vanity, I may say, that the long and particular acquaintance I have had with several tribes and nations, both in peace and war, has at least furnished me with materials to treat the subject with propriety.

As we have had many contradictory accounts of the two Floridas, part of our newly acquired territories; and as many of our readers may be at a loss what idea to form of those settlements, we shall present them with Major Rogers's account of them entire: which will likewise serve as a specimen of his brief way of mentioning the elder Colonies, most of which he has described with nearly the same brevity.

The country south of Georgia, and between that and the Mississippi river, an extent of about 600 miles, was by the Spaniards called Florida, which name it still retains; but is now divided by the English into two provinces, *viz.* East and West Florida.

East Florida is bounded north by Georgia, or St. John's river, which divides them; eastwardly and southward, by the gulf of Florida; south-west, by West Florida; and north-west, by the country of the Creek Indians.

The Spaniards attempted a settlement at St. Augustine in this province in 1512; however they were obliged to abandon this attempt, by reason of the savages, and other inconveniences, they not being properly supplied with necessaries to go through with it. In 1565 they again took possession, and erected a fort called St. Augustine, which commanded a convenient harbour for their ships trading between Spain and America; but there being a constant war between the Spaniards and Creek Indians, greatly prevented the enlarging their settlements here. They maintained their garrison (though several attempts were made to reduce it by the Carolinians, and afterwards by General Oglethorpe) till the conclusion of the late war, when the garrison and the whole territory of Florida was ceded to the crown of Great Britain, by the treaty of Fontainebleau, in 1762. His Britannic Majesty being absolute sovereign of the soil, has the appointment of the governors in both of the Floridas.

The soil of East Florida is not so good as that of Georgia in general; but the northerly part of it adjacent to Georgia is much like it, and may be improved to all the purposes that Georgia is, *viz.* for raising of corn, rice, indigo, silk, wine, &c. and again, in the west part of the province is some very good land, capable of being improved to great advantage.

The centre or Cape of Florida is a more sandy soil; however, there are some good settlements begun in this province, under the direction of Colonel Grant, the present Governor of it, and there is a prospect of it soon becoming a flourishing province; and as inhabitants are flocking to it from several countries in Europe, there is no doubt but in a short time it will be considerable.

Their exports at present are but small, the produce of their trade with the Indians being the chief they have to spare. As the country was three years since almost entirely uncultivated, and the number of inhabitants as yet but small, no great improvements and productions are at present to be expected; but, undoubtedly, this country is capable of producing rice, indigo, silk, wine, oil, and other valuable commodities in great abundance. As the country is new, it has great plenty of all kinds of wild game, common to the climate. The metropolis of the province is St. Augustine. The number of inhabitants, exclusive of his majesty's troops garrisoned there, is, as I am told, about 2000.

It may well be supposed, from its southerly situation, that the air and climate of this province is not more agreeable and healthy than that of Georgia, and that it is no less infested with poisonous and troublesome animals of various shapes and sizes.

— Thus far, relating to East-Florida.

West Florida was seized upon by the French, who began a settlement in it at Pensacola, in 1720, and they enjoyed it till the before mentioned treaty of Fontainebleau in 1762, when this was ceded to and formed into a government by his Britannic majesty. It is bounded, eastwardly, by East Florida; southwardly, by the Gulf of Mexico; westwardly, by the Mississippi river, and the Lake St. Pier; and northwardly, by the country of the Chikitaws.

The principal town is Pensacola; and as many of the French, who inhabited here before the treaty, have chose to become British subjects for the sake of keeping their estates, this will contribute to the speedy peopling this province, and no doubt render the settlements considerable very soon, especially as the land in this province is mostly very good, vastly preferable to the eastern province, its soil being capable of producing all the valuable commodities of rice, indigo, wine, oil, &c. in the greatest abundance; and its situation for trade is extremely good, having the river Mississippi for its western boundary.

They already carry on a very considerable trade with the Indians, and export great quantities of deer-skins and furs. The French inhabitants here raise considerable quantities of rice, and build some vessels.

There are at present, as I am told, about 6000 inhabitants in this province, which increase very fast, it being much more healthy and inviting than East Florida; especially the western parts upon the banks of the Mississippi, where it is said to be agreeable enough to English constitutions. In short, it is not to be doubted but that in a few years this will be a rich and flourishing province nature having denied it nothing that is necessary to make it so.

How far our Author's account of these two settlements may, in every circumstance, be depended upon, is a point not perfectly clear to us, as we are not precisely informed whether he hath related all of them from his own personal acquaintance with those provinces; or whether he hath not chiefly made his report from the information of others. He appears, however, to be so honest a Writer, that we do not suspect him to be capable of any intention to mislead his Readers, in any respect whatever.

In our Author's description of the manners and customs of the Indians, particularly those called the Five Nations, are many curious particulars; some of which may serve as a proper supplement to the account extracted, in the preceding article, from Lieutenant Timberlake's *Memoirs*: and the observations of both these writers may, perhaps, be considered by the judicious Readers as a valuable addition to the more elaborate performance[3] of Cadwallader Colden Esq; published not long before the commencement of our Review.

---

3. The history of the Five Indian Nations of Canada; *viz*. The Mohawks, Oneydoes, Onondagas, Cayugas, and Senekas; to whom are also added, as a sixth nation, the Tuscaroras. The Necariages of Misil makinac, have also been received as a seventh nation.

These five nations, are, beyond all the other Indian tribes, the most distinguished for their understanding, their valour, and above all, for their glorious spirit of liberty: in which respect even Britons may be proud to call them their brethren. Of these, again, the Mohawks are the first in rank, (in regard to the aforementioned virtues) though at present the smallest in number: to which circumstance they have been reduced, from being the most numerous, by their continual wars. The union of the five nations, somewhat resembles that of the Dutch United Provinces; and this republican league, or confederacy, in which no one nation hath any superiority over the other, have subsisted so long, that the Europeans, says Mr. Colden, know nothing of its origin. Their most northern settlement, says Mr. Rogers:

> . . . . is a town called Chockonawago, on the south of the river St. Lawrence, opposite to Montreal; but their largest settlements are between Lake Ontario and the provinces of New York and Pennsylvania, or the heads of the Mohock, Tanesee, Oneoida and Onondaga rivers. They claim all the country south of the river St. Lawrence to the Ohio, and down the Ohio to the Wabach, from the mouth of the Wabach to the bounds of Virginia; westerly, to the Lakes Ontario and Erie, and the river Miamee; their eastern boundaries are lake Champlain, and the British colonies. When the English first settled in America, they could raise 15,000 fighting men; but now, including the Delawares and Shawanees, they do not amount to more than between three or four thousand, having been thus reduced by the incessant wars they have maintained with the other Indians, and with the French, in Canada.

Speaking of the great military exploits of the Mohawks, our Author assures us, that they have been inveterate enemies to the French, ever since their first settlement in Canada; that they once burned the city of Montreal; and that they are almost the only Indians within may hundred miles, that have been proof against the solicitations of the French to turn against us; but the greatest part of them have maintained their integrity, and been our steadfast friends and faithful allies.—As to their persons, Mr. Rogers remarks, that there is rarely found, among the Indians, a person that is any way—

.... deformed, or that is deprived of any sense, or decrepit in any limb, notwithstanding the little care taken about the mother in the time of her pregnancy, the neglect the infant is treated with when born, and the fatigues the youth is obliged to suffer; yet generally they are of a hale, robust, and firm constitution; but spirituous liquors, of which they are insatiably fond, and the women as well as the men, have already surprisingly lessened their numbers, and will, in all probability, in one century more nearly clear the country of them.

How greatly have these untutored people the advantage over us, in respect to what is observed, in the beginning of this last quotation! To what can it be owing that, among us, so many are found deformed, or deprived of one or other of their senses? To what more than the spirit of Quackery[4] which, for many ages past, hath taken possession of us, instead of the simplicity of former times? Quackery seems, indeed, to have vitiated our whole National Constitution and character: it hath infected our government, our religion, our laws, nay our very nurseries! Everything appears to be over-done, among us; and, (anxious mortals that we are) we act as though afraid of trusting to Providence, or leaving anything to the unerring direction of nature.

---

4. This term may be used in a religious, moral, political or economical, as well as in a medical sense.

Hence, each succeeding generation is continually busied in undoing what was done by their predecessors: hence the perpetual changes and revolutions of all our systems; and, hence, perhaps, the fatal necessity for so many repeals of the solemn acts and decrees even of senatorial wisdom! But to our Author.

Among other virtues possessed by the Indians, Mr. Rogers extols their surprising patience and equanimity of mind. They have, says he, a—

> . . . . command of every passion, except revenge, beyond what philosophers or Christians usually attain to. You may see them bearing the most sudden and unexpected misfortunes with a calmness and composure of mind, without a word, or change of countenance; even a prisoner, who knows not where his captivity may end, or whether he may not in a few hours be put to a most cruel death, never loses a moment's sleep on this account, and eats and drinks with as much cheerfulness as those into whose hands he has fallen.
>
> Their resolution and courage under sickness and pain is truly surprising. A young woman will be in labour a whole day without uttering one groan or cry; should she betray such a weakness, they would immediately say, that she was unworthy to be a mother, and that her offspring could not fail of being cowards. Nothing is more common than to see persons, young and old of both sexes, supporting themselves with such constancy under the greatest pains and calamities, that even when under those shocking tortures which prisoners are frequently put to, they will not only make themselves cheerful, but provoke and irritate their tormentors with most cutting reproaches.

Their method of declaring war is very solemn, and attended, says our Author 'With many ceremonies of terror.' In the first place, they call an assembly of the *sachems* (old men) and warriors to deliberate on the affair; in which congress the women have a voice as well as the men. Take our Author's farther account in his own words.

When they are assembled, the president or chief *sachem* proposes the affair they have met to consult upon, and, taking up the hatchet (which lies by him) says, who among you will go and fight against such a nation? Who among you will go and bring captives from thence, to replace our deceased friends, that our wrongs may be avenged, and our name and honour maintained as long as rivers flow, grass grows, or the sun and moon endure? He having thus said, one of the principal warriors rises, and harangues the whole assembly; and then addresses himself to the young men, and inquires, who among them will go along with him and fight their enemies? when they generally rise, one after another, and fall in behind him, while he walks round the circle or parade, till he is joined by a sufficient number.

Generally at such a congress they have a deer or some beast roasted whole; and each of them, as they consent to go to war, cuts off a piece and eats, saying, This way will I devour our enemies, naming the nation they are going to attack. All that chuse, having performed this ceremony, and thereby solemnly engaged to behave with fidelity and as a good warrior, the dance begins, and they sing the war-song; the matter of which relates to their intended expedition and conquest, or to their own skill, courage and dexterity in fighting, and to the manner in which they will vanquish and extirpate their enemies; all which is expressed in the strongest and most pathetic manner, and with a tone of terror.

So great is the eloquence or influence of their

women in these consultations, that the final result very much depends upon them. If any one of these nations, in conjunction with the chiefs, has a mind to excite one, who does not immediately depend upon them, to take part in the war, either to appease the manes of her husband, son, or near relation, or to take prisoners, to supply the place of such as have died in her family, or are in captivity, she presents, by the hands of some trusty young warrior, a string of *wampum* to the person whose help she solicits; which invitation seldom fails of its desired effect. And when they solicit the alliance, offensive or defensive, of a whole nation, they send an embassy with a large belt of *wampum*, and a bloody hatchet, inviting them to come and drink the blood of their enemies. The *wampum* made use of upon these and other occasions, before their acquaintance with the Europeans, was nothing but small shells, which they picked up by the sea-coasts and on the banks of the lakes; and now it is nothing but a kind of cylindrical beads, made of shells white and black, which are esteemed among them as silver and gold are among us. The black they call the most valuable, and both together are their greatest riches and ornaments; these among them answering all the ends that money does among us. They have the art of stringing, twisting, and interweaving these into their belts, collars, blankets, mogasons, &c. in ten thousand different sizes, forms and figures, so as to be ornaments for every part of dress, and expressive to them of all their important transactions.

They dye the *wampum* of various colours and shades, and mix and dispose them with great ingenuity and order, and so as to be significant among themselves of almost anything they please; so that by these their records are kept, and their thoughts communicated to one another, as ours are by writing. The belts that pass from one nation to another, in all treaties, declarations, and important transactions, are carefully preserved in the palaces or cabins of their chiefs, and serve, not only as a kind of record or history, but as a public treasure. It must, however, be an affair of national importance in which they use collars or belts, it being looked upon as a very great abuse and absurdity to use them on trifling occasions. Nor is the *calumet* or pipe of peace of less importance, or less revered among them in many transactions, relative both to war and peace. The bowl of this pipe is made of a kind of soft red stone, which is easily wrought and hollowed out; the stem is of cane, elder, or some kind of light wood, painted with different colours, and decorated with the heads, tails, and feathers of the most beautiful birds, &c. The use of the *calumet* is, to smoke either tobacco, or some bark-leaf, or herb, which they often use instead of it, when they enter into an alliance, or on any serious occasion, or solemn engagements; this being among them the most sacred oath that can be taken, the violation of which is esteemed most infamous, and deserving of severe punishment from heaven.

When they treat of war, the whole pipe and all its ornaments are red; sometimes it is red only on one side, and by the disposition of the feathers, &c. one acquainted with their customs will know, at first sight, what the nation who presents it intends or desires. Smoking the *calumet* is also a religious ceremony upon some occasions, and in all treaties is considered as a witness between the parties; or rather as an instrument by which they invoke the sun and moon to witness their sincerity, and to be, as it were, guarantees of the treaty between them. This custom of the Indians, though to appearance somewhat ridiculous, is not without its reasons; for, they finding smoking tended to disperse the vapours of the brain, to raise the spirits and qualify them for thinking and judging properly, introduced it into their counsels, where, after their resolves, the pipe was considered as a seal of their decrees, and, as a pledge of their performance thereof, it was sent to those they were consulting an alliance or treaty with: so that smoking among them in the same pipe is equivalent to our drinking together, and out of the same cup.

Here we cannot help observing what a noble and consistent spirit of liberty prevails among these Indians, with respect to the method used by their chiefs of inviting, not impressing, the people to accompany them to the wars. What a striking contrast does this afford, to our tyrannical practice of seizing our fellow-subjects by brutal force, imprisoning and transporting them like felons and Newgate convicts; and, after such base treatment, compelling them to go forth with our fleets and armies, to fight in defence of the rights and liberties of their country!

In short, says our Author, the great and fundamental principles 'of their policy are, that every man is naturally free and independent; that no one or more on earth has any right to deprive him of his freedom and independancy, and that nothing can be a compensation for the loss of it.' Describing the other Indian nations, still farther to the westward, *viz.* those bordering on the great lakes, Mr. Rogers hath introduced some account of the famous Pondiac, or Ponteack, according to our author.

The Indians on the lakes, says he, are generally at peace with one another, having a wide extended and fruitful country in their possession. They are formed into a sort of empire, and the emperor is elected from the eldest tribe, which is the Ottawawas, some of whom inhabit near our fort at Detroit, but are mostly further westward towards the Mississippi. Ponteack is their present King or Emperor, who has certainly the largest empire and greatest authority of any Indian chief that has appeared on the continent since our acquaintance with it. He puts on an air of majesty and princely grandeur, and is greatly honoured and revered by his subjects. He not long since formed a design of uniting all the Indian nations together under his authority, but miscarried in the attempt.

In the year 1760, when I commanded and marched the first detachment into this country that was ever sent there by the English, I was met in my way by an embassy from him, of some of his warriors, and some of the chiefs of the tribes that are under him; the purport of which was, to let me know, that Ponteack was at a small distance, coming peaceably, and that he desired me to halt my detachment till such time as he could see me with his own eyes. His ambassadors had also orders to inform me, that he was Ponteack, the King and Lord of the country I was in.

At first salutation when we met, he demanded my business into his country, and how it happened that I dared to enter it without his leave? When I informed him that it was not with any design against the Indians that I came, but to remove the French out of his country, who had been an obstacle in our way to mutual peace and commerce, and acquainted him with my instructions for that purpose. I at the same time delivered him several friendly messages, or belts of *wampum*, which he received, but gave me no other answer, than that he stood in the path I travelled in till next morning, giving me a small string of wampum, as much as to say, I must not march further without his leave.

When he departed for the night, he enquired whether I wanted anything that his country afforded, and he would send his warrior to fetch it? I assured him that any provisions they brought should be paid for; and the next day we were supplied by them with several bags of parched corn, and some other necessaries. At our second meeting he gave me the pipe of peace, and both of us by turns smoaked with it; and he assured me he had made peace with me and my detachment; that I might pass through his country unmolested, and relieve the French garrison; and that he would protect me and my party from any insults that might be offered or intended by the Indians; and, as an earnest of his friendship, he sent 100 warriors to protect and assist us in driving 100 fat cattle, which we had brought for the use of the detachment from Pittsburgh, by the way of Presque Isle. He likewise sent to the several Indian towns on the southside and west-end of lake Erie, to inform them that I had his consent to come into the country.

He attended me constantly after this interview till I arrived at Detroit, and while I remained in the country, and was the means of preserving the detachment from the fury of the Indians, who had assembled at the mouth of the strait with an intent to cut us off.

I had several conferences with him, in which he discovered great strength of judgment, and a thirst after knowledge. He endeavoured to inform himself of our military order and discipline. He often intimated to me, that he could be content to reign in his country in subordination to the King of Great Britain, and was willing to pay him such annual acknowledgement as he was able in furs, and to call him his uncle. He was curious to know our methods of manufacturing cloth, iron, &c. and expressed a great desire to see England, and offered me a part of his country if I would conduct him there. He assured me, that he was inclined to live peaceably with the English while they used him as he deserved, and to encourage their settling in his country; but intimated, that, if they treated him with neglect, he should shut up the way, and exclude them from it; in short, his whole conversation sufficiently indicated that he was far from considering himself as a conquered Prince, and that he expected to be treated with the respect and honour due to a King or Emperor, by all who came into his country, or treated with him.

In 1763, this Indian had the art and address to draw a number of tribes into a confederacy, with a design first to reduce the English forts upon the lakes, and then make a peace to his mind, by which he intended to establish himself in his imperial authority; and so wisely were his measures taken, that, in fifteen days time, he reduced or took ten of our garrisons, which were all we had in his country, except Detroit; and had he carried this garrison also, nothing was in the way to complete his scheme. Some of the Indians left him, and by his consent made a separate peace; but he would not be active or personally concerned in it, saying, that when he made a peace, it should be such an one as would be useful and honourable to himself, and to the King of Great Britain: but he has not as yet proposed his terms.

In 1763, when I went to throw provisions into the garrison at Detroit, I sent this Indian a bottle of brandy by a Frenchman. His counsellors advised him not to taste it, insinuating that it was poisoned, and sent with a design to kill him; but Ponteack, with a nobleness of mind, laughed at their suspicions, saying it was not in my power to kill him, who had so lately saved my life.

In the late war of his, he appointed a commissary, and began to make money, or bills of credit, which he hath since punctually redeemed. His money was the figure of what he wanted in exchange for it, drawn upon bark, and the shape of an otter (his arms) drawn under it. Were proper measures taken, this Indian might be rendered very serviceable to the British trade and settlements in this country, more extensively so than any one that hath ever been in alliance with us on the continent.

As our readers are, perhaps, by this time, fully satisfied with regard to these free-born sons of the vast American wilderness, we shall conclude the present article, with a remark or two, borrowed from Mr. Colden, in respect to the Five nations.

They are called a barbarous people, bred under the darkest ignorance; and yet a bright and noble genius shines through these black clouds. None of the Roman heroes have discovered a greater love to their country, or a greater contempt of death, than these people called barbarians have done, when liberty came in competition. Indeed I think,' continues that learned and sensible historian, 'our Indians have outdone the Romans in this particular. Some of the greatest of those have murdered themselves to avoid shame or torments ; but the Indians have refused to die meanly, or with but little pain, when they thought their country's honour would be at stake by it; but have given their bodies, willingly, to the most cruel torments of their enemies, to show, as they said, that the Five Nations consisted of men whose courage and resolution could not be shaken.—They greatly sully, however, these noble virtues, by that cruel passion, revenge; this, they think, is not only lawful, but honourable; and for this only

it is that they can deserve the name of barbarians.
— But what, alas! have we Christians done, to make
them better?

We have, indeed, reason to be ashamed that these in-
fidels, by our conversation and neighbourhood, are
become worse than they were before they knew us.
Instead of virtues, we have only taught them vices,
which they were entirely free from before that time.

In another place he observes, on the same subject, that this
cruelty of revenge, is not peculiar to the Five Nations, but
is common to all the other Indians. To blunt, however, the
keenness of that censure we might be apt to cast on them,
upon this account, he hath the following just reflection:

It is wonderful, how custom and education are able
to soften the most horrid actions, even among a po-
lite and learned people. Witness the Carthaginians
and Phoenicians burning their own children alive in
sacrifice; and several passages in the Jewish history;
— and witness, in later times, the Christians burning one another for God's sake!

Journals of Major Robert Rogers (From *The Monthly Review;*
or, *Literary Journal:* By several hands. Vol. 34. London: 1766. For
January, 1766.)

Art. 32. *Journals of Major Robert Rogers;* containing an account of the several excursions he made, under the generals who commanded on the continent of America, during
the late war. From which may be collected the most material circumstances of every campaign on that continent,
from the commencement to the conclusion of the war.
8vo. 4s. Millan.

This is but the first part of the journals of this noted American partisan. It commences in 1755, and terminates with
the year 1760. The second part, which is to be printed
by subscription of one guinea, will contain the Author's

travels among the Cherokees and the southern Indians; his second tour into the interior country, upon the great lakes; and the Indian wars in America, since 1760: together with correct plans of all the British forts upon the continent.

From the specimen of the work now before us, it appears, that the accounts published by Major Rogers may be depended upon by the public; they are undoubtedly as authentic as they are important and necessary, to those who would acquire a thorough understanding of the nature and progress of the late military operations in North-America. The Author writes like an honest, a sensible, and a modest man; and he has given, throughout his whole conduct, undoubted proofs, that he is a brave and a skilful officer. For a farther idea of this gentleman, in his literary capacity, see our review of his *Account of North America,* in the preceding part of our No. for the present month.

The Battle of Lake George

by
Henry T. Blake

The Battle of Lake George

At the southern end of Lake George there stands a monument which was erected in 1903 by the New York Society of Colonial Wars to commemorate one of the most desperate battles and important victories in our colonial history. The monument consists of a massive granite pedestal surmounted by two life-size figures in bronze which represent a colonial military officer in conference with an Indian chief, and the principal inscription on the pedestal reads as follows:

1903

The Society of Colonial Wars erected this monument to commemorate the victory of the colonial forces under General William Johnson and their Mohawk allies under Chief Hendrick over the French Regulars commanded by Baron Dieskau with their Canadian and Indian allies.

The impression which this inscription suggests to the ordinary reader is that both Johnson and Hendrick were in command during the battle and that the victory was gained under their leadership. Neither of these inferences is correct. Chief Hendrick had been killed several hours before the battle was fought and several miles distant from its locality. Johnson had been wounded at the very commencement of the action and retired to his tent, leaving his second in command to manage the battle and he alone conducted it to its successful result. These are the undisputed facts of history. Moreover, it is universally agreed that Johnson's gross military neglect in making no preparations for the attack almost caused a defeat, and that his equally censurable refusal to permit a pursuit of the routed enemy rendered the victory incomplete and valueless. All authorities concur in these points, and they also agree that the real heroes of the day were: First, Lieutenant Colonel Whiting of New Haven, Conn., who in the preliminary morning fight after the death of Colonel Williams and Chief Hendrick took command of their panic-stricken followers and not only saved them from destruction but incidentally the rest of Johnson's army also; and, Second, General Phineas Lyman of Suffield, Conn., to whom, as already stated, Johnson turned over the command almost at the outset of the battle and who personally directed it for more than five hours thereafter till it ended in victory.

My subject, therefore, possesses a local interest for us, not only as sons of Connecticut but also as citizens of New Haven. Thousands of visitors from our State and hundreds from our near vicinity annually visit the beautiful and historic region where the monument referred to is situated, and others will do so down to the end of time, to most of whom the battle it commemorates is either entirely unknown or is dim and vague as a prehistoric legend. Not only on this, but on general grounds it devolves upon this, as on all other Historic Associations, to protest against misleading public records or inscriptions which tend to perpetuate injustice toward heroes of the past, whose names are already almost forgotten. For these reasons I have devoted the paper of this evening to an account of the battle of Lake George and the men who won it.

The three personages with whom our story will principally deal are General (afterwards Sir) William Johnson, General Phineas Lyman and Lieutenant Colonel Nathan Whiting; and it will be proper to begin it with some account of the previous history of these three individuals.

Sir William Johnson (to give him prematurely the title by which he is generally known) was born in Ireland and came to this country in 1735 at the age of twenty, to manage the large landed estates of his uncle, Admiral Johnson, in the Mohawk Valley. For this purpose and also for the purpose of trading on his own account he established himself on the edge of the vast Indian territory which then extended indefinitely toward the north, south, and west of the continent. Being shrewd and ambitious and possessing the genial adaptability of his race to all conditions of life, and to all sorts of men, he neglected no method of ingratiating himself with his savage neighbours and of gaining their respect and confidence. Accordingly he observed strict honesty and firmness in his dealings with them, kept open house for them at all times, and often lived with them in their wigwams, where he wore their garb, greased and painted his face after their fashion, and in whooping, yelling, dancing and devouring roast dog became a recognized champion. By these and other accomplishments he so won their hearts that he was formally adopted into the Mohawk tribe and accompanied them as a member, greased, painted and befeathered, to an important conference with the whites at Albany. Owing to his influence with the Indians he was appointed, in 1750, by the Colonial Government of New York, a member of the Governor's Council, which involved a residence for a considerable part of the year in the City of New York.

There he mingled with the best social circles, which doubtless conduced to amenity and polish in his manners; there also he became intimately identified with New York politics, which were as bitter and strenuous then as now, and which did not then any more than now conduce to the purity or magnanimity of a politician's personal character.

In 1755, when war was declared between England and France, a colonial movement was planned to capture Crown Point on Lake Champlain, then in possession of the French. In this expedition the Colonies of New York, Massachusetts and Connecticut agreed to unite, and Johnson was commissioned by each of them a Major General to be in command of their combined forces. This appointment was made, not on account of his military reputation, for up to that time he had had no experience as a soldier ; but partly on account of the influence it was likely to have in holding the New York Indians to the English side, and partly to the supposition that no one else could be put in the general command without exciting local jealousy. For both these reasons the appointment was judicious and attended with good results. Through Johnson's efforts the Mohawks agreed to fight on the English side, and most of them afterwards did so, though others, and all the tribes near Canada, allied themselves with the French.

In connection with this appointment of Johnson as Commander-in-Chief of the Provincial forces for the proposed expedition, the three Colonies also united in appointing Phineas Lyman of Connecticut to be second in command. Like Johnson, Lyman had had no previous military experience except as captain of a militia company in Suffield, and his selection was doubtless due not only to his prominence as a citizen but to a recognition of those abilities and soldierly qualities which were afterwards displayed in a distinguished military career. He was born in Durham, Conn., in 1716. He graduated at Yale College in 1738 and married into a prominent Massachusetts family, his wife being an aunt of Timothy Dwight, who was afterwards President of Yale College. After graduation he became a lawyer and settled in Suffield, which, at that time, through an error in the laying out of the Colony's boundary line, was included in Massachusetts, but was after wards, through his efforts, conceded to Connecticut where it belonged. He was for several years a member of the Connecticut General Assembly; at first in the lower house and afterwards in the upper branch, and his law practice is said to have been the largest in Connecticut. This practice General Lyman relinquished immediately after his military appointment, and proceeded to Albany, which had been selected as the rendezvous for all the troops and supplies for the proposed expedition.

The third one of the persons with whom we are now principally concerned was Colonel Nathan Whiting, who was born in Windham, Conn., but had resided from boyhood in New

Haven, being connected with the family of President Clap of Yale College. He graduated from Yale College in 1743, and in 1745 he took part in the expedition to Louisburg, where he so distinguished himself that he was promoted to a lieutenancy in the British army. After his return he engaged in business in New Haven, but when war broke out in 1755 his martial ardour revived and he accepted a Colonial commission as Lieutenant Colonel with the command of the Second Connecticut Regiment, which was raised for the movement on Crown Point. The regiment, which was made up partly of volunteers and partly of drafted militiamen, was assembled at New Haven, and on May 25, 1755, being about to depart for Crown Point, it marched, with Colonel Whiting at its head, into Rev. Mr. Noyes meeting house on the Green to hear a discourse by the Reverend Isaac Stiles on the character and duty of soldiers.

Some copies of the sermon still survive and show that the eloquent Divine did full justice to his subject and the occasion. He adjured his hearers to "file off the rust of their firelocks, that exquisitely contrived and tremendous instrument of death," also "to attend to the several beats of that great warlike instrument the drum, and to the language of that shrill high-sounding trumpet, that noble, reviving and animating sound"; he depicted their foes as "lying slain on the battle field with battered arms, bleeding sculls and cloven trunks," "while the good soldiers of Jesus Christ were all the while shining with all the beauty and lustre that inward sanctity and outward charms lend to the hero's look." Fired with enthusiasm by these encouraging prospects, the youthful warriors departed for the seat of war and in due time arrived at Albany, where, by the middle of July, about 3,000 provincials were encamped. A large part of the Mohawk tribe had also arrived, warriors, squaws and children, among whom Major General Johnson, with painted face, danced the war dance, howled the war whoop, and with his sword cut off the first slice of the ox that had been roasted for their entertainment.

After various delays, a part of the motley army, under command of General Lyman, moved about twenty-five miles up the Hudson River to The Great Carrying Place, from which there was a trail to Wood Creek, a feeder of Lake Champlain, on which Crown Point is situated. Here Lyman proceeded to build a fortified storehouse, which the soldiers called Fort Lyman, but which Johnson, with a politician's instinct, after wards called Fort Edward, as a compliment to the then Duke of York, and this name still clings to the important village which has since grown up at that place.

On the 12th of August, Johnson arrived with the rest of the militia and about 250 Mohawks out of the multitude who had been feasting and dancing at Colonial expense for a month at Albany. These were led by their principal sachem, Hendrick, commonly called King Hendrick, an aged chief of great renown both as warrior and orator, who had been to England twice, and wore a gorgeous uniform which had been presented to him by King George in person.

After consultation, it was decided not to approach Crown Point by way of Wood Creek but through Lake George; and to reach Lake George, fourteen miles distant, it was necessary to cut a road through the forest for the transportation of artillery, boats and stores. This task was accomplished in about a fortnight and on August 28, Johnson with 3,400 men, including Indians, arrived and encamped at the southern end of the lake. Six days later, September 3, Lyman joined him with 1,500 militiamen, 500 having been left to occupy Fort Lyman. Some of the cannon, bateaux and other war material had also reached the lake and the rest was slowly following in wagons along the newly-cut road. Not expecting any enemy, all these equipments and supplies as they arrived at Lake George were deposited along the shore of the lake in preparation for embarking them when everything needed should have come up. No action was taken to fortify the camp, though the erection of a permanent fort (afterwards called Fort William Henry) was begun with a view to establishing a future military post at that point.

Meantime, the enemy in Canada had been neither asleep nor

idle. While Johnson's army had been slowly cutting their forest road to Lake George, Baron Dieskau, the commander-in- chief of all the French armies in America, a soldier of great distinction and activity, whose motto was "Audacity Wins," had advanced from Crown Point to Ticonderoga with a force of 1,500 men consisting of 1,200 Canadians and Indians and 300 French Regulars. On the 2nd of September he had left Ticonderoga by way of Lake Champlain and Wood Creek, and was now (September 4th) on the other side of the ridge which separates Lake George from Wood Creek pushing his way southward up that stream, his objective point being Fort Lyman.

This post he expected to surprise and carry by assault, thus getting in the rear of Johnson, capturing the greater part of his stores and munitions and cutting him off from all future supplies and reinforcements. This he could easily have done, as Fort Lyman was held by only 500 raw militiamen and his approach was entirely unsuspected by the garrison as well as by Johnson himself. On the evening of September 7, Johnson first learned from a scout that a large body of men had been discovered about four miles above Fort Lyman and marching toward it. He immediately despatched a messenger with a letter warning the garrison of its danger and called a council of war to consider the situation. His own suggestion was to send 500 men the next morning to reinforce Fort Lyman, and 500 more across the country toward Wood Creek in order to seize Dieskau's boats and cut him off from a retreat.

Old King Hendrick, however, repelled this proposal with an Indian's mode of argument by taking two sticks and showing that they could be more easily broken when separated than when combined. Relinquishing this plan, therefore, Johnson decided to send 1,200 men the next morning in a single body to Fort Lyman to cooperate with the garrison in its defence. The old chief still demurred, declaring that if they were sent to be killed there would be too many, but if to fight there would be too few. Nevertheless, this plan was adhered to and an order was issued that 1,000 men from the Massachusetts and

Connecticut regiments, under command of Colonel Ephraim Williams and Lieut. Colonel Nathan Whiting, and 200 Indians commanded by Hendrick, should march to the aid of Fort Lyman early next morning.

While these discussions were going on in Johnson's camp, his messenger to Fort Lyman had been killed by Dieskau's scouts and the letter of warning found in his pocket. At about the same time, two of Johnson's wagoners had been captured on their way to Lake George, and from them it was learned that Fort Lyman was defended by cannon, while Johnson's camp was unprotected even by breastworks, and that his artillery was lying unmounted on the shore of the lake. No sooner were these facts known to the Canadians and Indians than they protested with one voice against Dieskau's plan of assaulting Fort Lyman the next morning and insisted on making the camp at Lake George the object of attack. The ground of this preference was the invincible repugnance of militiamen and Indians to face artillery, and they could neither be cajoled nor reasoned out of such an excusable prejudice. In vain did Dieskau argue, threaten and implore; it was Lake George or nothing, and in the end he consented, with infinite disgust, to march against Johnson's camp in the morning.

Soon after eight o'clock, therefore, on the morning of September 8, two hostile armies were marching towards each other, one south, the other north, along Johnson's road. As the Canadian force was the first to start, we will follow their movement first. Moving from a point near Glens Falls, three or four miles north of Fort Lyman, they had advanced about five miles when they reached a narrow ravine between two steep, wood-covered heights, at the bottom of which ran the road and alongside of it a little trickling brook. The general appearance of the locality is almost unchanged today, though a railroad now runs through the bottom of the ravine and a high way and trolley track skirt its western side. At this point the Indian scouts announced that a large force was approaching from the direction of Johnson's camp and Dieskau immediately prepared an ambuscade to receive it. The Indians and Canadians were distributed for half a mile among the woods on the two sides of the ravine and the Regulars were posted across it at the lower end; thus forming a cul-de-sac of savages and militiamen, who then in complete concealment and perfect silence awaited the approach of their unsuspecting enemy. Strict orders had been given not to fire a gun until the English should become completely enveloped in the trap.

The party from the camp had started a little after eight o'clock, the Mohawks being in front, headed by Old Hendrick, who was so heavy and infirm that he chose to ride a horse which had been lent to him by Johnson. Then followed Colonel Williams with the Massachusetts men; and Colonel Whiting with the Connecticut Militia brought up the rear. The whole column, however, was somewhat promiscuously intermingled and proceeded with surprising recklessness in a helter-skelter fashion without the usual precaution of sending scouts at least a mile in advance. Thus proceeding, the head of the column reached the ravine and had advanced some distance into it when Old Hendrick's olfactories recognized a familiar odour and he called out "I smell Indians!" Just then came the crack of a gun from among the bushes and in an instant the air was alive with horrible yells, as if ten thousand devils had broken loose mingled with the din of musketry, which flashed and smoked and rained deadly bullets on the bewildered, staggering and falling provincials. As Dieskau described it later in his official report: "the head of the column was doubled up like a pack of cards."

At the first fire Old Hendrick fell dead from his horse, and the Mohawks fled howling to the rear, spreading confusion and panic through the whole body. Colonel Williams sprang to the top of a large boulder to rally his men and was immediately shot through the head. And now the French regulars advanced, pouring murderous volleys into the huddled mass of militiamen, who crowded on each other in frantic efforts to escape the withering fire. To most of the Yankee boys it was their first experience of war, and if they thought of Parson Stiles sermon, with its allusions to "battered arms, cloven sculls and severed bodies" the application to the case in hand was less promotive of "the hero's look" than a longing for home and mother. The situation is thus described by Parkman:

> There was a panic; some fled outright and the whole column recoiled. The van now became the rear and all the force of the enemy rushed upon it, shouting and screeching. There was a moment of total confusion, but a part of Williams' regiment rallied under command of Whiting and covered the retreat, fighting behind trees like Indians and firing and falling back by turns, bravely aided by some Indians and by a detachment which Johnson sent to their aid.

As this detachment was not sent out until after the firing had been for some time heard at the camp to be approaching, thus giving notice of a defeat, and then had two or three miles to cover before it reached the scene of action, it is evident that Whiting must have had the matter well in hand before it came up. A New York historian says:

> After the death of Colonel Williams the command devolved on Lieutenant Colonel Whiting of Connecticut, who, with signal ability, conducted a most successful retreat. On account of the spirited resistance made by Colonel Whiting the enemy were an hour and a half driving the fugitives before them.[1]

Governor Livingston of New York, in a letter written shortly afterwards, says:

> The retreat was very judiciously conducted, after the death of Colonel Williams, by Lieutenant Colonel Whiting of Connecticut, an officer who gained much applause at the reduction of Louisburg.

Johnson, in his official report, says (without mentioning Whiting's name): "The whole party that escaped came in, in

---

1. *N.Y. State Hist. Assoc. Proceedings*, Vol. 2, p. 18.

large bodies," (a practical acknowledgement that the retreat had been well conducted,) and he also concedes that the delay which had been effected was of vital importance by giving time to put the camp in a posture of defence. Baron Dieskau, after his capture, expressed his admiration of Whiting's achievement, declaring that a retreat was never better managed; and Vaudreuil, the French Governor General of Canada, in a communication to his own government, admits that Whiting baffled an essential part of Dieskau's plan. This was to drive the routed provincials in confusion back upon an unprotected camp, and to rush in with them, spreading the panic, in which case he felt sure that his disciplined regulars, supporting the wild onslaught of his Canadian and Indian allies, would make victory certain.

That this plan, but for Whiting's leadership, would have been realized and would have succeeded, there can be little doubt. It was not until the firing was heard to be approaching the camp, thus evincing that "the bloody morning scout" (as it was long afterwards called) had been defeated, that any vigorous preparation was made for protection by any kind of barricade. The time was short, indeed, less than an hour and a half, for getting ready, but life and death were at stake, and in those few minutes the men worked in a frenzy. Trees were felled and laid end to end, bateaux, wagons, and other materials brought up from the lake and piled in heaps, and three or four heavy cannon dragged behind the barrier, where they were hurriedly mounted and placed in position. The fugitives were already swarming in. The more orderly bodies followed quickly after, and were rapidly assigned places among those who had been previously disposed at different points for the defence.

Then and before the arrangements were fully completed, the savage pursuers came whooping and yelling through the forest, brandishing their weapons and making straight for the slight barricade, already exulting in an assured victory and massacre. They were checked for a moment by a volley of musketry, and immediately after the unexpected roar of artillery and the crashing of cannon balls and grapeshot through the trees around them sent them scattering in consternation through the forest, where behind such shelter as they could get they pushed as near to the barricade as they dared and shot at the defenders as they could get opportunity. And now the French regulars were quickly seen advancing in solid columns down the road, their white uniforms and glittering bayonets showing through the trees in what seemed to be an interminable array. The inexperienced militia behind the barricade grew uneasy, but the officers, sword in hand, threatened to cut down any man who should desert his post.

Dieskau felt sure that if he could hold his forces together for a combined assault he could carry the breastwork; but the Canadians and Indians were scattered through the woods, each man fighting on his own account and could not be collected or controlled. With his regulars, therefore, and such few others as he could gather, he made charge after charge against the defences, now upon this side and now upon that but only to be repulsed at every point. The fighting spirit had begun to be developed in the defenders and the battle became one of promiscuous musketry for the most part, though the artillery was also vigorously served, now scattering a band of Indians who had collected in an exposed position, and now pouring balls and grapeshot at random through the forest, the crashing of which among the trees effectually encouraged the savages to keep at a respectful distance.

In the very beginning of the fight Johnson had been hit by a musket ball in the fleshy part of his thigh, but was able to walk to his tent, where he remained throughout the day, taking no further part in the action. General Lyman being thus left in command directed practically the entire course of the battle, and in the words of Dr. Holden of the New York Historical Society: "conducted what is considered by all experts to be one of the most important Indian fights in history to a successful termination." To quote again from Parkman:

General Lyman took command, and it is a marvel that he escaped alive, for he was for four hours in the heat of the fire, directing and animating his men.

"It was the most awful day my eyes ever beheld," wrote Surgeon Williams to his wife; "there seemed to be nothing but thunder and lightning and pillars of smoke." Governor Livingston in the letter already quoted says:

Numbers of eye witnesses declare that they saw Lyman fighting like a lion in the hottest of the battle not to mention a gentleman of undoubted veracity to whom General Johnson two days after the action acknowledged that to Lyman was chiefly to be ascribed the honour of the victory.

Whether such an admission was correctly attributed to Johnson or not there is but one voice among historians on the subject and that is that Lyman, and Lyman alone, fought the battle as the officer in command, and that to him alone as the directing spirit is due the credit for its result.

Towards five o'clock in the afternoon the fight began to slacken. The Canadians and Indians had lost their interest, as well as most of their ammunition, and were generally acting on an informal vote to adjourn. The regulars had been half annihilated; their ammunition also was exhausted and further efforts were hopeless. The provincials quickly perceived the situation and jumping over the breastwork with shouts pursued the retreating enemy. Dieskau was found on the ground partly resting against a tree, having been three times shot through the legs and body and left on the field by his own positive order, declaring that that was as good, a place to die as anywhere. He was carried to Johnson's tent, where he was courteously received and his wounds attended to by the surgeons. It was with some difficulty that he was prevented from being murdered by the Mohawks, who were enraged at the losses they had suffered in the morning's scout, and especially by the death of Hendrick. As soon as his wounds would permit he was sent to Albany, and thence to New York, and afterwards to England, where he remained on parole to the end of the war. He then returned to France and died there in 1767.

The enemy having been routed it only remained to complete the victory by a vigorous pursuit in force, in order to cut them off from their boats and thus prevent their escape back to Canada. This course was, however, forbidden by Johnson, though urged by Lyman with unusual warmth, and for his refusal he was censured by his contemporaries as well as since by all later critics. But what he disallowed to Lyman was partially accomplished without his knowledge on the same day by a party from the garrison at Fort Lyman. These having heard the firing in the direction of the lake had sallied out to discover the cause of it, and proceeding cautiously through the forest late in the afternoon had come upon some 300 Canadians and Indians, skulkers and fugitives from Dieskau's army, near a small pond by the side of the road and just beyond the scene of the morning's ambush. These they suddenly attacked, though themselves much inferior in number, and defeated them with great loss after a stubborn resistance. The bodies of the slain were afterwards thrown into the pond and it bears the appellation of "Bloody Pond" to this day. The scattered fugitives from this and the preceding conflicts of the day made their way as best they could to the boats which they had left at Wood Creek and returned through Lake Champlain, a worn-out and half-starved remnant, to Crown Point.

Johnson excused his refusal to permit a pursuit on the ground that he expected another attack, Dieskau having cunningly informed him that there was a large French force in reserve; his object no doubt being to give his routed followers a chance to escape. It seems incredible that Johnson should have given any credence to so flimsy a deception in face of the fact that Dieskau had allowed his troops to be defeated and half exterminated, and himself to be captured, without calling up his pretended reserves, and this excuse must be dismissed as insincere. Johnson also declared that his men were fatigued and disorganized by the events of the day and were not in a condition to pursue; but as he had been confined to his tent throughout the battle he could have known very little on this point in comparison with Lyman, who thought differently.

In view of these considerations and his subsequent conduct all writers agree that Johnson was actuated by jealousy of Lyman who had already been the chief figure of the engagement, and by the idea that if any more glory were achieved that day it would be difficult to monopolize it for himself. As Shakespeare puts it:

> *Who in the wars does more than his captain can*
> *Becomes his captain's captain; and ambition*
> *The soldier's virtue, rather makes choice of loss*
> *Than gain which darkens him.*
>
> Ant. and Cleo., Act 3, Sc. 1.

However this may be it is certain that he promptly determined to secure for himself all the glory of the victory and also all its substantial reward, for his official reports not only omit all mention of Lyman but clearly imply that the whole battle had been fought under his own personal supervision and direction. In them he says not a word about his early retirement from the fight but circumstantially recounts all the details of its progress in the manner of an eye-witness, commending by name the English officer Captain Eyre, "who," he says, "served the artillery through the whole engagement in a manner very advantageous to his character and those concerned in the management of it." After giving other particulars, he adds: "About four o'clock our men and Indians jumped over the breastwork, pursued the enemy, slaughtered numbers, and took several prisoners, including General Dieskau, who was brought into my tent just as a wound I had received was dressed."

As Johnson's wound had been dressed at least six hours before Dieskau was brought into his tent, it is impossible to acquit him of the deliberate intent to convey a false impression when he thus connects the time of receiving it with the very end of the battle. Nor is this conviction weakened when we read a semi-official despatch written the next day by his military secretary, Wraxall, to Governor Delancey, in which no mention whatever is made of either Lyman or Whiting, and he says in a postscript, "Our general's wound pains him; he begs his salutations; he behaved in all respects worthy his station and is the idol of the army."

A side light is shed on the animus of these despatches by a fact which is mentioned by Governor Livingston and President Dwight. This is that there existed among some of Johnson's officers a cabal against Lyman, which was spreading disparaging reports of his conduct during the battle; reports so obviously false and malicious and so completely refuted by overwhelming testimony that they seem to have fallen flat at the time, and to have been never heard of afterwards.

On September 16, or more than a week after the battle, Johnson made an official report of the events of September 8 to the Colonial governors, in which again Lyman's name and services are completely ignored. In connection with the morning's conflict he mentions Lieutenant Colonel Whiting as "commanding one division of the scouting party," but makes no allusion to his management of the retreat. The following passage, however, is significant: "The enemy," he says, "did not pursue vigorously or our slaughter would have been greater and perhaps our panic fatal. This gave us time to recover and make dispositions to receive the approaching enemy."

The statement that the pursuit was not vigorous would have been repelled by Dieskau, whose motto was always "Audacity Wins," and who had certainly pursued as vigorously as the resistance led by Whiting would permit; but notwithstanding this misrepresentation to Whiting's disparagement the acknowledgement clearly appears that the checking of the pursuit saved both the camp and the army from destruction. Considering that the report was being made to those Colonial authorities who were especially interested in Lyman and Whiting, the studious neglect to give either of them credit for the slightest service throughout the day bespeaks a spirit in its author which was anything but just, generous or honourable.

The magnitude, as well as the importance of the victory at Lake George was greatly overestimated, not only by the public at large but also by the British Government, both on account of the depression that had been caused by Braddock's defeat only two months previously, and also by the fact that it was the only gleam of success that enlivened the English cause in the Colonies that year. Johnson's reports, therefore, aroused great enthusiasm in England, and he was hailed as a conquering hero worthy of distinguished honours from a grateful country. Accordingly, soon after its receipt in London, he was created a baronet by the Crown, and Parliament voted him a reward of 5,000. Captain Eyre, the only officer named in the report, was promoted to be major, and Wraxall, whose only apparent military achievements were to accompany Johnson when he walked to his tent soon after the battle commenced, and to call him "The idol of the army" when it was over, was given a captain's commission.

Lyman and Whiting received nothing except the applause of their own countrymen, who speedily learned the facts and placed the credit for the victory where it belonged. Their example has been followed by all historians. The New York Society of Colonial Wars alone has sanctioned Johnson's injustice by erecting a monument which ascribes to him alone the conduct and success of the battle, and consigns Lyman and Whiting to permanent oblivion.

Johnson took no step forward after the victory, though strongly urged by Lyman to seize and fortify Ticonderoga, then unoccupied, but continued to talk about advancing on Crown Point, and called for reinforcements and additional supplies for that purpose. These were sent him through the months of September and October and into November, but during all that period his army of more than 4,000 men lay inactive except for the work they did in erecting Fort William Henry. Meantime the weather was growing colder and the preliminary storms of winter became more frequent and severe. The soldiers, insufficiently sheltered and clothed, badly fed, and decimated by sickness, were all the time on the verge of mutiny and were deserting in large numbers. Finally, on November 27, it was resolved to break up the camp, and there upon, a few men being left to garrison the half-finished fort, the rest of the army were dismissed to their homes. Parkman says: "The expedition had been a failure, disguised under an incidental success." Vaudreuil, the Governor of Canada, presents the same view to the French Government in a despatch dated October 3:

> M. Dieskau's campaign though not so successful as expected, has nevertheless intimidated the English who were advancing in considerable force to attack Fort Frederick (Crown Point) which could not resist them.

If this statement was well founded, it supplies a strong comment on Johnson's inactivity after Dieskau's defeat, for it indicates that had his army, flushed with victory, been pushed rapidly forward to Crown Point they might easily have captured the post and ended the English campaign with complete success. The actual outcome of it was that the close of the year found the French established at Ticonderoga in a better and stronger position than they had had at Crown Point, and fifteen miles nearer to the English settlements.

As this paper relates not merely to the Battle of Lake George, but also to the men who won it, it will properly conclude with a brief sketch of the subsequent lives of General Lyman and Colonel Whiting. But before dismissing Sir William John son from consideration it is only just to say that his career after the Battle of Lake George developed nothing which reflects discredit on his military capacity, or his personal honour. During the continuance of the French War his influence with the Indian tribes was invaluable to the Colonies, and his efforts unceasing to maintain friendly relations between the two parties on a basis of justice and humanity.

He was engaged in no other important military operations till 1759, when he went with a band of 900 Indians, as the second in command, under General Prideaux, on an expedition against Fort Niagara, and after the accidental death of Prideaux he succeeded to the chief command. In this capacity he conducted the siege of the fort with vigour, skill and courage. He fought a successful battle against a French relieving force, and after the capture of the fort firmly protected the garrison from his savage allies. He also, with his Indians, accompanied Amherst in the following year to Montreal and assisted in the investment and capture of that last stronghold of the French in Canada. This was his last important military service, but his influence with the Indian tribes of New York and Ohio continued to be beneficially exerted till the close of his life, which occurred in 1774. As an important factor in the making of American history he will always occupy a prominent and, on the whole, an honourable place.

As already stated, notwithstanding Johnson's studious concealment of General Lyman's part in the Battle of Lake George, which was successful so far as the British government was concerned, the true story was well known throughout the Colonies, and this was evinced in the following year by the renewal of his commission as Major General, which rank he continued to hold throughout the war. He was also repeatedly entrusted with important commands and took part in various campaigns against the French in Canada. In 1758 he commanded 5,000 Connecticut troops in the disastrous attack by General Abercrombie on Fort Ticonderoga, where he was among the foremost assailants and was with Lord Howe when he fell. Again in 1759, at the head of 4,000 men, he accompanied Lord Amherst in his successful expedition against Ticonderoga and Crown Point, and in 1760 assisted with 5,000 Connecticut troops in the capture of Montreal.

In 1761 he was again in Canada in command of 2,300 Connecticut soldiers, helping to complete the English conquest of that Province. After hostilities had ceased in Canada the seat of war was removed to the West Indies, and an expedition having been fitted out to capture Havana, Lyman was by the joint action of all the Colonies placed in command of the whole Provincial force of 10,000 men which accompanied it. The ex-

pedition sailed from New York in November, 1761, and in co-
operation with another fleet and army sent out from England,
struck the finishing blow of the war, Havana being taken and
several French Islands conquered and occupied by the English
during the year

· 1762. This was the last of Lyman's military experiences, as
the war was ended by the Treaty of Paris in February, 1763.
Throughout his active career in the army he had held the confidence not only of the public but of his brother officers, as a man
of superior ability, integrity and wisdom, as well as of military
skill, but unhappily, this confidence was the indirect cause of the
disappointments and misfortunes which ruined his future life.

After the conclusion of peace, a considerable number of the
officers and soldiers who had served in the Colonial armies,
formed an association which they called "The Company of
Military Adventurers," whose purpose was to secure from the
British Government a grant of lands in the new western territory which had just been wrested from France largely through
their own personal efforts and often (as in Lyman's case) at the
sacrifice of their private fortunes. General Lyman was selected
by this organization as their agent to proceed to London, and
there prosecute the claims and objects of the company.

In pursuance of this appointment, Lyman relinquished the
idea of resuming his legal practice and went to England in 1763,
where for eleven long years he pursued a weary and discourag-
ing struggle with the officials in power to obtain their consent
to the reasonable request which he brought to their notice. As
Dr. Dwight remarks:

> It would be difficult for a man of common sense to invent
> a reason why a tract of land in a remote wilderness, scarce-
> ly worth a cent an acre, could be grudged to anybody of
> men who were willing to settle upon it.

Especially so when the petitioners were a body of veterans
who had gained the victories by which the land was obtained,
and whose occupation of it would be important for its future

274

protection. Nevertheless, during all this time Lyman's appeals were met with indifference and treated with neglect. Appointments were made only to be forgotten, and promises, which were never fulfilled. Ashamed to return home without success, he lingered on, hoping against hope and striving against continuous discouragement, until, as Dr. Dwight expresses it:

> .... he experienced to its full extent that imbecility of mind which a crowd of irremediable misfortunes, a state of long-continued anxious suspense, and strong feelings of degradation invariably produce. His mind lost its elasticity and became incapable of anything beyond a seeming effort.

And under such conditions the best eleven years of his life were frittered away.

At length, about 1774, the petition in some form or other was granted. Still General Lyman, apparently unable to form new resolutions, failed to return home. His wife, distressed at his long absence, and by the privations which his family suffered in consequence, then sent his second son to England to bring him back. The appeal was successful and Lyman returned in 1774, bringing the grant of land to the petitioners, and for himself the promise of an annuity of 200 sterling. As for the grant of land, many of the beneficiaries were dead and others too old to avail themselves of it. The storm cloud of the Revolution also was now gathering fast and the younger part of his generation had other things to think of than that of settling a western wilderness. For these reasons the land grant proved practically valueless for its intended purpose; and as for his personal annuity, the speedy outbreak of Colonial rebellion, if no other reason, prevented its ever being paid.

The tract of land in question was situated on the Mississippi River, and was part of the territory then known as West Florida. It included the present site of Natchez, where a French fort had been built and afterwards abandoned.

To this malarious and fever-stricken region in 1775, General Lyman, then a broken-down man of fifty-nine, betook himself by a thousand-miles journey over road-less mountains and bridge-less rivers, accompanied by a few companions, among whom was his eldest son, who was feeble both in body and mind. The son died soon after their arrival and shortly afterward the worn-out father followed him to the grave. Dr. Dwight says:

> Few persons began life with a fairer promise of prosperity than General Lyman. Few are born and educated to brighter hopes than those cherished by his children. None within the limits of my information have seen those hopes, prematurely declining, set in deeper darkness. For a considerable time no American possessed a higher or more extensive reputation; no American who reads this subsequent history will regard him with envy.

This allusion to the happy prospects of General Lyman's family in early life, suggests that a few words be given to their pathetic fate. The story is related somewhat circumstantially by Dr. Dwight.

General Lyman's second son, who brought his father home from England, accepted, while there, a lieutenant's commission in the British army. In 1775, while in Suffield, he was ordered to join his regiment in Boston, which he did and served on the British side till 1782. It was probably the painful relations with their neighbours which this situation brought to the family in Suffield which caused Mrs. Lyman, in 1776, to remove, with the rest of her children, consisting of three sons and two daughters, to West Florida. Her elder brother accompanied them on the sad and toilsome journey. Within a few months Mrs. Lyman and her brother both died. The children remained in the country till 1782, when the settlement was attacked by the Spaniards.

The little colony took refuge in the old fort and resisted the invaders until compelled to surrender on terms; but the terms were at once outrageously violated. In desperation the victims rose upon their conquerors and drove them from the settlement, but learning soon afterward that a larger force was coming up the river to punish them, and fearing the worst of cruelties, the whole colony fled to the wilderness, aiming to reach Savannah, which was then in possession of the British. On their way they endured innumerable hardships and perils, suffering continually from hunger, thirst, fatigue and sickness. Once they were captured by a hostile band of savages, who were about to torture and scalp them, when they were miraculously rescued by the intervention and address of a friendly negro; but those who survived the terrible journey reached Savannah after wandering a distance of over 1,300 miles, through a period of 150 days.

As a result of these experiences the two daughters died at Savannah. The three sons remained there until the war was over and then accompanied the departing British troops. One of them was afterwards in Suffield for a short time but soon disappeared, and what finally became of him and his two brothers, Dr. Dwight, although they were his cousins, was never able to learn.

As to the second son, he continued in the British service till 1782. At that time nearly torpid with grief and disappointment he sold his commission, but collected only a part of the purchase money, and that he speedily lost. He returned to Suffield penniless and almost an imbecile. Friends there endeavoured to revive his courage and restore his mental balance, but in spite of all efforts he sank into listlessness and unkempt pauperism and in this condition he died. Truly, the comment of Dr. Dwight was well applied when he called his narrative *The History of an Unhappy Family.*

The record of Colonel Whiting will be shorter and more cheerful. As we have seen, he held, during the campaign of 1755, the rank of lieutenant colonel only, but the next year the General Assembly voted him a colonel's commission, with its thanks, for the skill, courage and ability which "he had displayed at the Battle of Lake George and on other occasions." He took part in all the subsequent campaigns of the war, highly commended by both British and Americans as an officer of uncommon merit, and when peace returned resumed his mercantile business at New Haven. In 1769 he represented New Haven in the Lower House of the General Assembly, and in 1771 was nominated for the Upper House, to which he would undoubtedly have been elected but for his death, which occurred in that year at the early age of 47.

Dr. Dwight described Colonel Whiting as "an exemplary professor of the Christian religion, and for refined and dignified manners and nobleness of mind rarely excelled." And Professor Kingsley in his Centennial Discourse of 1838 speaks of him as one of those citizens for whom New Haven had especial reason to be proud.

He was buried in the ancient burial ground on New Haven Green, but where, no living man can tell. In the Grove Street Cemetery can be found the mutilated fragment of a time-worn slab, leaning against the tombstone of President Clap, in whose family Whiting's boyhood was passed. The name has been broken off, but the inscription which remains records that the deceased died in "New Haven, full of Gospel Hope, April 9th An Dom 1771. Act 47," and the stone is thus identified as having once marked the resting place of Colonel Nathan Whiting.

And thus it happens that Lyman and Whiting, the men who won the Battle of Lake George together, and who suffered the same injustice in connection with that achievement, and who have been alike ignored in the only structure which commemorates the victory they won, are alike sharers in this fate also, that they both rest in unknown graves.

LEONAUR

ALSO FROM LEONAUR
AVAILABLE IN SOFTCOVER OR HARDCOVER WITH DUST JACKET

CAMP-FIRE AND COTTON-FIELD by *Thomas W. Knox*—A New York Herald Correspondent's View of the American Civil War.

SERGEANT STILLWELL by *Leander Stillwell*—The Experiences of a Union Army Soldier of the 61st Illinois Infantry During the American Civil War.

STONEWALL'S CANNONEER by *Edward A. Moore*—Experiences with the Rockbridge Artillery, Confederate Army of Northern Virginia, During the American Civil War.

CONFEDERATE BLOCKADE RUNNER by *John Wilkinson*—The Personal Recollections of an Officer of the Confederate Navy.

THE SIXTH CORPS by *George Stevens*—The Army of the Potomac, Union Army, During the American Civil War.

THE RAILROAD RAIDERS by *William Pittenger*—An Ohio Volunteers Recollections of the Andrews Raid to Disrupt the Confederate Railroad in Georgia During the American Civil War.

CITIZEN SOLDIER by *John Beatty*—An Account of the American Civil War by a Union Infantry Officer of Ohio Volunteers Who Became a Brigadier General.

COX: PERSONAL RECOLLECTIONS OF THE CIVIL WAR--VOLUME 1 by *Jacob Dolson Cox*—West Virginia, Kanawha Valley, Gauley Bridge, Cotton Mountain, South Mountain, Antietam, the Morgan Raid & the East Tennessee Campaign.

COX: PERSONAL RECOLLECTIONS OF THE CIVIL WAR--VOLUME 2 by *Jacob Dolson Cox*—Siege of Knoxville, East Tennessee, Atlanta Campaign, the Nashville Campaign & the North Carolina Campaign.

THE RELUCTANT REBEL by *William G. Stevenson*—A young Kentuckian's experiences in the Confederate Infantry & Cavalry during the American Civil War.

KERSHAW'S BRIGADE VOLUME 1 by *D. Augustus Dickert*—Manassas, Seven Pines, Sharpsburg (Antietam), Fredricksburg, Chancellorsville, Gettysburg, Chickamauga, Chattanooga, Fort Sanders & Bean Station.

KERSHAW'S BRIGADE VOLUME 2 by *D. Augustus Dickert*—At the wilderness, Cold Harbour, Petersburg, The Shenandoah Valley and Cedar Creek.

LEONAUR

ALSO FROM LEONAUR
AVAILABLE IN SOFTCOVER OR HARDCOVER WITH DUST JACKET

CAPTAIN OF THE 95th (Rifles) *by Jonathan Leach*—An officer of Wellington's Sharpshooters during the Peninsular, South of France and Waterloo Campaigns of the Napoleonic Wars.

BUGLER AND OFFICER OF THE RIFLES *by William Green & Harry Smith* With the 95th (Rifles) during the Peninsular & Waterloo Campaigns of the Napoleonic Wars

BAYONETS, BUGLES AND BONNETS *by James 'Thomas' Todd*—Experiences of hard soldiering with the 71st Foot - the Highland Light Infantry - through many battles of the Napoleonic wars including the Peninsular & Waterloo Campaigns

THE ADVENTURES OF A LIGHT DRAGOON *by George Farmer & G.R. Gleig*—A cavalryman during the Peninsular & Waterloo Campaigns, in captivity & at the siege of Bhurtpore, India

THE COMPLEAT RIFLEMAN HARRIS *by Benjamin Harris as told to & transcribed by Captain Henry Curling*—The adventures of a soldier of the 95th (Rifles) during the Peninsular Campaign of the Napoleonic Wars

WITH WELLINGTON'S LIGHT CAVALRY *by William Tomkinson*—The Experiences of an officer of the 16th Light Dragoons in the Peninsular and Waterloo campaigns of the Napoleonic Wars.

SURTEES OF THE RIFLES *by William Surtees*—A Soldier of the 95th (Rifles) in the Peninsular campaign of the Napoleonic Wars.

ENSIGN BELL IN THE PENINSULAR WAR *by George Bell*—The Experiences of a young British Soldier of the 34th Regiment 'The Cumberland Gentlemen' in the Napoleonic wars.

WITH THE LIGHT DIVISION *by John H. Cooke*—The Experiences of an Officer of the 43rd Light Infantry in the Peninsula and South of France During the Napoleonic Wars

NAPOLEON'S IMPERIAL GUARD: FROM MARENGO TO WATERLOO *by J. T. Headley*—This is the story of Napoleon's Imperial Guard from the bearskin caps of the grenadiers to the flamboyance of their mounted chasseurs, their principal characters and the men who commanded them.

BATTLES & SIEGES OF THE PENINSULAR WAR *by W. H. Fitchett*—Corunna, Busaco, Albuera, Ciudad Rodrigo, Badajos, Salamanca, San Sebastian & Others

LEONAUR

ALSO FROM LEONAUR
AVAILABLE IN SOFTCOVER OR HARDCOVER WITH DUST JACKET

LIGHT BOB by *Robert Blakeney*—The experiences of a young officer in H.M 28th & 36th regiments of the British Infantry during the Peninsular Campaign of the Napoleonic Wars 1804 - 1814.

NAPOLEON'S RUSSIAN CAMPAIGN by *Philippe Henri de Segur*—The Invasion, Battles and Retreat by an Aide-de-Camp on the Emperor's Staff

SWORDS OF HONOUR by *Henry Newbolt & Stanley L. Wood*—The Careers of Six Outstanding Officers from the Napoleonic Wars, the Wars for India and the American Civil War. Illustrated.

HUSSAR IN WINTER by *Alexander Gordon*—A British Cavalry Officer during the retreat to Corunna in the Peninsular campaign of the Napoleonic Wars.

THE LIFE OF THE REAL BRIGADIER GERARD VOLUME 1 THE YOUNG HUSSAR 1782 - 1807 by *Jean-Baptiste De Marbot*—A French Cavalryman Of the Napoleonic Wars at Marengo, Austerlitz, Jena, Eylau & Friedland.

THE LIFE OF THE REAL BRIGADIER GERARD VOLUME 2 IMPERIAL AIDE-DE-CAMP 1807 - 1811 by *Jean-Baptiste De Marbot*—A French Cavalryman of the Napoleonic Wars at Saragossa, Landshut, Eckmuhl, Ratisbon, Aspern-Essling, Wagram, Busaco & Torres Vedras.

THE LIFE OF THE REAL BRIGADIER GERARD VOLUME 3 COLONEL OF CHASSEURS 1811 - 1815 by *Jean-Baptiste De Marbot*—A French Cavalryman in the retreat from Moscow, Lutzen, Bautzen, Katzbach, Leipzig, Hanau & Waterloo.

RIFLEMAN COSTELLO by *Edward Costello*—The adventures of a soldier of the 95th (Rifles) in the Peninsular & Waterloo Campaigns of the Napoleonic wars.

WITH THE LIGHT DIVISION by *John H. Cooke*—The Experiences of an Officer of the 43rd Light Infantry in the Peninsula and South of France During the Napoleonic Wars.

COLBORNE: A SINGULAR TALENT FOR WAR by *John Colborne*—The Napoleonic Wars Career of One of Wellington's Most Highly Valued Officers in Egypt, Holland, Italy, the Peninsula and at Waterloo.

A VOICE FROM WATERLOO by *Edward Cotton*—The Personal Experiences of a British Cavalryman Who Became a Battlefield Guide and Authority on the Campaign of 1815.

LEONAUR

ALSO FROM LEONAUR

AVAILABLE IN SOFTCOVER OR HARDCOVER WITH DUST JACKET

WELLINGTON AND THE PYRENEES CAMPAIGN VOLUME I: FROM VITORIA TO THE BIDASSOA *by F. C. Beatson*—The final phase of the campaign in the Iberian Peninsula.

WELLINGTON AND THE INVASION OF FRANCE VOLUME II: THE BIDASSOA TO THE BATTLE OF THE NIVELLE *by F. C. Beatson*—The second of Beatson's series on the fall of Revolutionary France published by Leonaur, the reader is once again taken into the centre of Wellington's strategic and tactical genius.

WELLINGTON AND THE FALL OF FRANCE VOLUME III: THE GAVES AND THE BATTLE OF ORTHEZ by *F. C. Beatson*—This final chapter of F. C. Beatson's brilliant trilogy shows the 'captain of the age' at his most inspired and makes all three books essential additions to any Peninsular War library.

NAVAL BATTLES OF THE NAPOLEONIC WARS *by W. H. Fitchett*—Cape St. Vincent, the Nile, Cadiz, Copenhagen, Trafalgar & Others

SERGEANT GUILLEMARD: THE MAN WHO SHOT NELSON? *by Robert Guillemard*—A Soldier of the Infantry of the French Army of Napoleon on Campaign Throughout Europe

WITH THE GUARDS ACROSS THE PYRENEES by *Robert Batty*—The Experiences of a British Officer of Wellington's Army During the Battles for the Fall of Napoleonic France, 1813.

A STAFF OFFICER IN THE PENINSULA *by E. W. Buckham*—An Officer of the British Staff Corps Cavalry During the Peninsula Campaign of the Napoleonic Wars

THE LEIPZIG CAMPAIGN: 1813—NAPOLEON AND THE "BATTLE OF THE NATIONS" *by F. N. Maude*—Colonel Maude's analysis of Napoleon's campaign of 1813.

BUGEAUD: A PACK WITH A BATON by *Thomas Robert Bugeaud*—The Early Campaigns of a Soldier of Napoleon's Army Who Would Become a Marshal of France.

TWO LEONAUR ORIGINALS

SERGEANT NICOL by *Daniel Nicol*—The Experiences of a Gordon Highlander During the Napoleonic Wars in Egypt, the Peninsula and France.

WATERLOO RECOLLECTIONS by *Frederick Llewellyn*—Rare First Hand Accounts, Letters, Reports and Retellings from the Campaign of 1815.

Printed in the United Kingdom by
Lightning Source UK Ltd., Milton Keynes
140830UK00001B/158/P